The

Sea-Board *of* Mendip

An Account of the History, Archæology, and Natural History of the Parishes of Weston-super-Mare Kewstoke, Wick St. Lawrence, Puxton Worle, Uphill, Brean, Bleadon, Hutton Locking, Banwell, and of the Steep and Flat Holms

BY

FRANCIS A. KNIGHT

AUTHOR OF "BY LEAFY WAYS," "RAMBLES OF A DOMINIE"
"IN THE WEST COUNTRY," ETC. ETC.

WITH NUMEROUS ILLUSTRATIONS

1902
LONDON
J. M. DENT & CO.

Printed by BALLANTYNE, HANSON & Co.
At the Ballantyne Press

Introduction to the 1988 edition

For many years 'The Seaboard of Mendip' by Francis A Knight has been rightly regarded as the cornerstone of all research into the history of Weston-super-Mare and the surrounding area. It is surprising that since its original publication in 1902 there has been no re-print before now. In recent years other books have been published on the history of Weston-super-Mare, but all have acknowledged their debt to F A Knight, and much information in this book is not available elsewhere. In addition no substantial work has been published on the surrounding area, and this reprint makes available once more a storehouse of information on Kewstoke, Wick St Lawrence, Puxton, Worle, Uphill, Brean, Flat and Steep Holm, Bleadon, Hutton, Locking and Banwell.

Francis A Knight had a career as a Schoolmaster, teaching at Sidcot School and later setting up his own school 'Brynmelyn' in Weston-super-Mare. He was a prolific writer contributing articles to the Daily News and other national magazines on nature subjects, as well as writing a number of books many of which were firmly rooted in the West Country in general and the Mendips in particular. His two best-known books are 'Seaboard of Mendip' and its continuation 'Heart of Mendip' which deals with the Winscombe area. These books have been accurately described as 'always needful to the local scholar', and reflect Knight's love of the Mendip countryside and his pains-taking efforts to be accurate.

F A Knight was not born in the area but came to it as a boy and lived around the Mendips until his early death at the age of 63 in 1915. He was a quaker who held strong views on the demoralising influence of poor literature, and would allow no ephemeral magazines in his school. He died within a few weeks of the publication of 'Heart of Mendip', and it is a mark of the esteem in which he was held that as a memorial to F A Knight, Sidcot School sent three ambulances and old Brymelyn Boys sent a touring car for use by the Society of Friends Ambulance Unit in France and Belgium. A full account of the life of Francis A Knight written by Olive Hallam can be found in Avon Past No 10 Spring 1985.

The text of this edition has not been changed from that of the original publication, although the view of history in some areas has changed in the light of modern research. In particular, this history of Worlebury has been revised, and is best obtained from Jane Evans, '*Worlebury – story of the Iron Age fort*' published by Woodspring District Council in 1980. Other more recent books covering the Area and which maybe of interest include

The Archaeology of Avon, a review from the neolithic to the Middle Ages, edited by M Aston and R Iles, Avon County Council 1987.

The Archaeology of Somerset, a review to 1500 AD, edited by M Aston and I Burrow. Somerset County Council 1982.

J W Gough – Mines of Mendip, David and Charles, Rev Ed, 1967.

Mendip, a new study edited by R Atthill, David and Charles, 1976.

P Newman – Channel Passage, the area around Portishead, Clevedon, Weston-super-Mare and Burnham-on-Sea, Kingsmead 1976.

The Roman West Country, classical culture and celtic sorcery edited by K Branigan and P J Fowler, David and Charles, 1976.

Steep Holm: a case history in the study of evolution, edited by Kenneth Allsop Trust and J Fowles, Kenneth Allsop Memorial Trust 1978.

A small number of extra photographs taken at the time of the 1st publication of 'Seaboard of Mendip' have been included to give an idea of life in the area in 1902. Some of these have come from the collection of Avon Library and Information Service at Woodspring Central Library. We are also grateful to Woodspring Museum and its Curator Jane Evans for permission to reprint photographs from their collection, and the photograph of Francis A Knight is reproduced by permission of Chris Richards.

In the light of the vast development of the area, particularly in Weston-super-Mare since 1902, it is a real pleasure to be able to make available once again this invaluable work of reference 'The Seaboard of Mendip'.

John Loosley
Area Librarian, Woodspring
Avon Library and Information Service

PREFACE

THIS book is in some measure the fruit of the writer's forty years of residence in the Mendip Country, and of a considerable amount of research at the British Museum, the Record Office, and other depositories of ancient documents. But the work could never have been accomplished had it not been for the cordial assistance, not only of those who were already the author's friends, but of very many others on whose help he had no claim. Where so many have freely given time and labour it is almost invidious to mention names. But the writer wishes particularly to record his indebtedness to Ernest E. Baker, F.S.A., whose generous loan of extracts from Church Registers and Books of Parish Accounts, and of Notes on the Early History of Weston-super-Mare, has been of incalculable service. The author desires also to offer his most hearty thanks for the assistance rendered him by the clergy of the district, who indeed have, as a body, entered warmly into the work and have formed its chief support. The volumes of the Somersetshire Archæological and Natural History Society have been a mine of wealth in preparing the history of the various parishes; and some of the most interesting illustrations in the book have been taken, by kind permission of the Committee of the Society, from objects in the Museum at Taunton. The illustrations are in the main the work of the author's brother, Howard F. Knight, whose skilful photographs have received many happy touches from the brush of the author's friend, Edward T. Compton.

In spite of all these advantages it is only too certain that "The Sea-Board of Mendip" will be found to contain many errors and omissions. Already the writer is aware of points that might well have been included. But, as the late Mr. F. H. Dickenson said in his Essay on the Banwell Charters: "There are some things that can hardly be done at all except imperfectly: for if one waits for perfection one waits too long, and that which is imperfect at first is corrected afterwards by the help of others. This must be my excuse for the mistakes I have made." The writer to-day would make these words his own. He feels that, even after years of labour, he can offer to his readers but an imperfect sketch of one of the most interesting corners of one of the most interesting counties of England.

F. A. Knight

WINTRATH,
WINSCOMBE, SOMERSET,
October 1902.

CONTENTS

LIST OF ILLUSTRATIONS

List of additional illustrations in the 1988 edition.

The Sea-Board of Mendip

THE MENDIP COUNTRY

MENDIP COUNTRY is the name here given to a district, about thirty miles long and two hundred square miles in area, extending across the northern part of Somerset, from the shore of the Bristol Channel to the ancient town of Frome, including the Mendip Hills, together with a narrow fringe of the moorland at their feet. It is bounded on the north by the river Yeo and by the southern verge of the Radstock coal-field; while its frontiers on the south are the river Axe and the wide alluvial plain which covers so much of the central regions of the county. The hills which form its principal feature are part of a ridge—of which the western half reappears beyond the Bristol Channel, bordering the South Wales coal-field—formed, no doubt, by a shrinkage of the earth's crust. Their most characteristic and conspicuous geological formation is the Carboniferous or Mountain Limestone, the grey rock which is seen in so many cliffs and gorges; in the magnificent ravine of Cheddar, for example, in the combes of Ebbor and Burrington, in the cliffs of Callow and Brean, in the rugged crest of Crook's Peak, and in the sea-girt bases of the Holms. But so much has been worn away by frost and rain and by the action of the sea, that there are places where the Mountain Limestone has entirely disappeared, and where the more ancient Old Red Sandstone stands now at a higher elevation than any existing part of the formation which once lay over it. Charterhouse Warren, 1024 feet above sea level, is on the Mountain Limestone. But Black Down, the highest summit of the range, 1068 feet above the sea, with Pen Hill and Priddy Nine Barrows, each just a thousand feet high, is on the older rock. Both formations were, it is believed, deposited in a shallow sea. But while the Old Red Sandstone, as we see it here, contains no fossils, the Mountain Limestone, in itself chiefly composed of coral, is crowded with remains of animal life. In times comparatively recent it has been hollowed by rain and running water into many caves and fissures, in which have been discovered the skeletons of animals long extinct. The Mendip bone caves are familiar to all geologists; while the beautiful stalactite caverns of Cheddar are almost as famous as the cliffs themselves.

Both the Old Red Sandstone and the Mountain

Limestone are formations of great antiquity, and were covered once by a vast thickness of other rocks. Professor Ramsey estimated that 5000 feet of strata had been worn away from the tops of the hills. Mr. Charles Moore believed that no less than 16,000 feet had in this way disappeared; in other words, that the Mendip Hills were at one time three miles higher than they are in these days. Among the beds which have been removed are the Coal Measures. The Mountain Limestone underlies the lowest seam of coal which has yet been discovered in these islands. And whatever may be the case to the south of the range, where the limestone dips under the moor, there can be no coal left on Mendip.

It is, however, the firm conviction of the country people that there is coal to be found among the hills. And the place is still pointed out, in Longbottom Valley near Shipham, where, in 1813, a shaft was sunk in search of coal. The attempt was, it is said, abandoned for want of money to erect pumping machinery. That there is any coal there is in the highest degree improbable. The valley is formed on one side by a ridge of Carboniferous Limestone, a formation which underlies the Coal Measures; and on the other by the still lower Old Red Sandstone. This much at least may be regarded as certain. Any fragments of coal which may have been found on the spot are not in their natural position, and can only have come there by accident. It is very interesting, in connection with this popular belief, to know that in the village of Banwell, three miles distant, there is a spring whose course the Shipham "dowsers," or water-finders, claim to have traced all the way from Longbottom, or near it, to Banwell, and which has been known to throw up pieces of coal. A somewhat similar thing happens at Wells, where the powerful spring that fills the moat of the Bishop's Palace occasionally brings up fragments of cinders from the lead-works at Priddy, on the top of Mendip, more than three miles away.

Round the edges of the hills and in hollows among their spurs there are in many places beds of Dolomitic Conglomerate, an ancient sea-beach, in which fragments of older rocks are embedded. Still lower down, along the skirts of the hills, are broad deposits of Red Marl. The low ground at the foot of the range, in some cases but little above the level of the sea, is Alluvial, and is composed mainly of peat earth, in which, at various points, have been found the remains of ancient forests. Igneous rock occurs in small masses in the neighbourhood of Weston-super-Mare. But on one of the highest parts of Mendip, to the north of Doulting and East Cranmore, there is a bed of it which extends east and west for a distance of nearly three miles. At the eastern end of the range the geological formations are complicated in the extreme; and it has been said that there are probably few places in the world where so many varieties of rock are to be seen within so small an area as in the neighbourhood of Frome.

The Mendips no longer rank among the mining centres of Britain. But from the period of the Roman Occupation, down to a time within the memory of persons still living, mining was the most important industry of a great part of the hill country. The ores which the miners sought for were chiefly those of lead and zinc—calamine, as the latter is always called in the district. Both iron and manganese have been worked at various points, though no mines of either metal are now in operation. Much of the iron ore was in the form of ochre, both brown and yellow, and was used in the manufacture of paint. The search for calamine has long been abandoned. Only a few old men remain who dug for it in the days of their youth. But there are wide areas among the Mendips where the ground is so seamed with old workings, and so honeycombed with long-deserted shafts, as to be valueless except for grazing. The only work of the nature of mining now carried on among the hills is at Priddy, on the high ground between Cheddar and Wells, where about fifty men are employed in extracting lead from the imperfectly smelted refuse left by the earlier miners.

Various explanations have been attempted of the meaning of the word Mendip. Some writers have suggested that the first syllable is the Celtic *maen*, "a rock"; the same root that appears in

Bwlch-y-Maen, for example, and in the names of many headlands and isolated rocks round our coasts, such as The Deadman, and The Old Man of Hoy. Others have boldly asserted that Mendip is an altered form of Mine deep. No explanation has, however, yet been found which satisfies philologists, and the true derivation of the name remains unknown.

One remarkable survival from the old mining days is the use of the divining rod, which, once employed by diggers of lead and calamine, is now constantly used in finding springs of water. The dowser, as the man who has the power is called on Mendip, is almost invariably called in before the sinking of a well. There are still many dowsers in the Mendip Country; and the art of water-finding, which throughout England is now almost regarded as a profession, has been practised among these hills from time immemorial.

There is no single summit in the whole range of the Mendips which rises head and shoulders above the rest. The highest point, the broad top of Black Down, is only 1068 feet above sea level, and there is little about it to distinguish it from its neighbours. The much more conspicuous hill called Crook's Peak, which is such a bold feature in the landscape that it is used as a steering mark by coasting vessels in the Bristol Channel, is no more than 628 feet above the sea.

Besides its hills the Mendip Country has no striking

natural features. Its rivers make little show upon the map of England. To the Axe, however, whose muddy waters reach the sea near Brean Down, at the southern limit of the Mendip coast-line, there attaches no small historic interest. Uphill, at the mouth of it, was a Roman port. And the stream itself was long an important boundary-line, at a time when the country beyond it was still Wales, and in the hands of the Britons. Parts of the district are finely timbered; but there are scanty relics anywhere of the woods of which we read in Domesday Book. The Forest of Selwood, at the eastern end of the hills, where King Alfred assembled his army before the march to Ethandune, has practically vanished. The Mendip Forest, in which the English kings followed the chase both before and after the Norman Conquest, was probably by no means all covered with trees; and after the Perambulation of 1298, appears to have been mainly confined to the two manors of Axbridge and Cheddar. It must be admitted that, except for the magnificent Gorge of Cheddar, whose noble cliffs are without a rival in the kingdom, the features of Mendip scenery are quiet and unpretending, and set in sober key.

Quiet and peaceful is, in our time, the rural life of this corner of the west; yet there are few parts of England which can look back upon a record longer, or more varied, or more stirring, than these green hills, and the far-reaching levels at their feet. In the broad plain which stretches southward from the border of the Mendip Country are some of the most famous spots in Britain. And if the scenes of the most memorable passages in the history of Somerset lie beyond the limits of the hills, their story has from the earliest times been closely associated with that of the wider area of the shire.

At the time of the Roman invasion of Britain a large part of what we now call Somerset was colonised by the Belgæ, a Celtic tribe which, some centuries before, had, it is believed, crossed over from Gaul, and had dispossessed the earlier inhabitants. They were an offshoot, no doubt, of the warlike race alluded to by Cæsar, in the familiar opening words of his description of the Gallic War : "*Gallia est omnis divisa in partes tres ; quarum unam incolunt Belgæ.*" Of their still more primitive predecessors, a people of the later Stone Age, it is possible that we have traces in the Stone Circles of Stanton Drew, which, though far less imposing than those of Stonehenge, are much more perfect than those at Avebury ; in the lately discovered Lake Village near Glastonbury, one of the most remarkable vestiges of primitive man ever found in this or indeed in any country ; in the great tumulus of Stony Littleton, a few miles south of Bath ; and in the cromlech of Orchardleigh, not far from Frome, which is the only known monument of the Stone Age within the bounds of Mendip.

To the Belgic invaders, the conquerors of these Neolithic people, we may perhaps attribute the majority of the old camps which occupy so many points of vantage among the hills. It is thought that the Mendips formed the frontier of the Belgæ in Somerset. And in the thirty miles of hill-country there are at least twenty old encampments. Some of these are certainly of Roman origin, and were doubtless built to guard the road down which the produce of the Mendip mines was carried to the sea. Some again may have been the work of the Saxons, at the time when the hills marked the limit of their conquests. But it is probable that the greater number, at any rate, of these ancient military works are Belgic. One of the largest is Dolbury Camp, near the village of Churchill. Its defences, now mere heaps of loose stones, but at one time walls of dry masonry, enclose a space of twenty acres. But the most remarkable of the whole chain of forts is Worlebury, on the western end of the hill above Weston-super-Mare. The ramparts were of great strength, and within them are about a hundred pits, excavated in the rock. In these, together with rude implements and weapons, have been found parts of many skeletons, some of which showed marks of a desperate conflict. One skull, now in the museum at Taunton, bears the scars of seven sword-cuts.

There can be little doubt that the Belgæ worked the lead mines which were afterwards taken possession of by their conquerors. Wherever the old workings are disturbed there are found, together with clear traces of the Roman Occupation, rude pottery and weapons and implements of flint, which point to a period still more remote. It is believed that no British coins, bearing any lettering whatever, were struck before the landing of Cæsar; but, long before the Roman Conquest, gold pieces, rudely imitated from the stater of Philip II. of Macedon, and made probably in Gaul, were in circulation in the island. One of these coins, found at Churchill, is in the museum at Taunton.

If the traces of the more ancient inhabitants of the Mendip Country are but vague and indefinite, leaving much room for theory and conjecture, we have ample records of the Roman Occupation. The conquerors appear to have been attracted by the pleasant climate and the mineral wealth of Somerset as well as by the hot and health-giving springs of Aquæ Solis; and the district was evidently one of no small importance. Few towns in this country have yielded more Roman antiquities than Bath. At least twenty Roman villas have been discovered at various points in Somerset, while coins, gems, pottery, and other objects of antiquarian interest have been found in almost every corner of the county.

It is said that the Roman invasion of Britain was at least partly prompted by travellers' tales of the gold and pearls that were to be found in the island; and it is certain that the conquerors laid their hands upon the mining country of Mendip within a very few years after the landing of Claudius.[1] The entire line

[1] See page 12.

of the hills is traversed by a Roman road which ran from Old Sarum in Wiltshire to the little port of Uphill, at the mouth of the Axe, a distance of fifty-five miles, and was guarded, within the bounds of Somerset, by Roman camps at Brean Down, Uphill, Banwell, Burrington, Black Down, Charterhouse, and Newbury Hill. There are, also, British forts at Brean, Worlebury, Sand Point, Bleadon, Churchill, Banwell, Cadbury, Dolbury, Maesbury, Blacker's Hill, Leighton, Tedbury, and Wadbury. Some of these are near the Uphill road; and many of them, if we may judge from the coins and other objects found in them, were occupied by the Romans. The Fosse Way, the great road that crossed the island, from the south coast of Devonshire to Lincoln—a road whose Roman character, as Mr. Scarth observed, "is perhaps more decided than that of any other highway in the kingdom"—also ran through these hills, and crossed the Uphill road at right angles near Shepton Mallet. Along the lines of the great Roman roads that traverse Britain there are at least seventy places called Cold Harbour,[1] a name believed to point to the site of a ruined Roman villa, whose strong walls and numerous rooms would make it a convenient shelter for travellers. There are two Cold Harbours in the Mendips; one at Uphill, and one near Wookey Hole. There is a third at Dundry, at no great distance

[1] Isaac Taylor, "Words and Places."

from the hills. In addition to many more familiar place-names that indicate Roman occupation, there are in Somerset ten Silver Streets, a word in which silver is regarded as a corruption of the Latin *silva*, "a wood."[1] Of these there are examples in the Mendip Country, at Cheddar and at Congresbury.

One of the chief Roman mining stations was at Charterhouse-on-Mendip, two miles north of the head of Cheddar Gorge; on the site, no doubt, of a still earlier British settlement. Here have been discovered foundations of buildings, altars, coins, weapons, rings, brooches, inscribed leaden tablets, with abundance of Samian and other pottery. Most significant of all, however, are the massive pigs of lead which have been brought to light from time to time among the hills, bearing the names of Claudius, Vespasian, Antonine, Britannicus, and Hadrian. The inscriptions on two of these show that they were probably cast as early as the year 49, or only six years after the conquest under Claudius.

Among the many camps or hill-forts in Somerset there are three called Cadbury; one in the Mendip Country, near Yatton, another near Clevedon, and a third half-way between Wincanton and Ilchester. This last is by some authorities regarded as no other than the actual Camelot of King Arthur. It is remarkable that in the immediate neighbour-

[1] "Som. Arch. Pro.," vol. xxiv.

hood of it are places bearing the names Queen Camel, West Camel, and Camel Hill. Associated with the story of King Arthur is the Abbey of Glastonbury, which, founded in British times, alone of all the great religious houses survived the Saxon Conquest, and attained to great importance under the early English kings. In later ages the Abbey became the largest, the most wealthy, and the most powerful in England. There was, it is said, a time when its mitred head could summon to his standard a force of fifteen thousand fighting men.[1] Glastonbury is beyond the pale of the Mendip Country. But the Abbot was, by virtue of his office, one of the four Lords Royal of Mendip; and a number of manors in the district are set down in Domesday Book among the vast possessions of the Abbey. And from every point of vantage in the hills there shows, across the wide green plain to the southward, the solitary tower that looks down upon the Island Valley of Avilion; upon the spot where, according to the story long believed in all monastic houses, landed Joseph of Arimathæa and his companions; upon the ruin of the Abbey dowered by Ina and Canute, the Abbey where Dunstan ruled, and where, according to old tradition, mouldered the bones of Guinivere and Arthur.

In Saxon times Somerset was the scene of much fighting. After his great victory over three

[1] The Rev. F. Warre, "Som. Arch. Pro.," vol. v.

British kings at Deorham, near Badminton, in 577,[1] the West Saxon conqueror, Ceawlin, is said to have established his frontier at the river Axe.[2] And in 658, Cenwalch, still pushing westward, carried the English border to the Parret.[3] On a spot hard by that slow-moving river, were fixed, two centuries later, the hopes of England. Not far from the Parret, a mile from the point where it is joined by its tributary the Tone, is a low green mound, an insignificant rising in the wide expanse of moor. This is all that remains of the Isle of Athelney, scene of one of the most famous episodes in history.

It was to this spot, then surrounded by sheets of water, by vast and impassable peat-bogs, and by forests of alder trees, that King Alfred, hard pressed by Guthrum and his Danes, retired for breathing-space—not, probably, as a solitary fugitive, but with his nobles about him, and with his army no farther away than the Forest of Selwood at the eastern extremity of the Mendip Country—before that May morning when he humbled his fierce antagonist on the hills at Ethandune. It was the opinion of the late Bishop Clifford that there is good reason to believe that the place of victory lies, not in Wiltshire, as is usually said, but in Somerset, at Edington, in the Polden Hills. It was in the church at Aller, four miles east of Athelney, that Guthrum

[1] Anglo-Saxon Chronicle. [2] Guest. Freeman.
[3] Anglo-Saxon Chronicle.

and thirty of his captains submitted to the rite of baptism; while at Wedmore, a few miles to the south of Cheddar Gorge, have been discovered the massy foundations of the summer palace where the victor entertained his beaten enemy. Of the monastery which King Alfred founded at Athelney in gratitude for his deliverance, and which survived until the overthrow of all monastic houses by Henry VIII., no trace remains beyond a few blocks of dressed stone built into the walls of the farm that stands upon the spot, and fragments of encaustic tiles which are at times turned up by the plough.

Guthrum has left his memory but not his mark in Somerset. But, as Bishop Clifford has shown,[1] there is some ground for thinking that three spots upon the coast, two of them in the Mendip Country, commemorate, with more or less of clearness, the name of another sea-rover, Hubba, who, while Alfred was at Athelney, landed at the mouth of the Parret, and who, after ravaging the neighbourhood, was surprised and slain by an Ealdorman of Devon. The little port of Uphill, on the Axe, is described in Domesday Book as Opopille. Pill is a west-country word for a creek; and, as Bishop Clifford suggested, Opopille may well be a corruption of Hubbapill. In Hobbs's Boat, higher up the river, the name is plainer still. Ten miles to the southward, near Combwich on the Parret, the Cimwich of Roger

1 "Som. Arch. Pro.," vol. xxi.

de Hoveden, the scene of Hubba's overthrow, there stands by the river a great tumulus, nameless indeed, but not far from a farm whose title suggests that this green barrow is the very mound of Hubbalowe, which his sorrowing followers raised over the dead sea-rover.[1]

Other records of the Norsemen may be read in the Scandinavian names of the Holms, the two islands in the Bristol Channel; in the names of some of the hamlets called Wick—Wick St. Lawrence, for example; and perhaps in the name Birnbeck, the little islet under Worlebury Hill.[2]

The Mendips were a favourite hunting-ground of the Saxon kings, and in Domesday Book is a list of Mendip manors which were included in the property of the Crown, and of which it is said, "They have never paid Danegeld, nor is it known how many hides there are there." Among the archives of the ancient town of Axbridge there is a document, compiled before the year 1413, no doubt from earlier records, which describes the government of the borough in the reigns of Athelstan, Edmund, Edred, Edgar, and St. Edward, and which relates how King Edmund, while hunting in the forest of "Minndep," as the kings were accustomed to do in the summer, was nearly carried by his horse over the brink of "Cedderclyff." If there were no mints in Somerset in British times, there were at least twelve places in the county where Saxon coins were struck. One of these is

[1] John of Brompton.

[2] See also the chapter on "Locking."

believed to have been Congresbury, for in the museum at Taunton is a silver penny of Edward the Confessor which bears on the reverse, together with the name of the moneyer, ELFWINE, the letters CONGR. After the Norman Conquest money was coined only at Bath, Ilchester, and Taunton.

It is recorded in the Saxon Chronicle that, in the year after the Battle of Hastings, King Harold's mother, Githa, "and the wives of many good men with her," took refuge for a time on the Steep Holm, until they were able to sail to Flanders. To the same island some centuries before, had, according to Leland, retired Gildas the historian. But his sanctuary was broken by the visits of pirates from Brittany, who no doubt found the Holm a convenient station from which to plunder both sides of the Channel, and he was driven at length to seek shelter within the walls of Glastonbury.[1]

In the year 918 some Danish sea-rovers, who had been beaten off from Watchet and Porlock, landed on one of the Holms; and there, to use the words of the Anglo-Saxon Chronicle, "they sat down . . . until such time as they were quite destitute of food; and many men died of hunger, because they could not obtain any food. Then they went thence to South Wales, and thence to Ireland." In the year 1067, one of the sons of Harold led a fleet of war-ships up the Avon, and ravaged the neighbourhood.

[1] Leland, *De Gilda Sapiente.*

But having failed in an attack upon Bristol, the marauders retired to Somerset, "where they went up the country."[1]

A conspicuous figure in the early history of Somerset was Ina, ablest of all the West Saxon kings, conqueror and law-giver, benefactor of the Abbey of Glastonbury, builder of Taunton Castle, and founder of the Cathedral of Wells. Wells Cathedral is not only the noblest building in the Mendip Country, but is perhaps the most beautiful, though one of the smallest, of all the English cathedrals. It is, moreover, the only one which is complete in all its parts. Freeman the historian considered that there was not in all Europe another such group of buildings as that on which the eye looks down from the Tor Hill, on the Shepton Mallet road: "the Cathedral as the great centre, the Palace, the Cloister, the Chapter House, the Vicars' Close, the detached houses of the canons, the more distant view of the Parish Church." No-where else have such buildings suffered so little from the hands of fanatics or restorers. The Cathedral is the Cathedral of six hundred years since. The Bishop lives in the Palace that was finished before the last Crusaders were driven from Jerusalem. The Dean inhabits the house that was rebuilt by Gunthorpe more than four centuries ago. The dwellings in the Vicars' Close, though more altered than the other

[1] Anglo-Saxon Chronicle.

Wells Cathedral

buildings, have been inhabited since the Battle of Cressy. And the Cathedral gates, the Chain Gate, the Dean's Eye, and the Penniless Porch, are the remains of fortifications erected during the Wars ot the Roses. The famous west front of the Cathedral was condemned by Freeman as a "sham, a sin against the first law of architectural design." There is no denying that both doors and windows are made but minor details in its plan. But there are many who, with Dean Plumptre, are "content to admire, reverence, and love a thing that is beautiful in itself, for the sake of its beauty.[1] Some of its hundreds of figures possessed, in the eyes of Flaxman, "a grace excelling modern productions." It is a work unsurpassed in Europe. And our wonder grows when we consider the time of its accomplishment; that all this was done with comparatively rude appliances, with the aid of few books, and with but little knowledge of anatomy, by command of a man who, side by side with Stephen Langton, faced King John at Runnymede.

There were not many Norman strongholds in Somerset, and there appears to have been only one in the Mendip Country—Rougemont, or, as it is usually called, Richmont Castle, near East Harptree, on the north side of the hills. In the struggle between Stephen and the Empress Maud, Sir William Harptree, like De Mohun of Dunster, took the side

[1] Dean Plumptre, "Wells Cathedral and its Deans."

of the Empress, and his castle was taken by storm by King Stephen himself. Rougemont was demolished by its owner, Sir John Newton, for the sake of its building materials, so long ago as the reign of Henry VIII., and little remains of it to-day except the foundations of its keep. The Castle of Nunney, not far from Frome, rather a fortified manor-house than a castle, in the ordinary sense of the word, was built in the reign of Richard II.

The Great Pestilence—which in modern times has been spoken of as the Black Death, one of the most awful plagues of which we have any record—first reached Europe in the autumn of 1347, having originated in the far East, where it had already caused a loss of life unparalleled in history. Thirteen millions of persons are said to have died in China alone; and the death-rate in Cairo, when things were at their worst, was as high as 15,000 a day. Two famous writers described its ravages in Italy. One of these was Boccaccio, whose light-hearted Story-Tellers fled from Florence to escape the Plague, from which 100,000 people had perished in that city alone; and the other was Petrarch, whose Laura died of it at Avignon, one out of 150,000 victims.

The Great Pestilence took a year to reach England. It was first heard of at Weymouth, in the later half of 1348, and it quickly swept across Dorset, Devon, and Somerset. Its ravages have been traced by the very extraordinary increase in the number of clergy who were appointed to livings in 1348 and 1349. Before the coming of the Plague the average number of such appointments made yearly by the king, in whose hands many livings were, was about 100. In 1349, between June and the middle of September, the number was 440, compared with 36 in the corresponding part of the year before. From January 25, 1349, to January 25, 1350, no fewer than 894 livings were filled up by King Edward III. alone. The changes are very marked in the towns on the coast. Bridgwater, Clevedon, Weston-super-Mare, Portishead, and Bristol were among the earliest places that suffered. And it is highly probable that the contagion was conveyed by a ship drifting up the Channel with plague-stricken corpses on board; a thing which is known to have happened elsewhere. In the summer of 1349, for instance, a ship left London, where the Plague was then raging. The whole crew died while the vessel was at sea, and the fatal bark was driven ashore on the coast of Norway. The Pestilence swept over the country. In one province where there were 479 churches, 466 priests are said to have perished of the Plague. Wide areas were not only completely devastated, but in some cases remained without inhabitants for whole generations, so that forests grew up round the ruins of deserted hamlets, and bears took possession of forgotten churches.

In Somerset the Pestilence was at its worst in December 1348, and in January and February 1349.

In those months the number of vacant livings filled up in this county were 32, 47, and 43 respectively. Two things may be gleaned from these brief records. One is that, since the proportion of priests to laymen was comparatively small, the total loss of life must have been very great indeed. The fate that befell the pastor must undoubtedly have overtaken a large part of his flock. The other is, that in spite of the deadly character of this, the most terrible of all pestilences of which any authentic history remains—in spite of the knowledge that they were going to almost certain death—there was, among those simple men of God, no lack of volunteers to fill the places of the fallen, to take charge of the sorely stricken parishes, and to do their best to minister to the needs of sick and dying.[1]

There was some fighting in Somerset during the Wars of the Roses. It was after the second Battle of St. Albans that Stogursey Castle was taken and burnt, and it has ever since remained a ruin. A few years later, in the reign of Edward IV., a dispute arose between the Prior of Green Ore and some of the Mendip miners, tenants of Lord Bonville; and the Prior having complained to the king, Lord Chief Justice Choke was sent down to settle the quarrel. The result of his mission is recorded on an ancient map entitled, "Meyndeep with its Adjacent Villages and Laws," which is of the highest

[1] "The Great Pestilence," Francis Aidan Gasquet, D.D., O.S.B.

interest, not only as showing the bounds of the Mining Forest, which were not the same as those of the Hunting Forest, but because it gives us some idea of the great importance of the mining industry of the Mendip Country in the closing years of the Wars of the Roses. "The said Lord Chocke," says one of the four ancient copies of the Laws, "sate upon a place of my Lord of Bathes, called the Fordge upon Meyndeepe, wherat he commanded all the commoners to appear, and in especiall ye four Lords Royale of Meyndeep. That is to say, my Lord Bishop of Bath and Wells, my Lord of Glastenbury, my Lord Bonvill, Lord of Chuton, and my Lord of Richmond, with all ye appearance to ye number of Ten Thousand People." [1]

During the reign of Henry VII., Somerset was crossed by two rebel armies. In the summer of 1497 an insurrection broke out in Cornwall, in consequence of a heavy war-tax, and the rebels, under Flamank and Lord Audley, marched up to London to lay their grievances before the king, passing through Wells on their way. They were beaten at Blackheath on the 22nd of June. In the same year, in the month of September, Perkin Warbeck, who declared himself to be the Richard, Duke of York, said to have been murdered in the Tower, landed in Cornwall, and again the Cornishmen rose in arms. Having been beaten off from Exeter, Warbeck made his way to Taunton. Here, at the approach

[1] "Som. Arch. Pro.," vol. xv.

of the royal troops under Lord Daubeny, the King's Chamberlain, the rebel commander abandoned his followers and fled, taking sanctuary in the Abbey of Beaulieu. King Henry, however, marched into Somerset, and by the end of September arrived at Bath with a force of 10,000 men. At Wells he was entertained at the Deanery by its builder, Gunthorpe. Thence he marched to Glastonbury, whose Abbey was then at the height of its power; thence to Bridgwater and then to Taunton, where he was probably lodged at the Priory. To Taunton Warbeck was brought from his sanctuary at Beaulieu, and there, after confessing his imposture, he received the royal pardon. The rebels were treated with singular lenity. The chief punishment inflicted on the county was in the shape of fines levied on those who had "aided and comforted" either the followers of Warbeck or the earlier Cornish insurgents; and from the list of those who were fined we can trace the route taken by the rebels. In addition to money payments, all of which were not discharged until nine years later, some of those who had shared in the rising gave substantial expression to their repentance by rebuilding and beautifying churches and abbeys at various places in the county.[1] One memorial of the time may be seen in the statue, usually said to represent King Henry VII., which looks down from

[1] "Som. Arch. Pro.," vol. xxv.

a niche in the western side of the tower of Axbridge Church.

No county in England is more rich than Somerset in ancient houses. It has been said that there is hardly a parish that does not possess a dwelling as old at least as the days of Queen Elizabeth. In many villages the manor-houses have been converted into farm buildings. But some of them, at any rate, still retain some traces of their ancient dignity in the shape of panelled rooms, carved chimney-pieces, or finely moulded ceilings, while the Bishop's Palace at Wells is the finest thirteenth-century residence in the whole island.

Scattered among the Mendips, as, indeed, in every corner of the county, are many ancient stone crosses, a few of which are older even than the Norman Conquest. Some of them were used, no doubt, as places from which proclamations were read, some were for the collecting of market dues, and some were probably centres of public worship, before the erection of parish churches. Some covered crosses have been destroyed on the ground that they were in the way of the traffic, as at Banwell and Axbridge. But two fine examples of such structures still remain, at Cheddar and Shepton Mallet.

The churches of Somerset present features of great interest. Though many of them were originally built at a much earlier time, and contain Norman and even Saxon work, a large proportion of them were rebuilt during the Perpendicular period, that is to say, between 1377 and 1547; and among the Somerset towers of that time are some of the finest in all England. Among the best in the Mendip Country are those of St. Cuthbert's at Wells, of Winscombe, Banwell, and Chewton Mendip. In some of the towers hang bells which are older even than the churches, and bear marks which point to their having been cast as early as the fifteenth century. Many of the Mendip bells were cast by the Bilbies, a family of bell-founders who lived at Chew Stoke, and who were distinguished in their craft from about 1700 to the year of Waterloo.

Church Registers were first established by order of Cromwell, the successor of Cardinal Wolsey, in 1536. And in some of the Mendip churches are still preserved the old records which were commenced within a few years of this date. Three villages possess books of Churchwardens' Accounts of great antiquity. Those of Banwell go back to 1516, those of Croscombe to 1474, and those of Yatton to 1440. These old records are extremely interesting, and throw much light upon the histories of their several parishes.

In the reign of Henry VIII. the antiquary Leland received a commission under the Great Seal to travel throughout England in search of antiquities, and with power to examine the libraries of all religious houses. He twice visited Somerset, in 1540 and 1542, and in the "Itinerary" which he compiled are most interesting pictures of the county as he saw it.

His descriptions of Bath are, to the archæologist at any rate, especially valuable; for in his time many Roman antiquities which have now disappeared were still to be seen, built into the town walls. The hot baths were even then evidently much frequented. After describing "2 Springs of whote Wather," Leland says: "The Colour of the water of the Baynes is as it were a depe blew Se Water, and rikith like a sething Potte continually, having sumwhat a sulphureous and sumwhat an onpleasant savor." Leland's travels in Somerset were after the dissolution of the monasteries. He does indeed speak of the information given him by the Prior of Bath. But such expressions as, "The late Priory of Blake Monkes" (Dundry); "There was a Priory of Nunnes" (Cannington); and "Ther was also late a House of Freres yn this Towne" (Ilchester), are significant of what had happened. Glastonbury was not yet wholly dismantled, and Leland describes many monuments, apparently as he saw them. The fall of this, the greatest of English abbeys, was among the striking events of the reign. Richard Whiting, the last of its long line of abbots, was, after a mock trial in the great hall of the Bishop's Palace at Wells, on a trumped-up charge of stealing the Abbey plate, dragged on a hurdle up the Tor Hill at Glastonbury, and there hanged, and his head was set up over the gate of the Abbey. In 1540 the monastery was disestablished, and its vast possessions became the property of the Crown. Ruthless hands were laid upon its plate and jewels, and on the costly vestments of the monks; the treasures of its library were scattered; its walls, which once enclosed a space of sixty acres, became a common quarry, until but a fragment remained of what had been for ages the richest and most powerful monastery in the world.

The fate of Glastonbury was the fate of many abbeys, great and small. And while the county contains some most picturesque remains of its old monastic houses, some, on the other hand, have entirely disappeared. Of the Abbey of Athelney, for example, not one stone stands upon another. Woodspring Priory, used first as a hospital, and later as a dwelling-house, alone of all the monasteries of the Mendip Country has escaped destruction. The ruin of the rest has been absolute and complete. Of the Priory which Aldhelm built at Frome nothing is left but a tradition. Of the nunnery which once occupied the site of Winscombe Court, not a stone remains: its history and the name of its founder are alike unknown. Of the Abbey of Banwell, which King Alfred gave to his friend and biographer, Asser, no trace is left: even the spot where it stood is uncertain. Of the little cell at Charterhouse-on-Mendip, the very site has been long since forgotten.

The great event in Somerset in Queen Elizabeth's reign was the preparation to meet the Armada. This preparation began many years before the sailing of the Spanish fleet. And most interesting records still exist giving the strength of the forces, and even the names of the efficient "Pykemen and Shotte." It is some evidence of the stationary character of the Somerset population that out of seventy-five names mentioned in the Hundred of Winterstroke, for example, a Hundred which includes a large part of the Mendip Country, at least fifty are still to be found in the district. Of 12,000 able-bodied men "certified" in the whole county, 4000 were, in 1588, reported as trained and armed, about half of them with muskets. And when the news came that the Armada had actually set sail from Corunna, the whole of these 4000, together with 50 lances and 100 light-horsemen, marched up to London to assist in defending the capital. Captain Owrde, who had reviewed the forces the year before, reported to the Government: "I founde beyonnde myne expectacon and vnto my greate comforte, the contrie so excellentlie furnished with all sorts of armor and weapons and that verie goode in suche pfecte redines, the men so well sorted and chosen, bothe for able bodies and comlye psonages, . . . that I assure Yo^r^ Lordshippes yt dothe exceede anie contrey that ever I came in." Nor was the county backward in its preparations for meeting the enemy at sea. Bridgwater provided a ship called the *William*. Chard had a share in fitting out the *Revenge* and the *Jacobe*. News of the near approach of the Armada was brought into Bridgwater on the 21st of July by a ship that, on its voyage from St. Jean de

Luz, had sighted the Spanish fleet only three days before.[1]

At the beginning of the struggle between the king and the Commons the Mendip Country, like the rest of Somerset, was all for the Parliament. At the end of the year 1642, after two trifling skirmishes and a brief siege of Wells, followed by the sack of the Bishop's Palace, and the wanton destruction of the Cathedral windows by Puritan fanatics, the whole district was in the hands of the Roundheads. But after the Royalist victory at Lansdowne, on the 5th of July 1643, the tables were turned, and throughout the following year the whole county was for the king. In 1643 Charles himself was at Mells, at the house of Sir John Horner, who the year before had armed his tenants and neighbours for the opposite side, and whose estates were in consequence sequestrated. There is still preserved at Wells a letter in which the king demanded from the Mayor £500, and a supply of boots and shoes. The city, however, had suffered severely from both sides, and all they could raise was £100, and 200 pairs of boots. In the summer of 1644 Taunton, after a brief siege, surrendered to the Parliamentarians. And although in October the town itself was retaken by the royal troops under Wyndham, Blake and his handful of heroes held out in the castle, "determined to stay there while they had breath, and ready to fast two

[1] Green, "Somerset and the Armada."

days in the week if needful." The siege was raised in December, at the approach of a relief column; but it was renewed again in the following April. In the interval Blake had done his best to strengthen the fortifications; and his gallant defence, behind wooden palisades and hastily constructed earthworks, is among the most stirring episodes of the war. After a month of desperate fighting Hopton sent to offer Blake fair terms if he would surrender. Blake replied that he had four pairs of boots left, and that he would eat three of them before he gave up the town. Five times the stormers were beaten back. And at length, when more than half the town was in ashes, when there remained only two barrels of powder in the magazine, the approach of Fairfax relieved Taunton for the second time. The Battle of Lansdowne, though not decisive, is regarded as a royal victory; but the fight at Langport, where Goring's army was wrecked beyond recovery, ranks high among the triumphs of the Parliament. It was the opinion of Fairfax that it was his best campaign. He was in command, but it was Cromwell himself who, when the royal ranks gave way, chased the flying cavaliers through the blazing streets of Langport. From Langport, Fairfax marched to Bridgwater, carrying with him to the siege the guns that he had taken from the king at Naseby only a few weeks before. Bridgwater, which had been reported impregnable, held out for only two days against the red-hot shot of the Parliamentary artillery. Its castle was dismantled by order of the Commons, and little remains of it now except the foundations. Nunney Castle, near Frome, which also withstood a siege of two days, was spared after its surrender, and its roofless ruin still stands, a most picturesque memorial of the war.

Until the reign of Charles II. there was no regular copper coinage in this country. Under the early Stuarts tokens were issued by private individuals, who held monopolies from the Crown. These monopolies lapsed under the Commonwealth, and in 1649 many tradesmen all over the country began to issue tokens of their own. This coinage continued until 1672, when farthings were struck in the Royal Mint, and the tradesmen's tokens fell gradually into disuse. The trade tokens of Somerset were very numerous, having been issued from more than sixty different towns and villages; and more than three hundred varieties are known. Sixty-five tokens at least were struck at Taunton, which issued more than any other Somerset town. Eleven places in the Mendip Country are represented in this coinage. Even so small a village as Winscombe had a token of its own. The frequent occurrence on these coins of implements connected with the woollen manufacture shows that the cloth trade, now confined to a few spots in the county, was at that time a very important industry. From 1787 to 1795 there was again a scarcity of copper coin, accompanied by a re-issue of private tokens. From 1811 to 1817 silver money as well as copper was coined by private firms, or by various corporations, in consequence of a scarcity of coin which was partly occasioned by heavy purchases, especially of silver, by France. Frome had a share in this later coinage, and issued silver pieces of the value of one and two shillings each respectively.

During Monmouth's brief rebellion his little army was at Wells, at Frome, and at Shepton Mallet. The bullet-marks of his followers can still be seen on the west front of Wells Cathedral, and the niches from which their sacrilegious hands tore down the effigies are vacant still. The Field of Sedgemoor, scene of the last battle fought on English ground, is but twelve miles, as the crow flies, from the southern slope of Mendip. And when, at the very beginning of the conflict, the drivers of the Duke's ammunition waggons, panic-stricken at the flight of Lord Grey's cavalry, left the doomed battalions to yet speedier and more certain overthrow, it was to these hills that they made their way. And when vengeance was taken on the unhappy rustics who, for the sake of faith and freedom, had followed the fortunes of King Monmouth, the Mendip villagers were among the worst sufferers at the hands of the merciless Jeffreys.

Three years after Sedgemoor another invader landed at Lyme; an invader of a very different standing, and bearing very different credentials. And it was in Somerset, near the town of Wincanton, in a sharp skirmish between a detachment of Mackay's regiment and some Irish troops under Sarsfield, that the first blood was shed in the short struggle between James II. and the Prince of Orange. It has been said that the cruel memories of Sedgemoor made the men of the West Country hesitate to join at once in another insurrection. They were not, however, wholly indifferent. And in this fight at Wincanton it was a false alarm that reinforcements were coming, given by the country people, which induced Sarsfield and his men to fall back.[1] The Prince did not pass through the Mendips. His route to London lay through Salisbury.

The chief interest of the Somerset of the eighteenth century lies outside the Mendip Country, and centres in the town of Bath, for many years the most fashionable resort in England. The singular reign of Beau Nash, whose word was law in all civic and social arrangements, was at its height from 1730 to 1740. Both before and after his day, Bath had many distinguished visitors. Members of our own Royal Family, and more than one sovereign of France, have been among its residents. Here for a time lived the two Pitts, Horace Walpole, John Wilkes. Here Burke died. In these streets Nelson, Clive, and Peterborough were once familiar figures. It was from Bath that Wolfe set out on his last campaign. It was from his house in this city that Herschel first saw the planet that, though

[1] Macaulay.

now called Uranus, was for a time named after the King and then after the great astronomer himself. Fielding and Smollett, Sheridan and Goldsmith, Wordsworth and Southey, Scott and Dickens, Gainsborough and Lawrence are some of Bath's remembered visitors. These, indeed, are to be looked upon but as birds of passage. Few of them were really natives of the county. But among those who were born in Somerset, or who lived long within its borders, are some who, for good or ill, have left their mark in history, and some at least of these have been closely associated with the Mendip Country. Dunstan, once the most powerful man in England, was born at Glastonbury. Roger Bacon, one of the most distinguished philosophers of his time, was a native of Ilchester. Many famous bishops have held the See of Bath and Wells. Among them were Jocelin, greatest of the builders of the Cathedral; Still, the reputed author of the earliest English comedy; Wolsey, the imperious; Laud, obstinate and ill-fated; and Ken, one of the Nonjurors, better known as the author of the Morning and Evening Hymns. The village of Stogursey, near the northern limit of the Quantocks, preserves the altered name of De Courci, the conqueror of Ulster. From his son, made Baron of Kinsale in 1223, is descended the present Lord Kingsale, who is thus the holder of the most ancient title in the United Kingdom which has been handed down in unbroken line. Nearer to Bridgwater is the hamlet of Cannington, where was born the beautiful Joan Clifford, the Fair Rosamond of the Plantagenet love-story. Pawlett, on the other side of the Parret, gave its name to Sir Amyas Poulet, who was one of the guards of Mary Queen of Scots. West Harptree, at the northern foot of Mendip, was the home of Sir Thomas Gournay, who stood by when King Edward II. was murdered at Berkeley; and who, having fled the country, was seized at Burgos and beheaded at sea.

The cottage at Wrington, where John Locke was born, has been demolished some years. But the birthplace of Admiral Blake is still shown at Bridgwater, and is probably much as he last saw it, in the heyday of his great renown. Hopton, the Royalist commander, who pressed Blake so hard at Taunton, was a Somerset man. Pym and Hollis, two of the Five Members, were Somerset men, though both sat for constituencies in Devon. John Bull, who wrote "God Save the King"; Speke, the explorer of the Nile; Crosse, the electrician; Queckett, the microscopist; Young, the decipherer of Egyptian hieroglyphics; and Fielding, the novelist, were all born in this county. Alexander Barclay, translator of the "Shyp of Folys," was Rector of Wookey in the reign of Henry VIII. Langhorne, the translator of Plutarch, was Incumbent of Blagdon. Wordsworth and Coleridge lived long in Somerset; and it was among the Quantocks that the latter wrote his finest poems. A house where he is said to have stayed is still pointed out in Clevedon. And at Clevedon, too, by "The little grey church on the windy hill," is the grave of Arthur Hallam—

> "the grave that has been wept above
> With more than mortal tears."

Barley Wood, the house where Macaulay, as a child, spent many happy days, still stands at Wrington; where, too, in the shadow of the noblest of Somerset church towers, lies the dust of Hannah More. The memory of her good deeds is still green in more than one of the Mendip villages, and old men still creep among us who remember her, and her labours of love on behalf of the rugged miners of the hills.

In a district so varied with hill and valley, marshland and sea-shore, the flora and the fauna—the plants, the birds and beasts, the insects and the shells—are of remarkable interest. Many rare birds have been recorded here. And among the plants are two that occur nowhere else in Britain. It has been said, too, by a distinguished geologist, that "the palæontology, the ancient natural history of the district, exceeds in interest that of any other district in England." [1]

The Mendip Country is nowhere the seat of any important manufacturing industry. The two insignificant tidal harbours of its scanty sea-board are visited only by small colliers and coasting smacks. Its most flourishing town has a population of barely

[1] Charles Moore.

twenty thousand. Its interests are mainly agricultural. And although Somerset dairy-farming has been famous for unnumbered generations, it is an occupation which lends to the inhabitants, no less than to the landscape, a sense of quietness and repose. The green heart of Mendip is, like the country about Aylmer's Field—

> "A sleepy land, where, under the same old wheel
> The same old rut would deepen year by year."

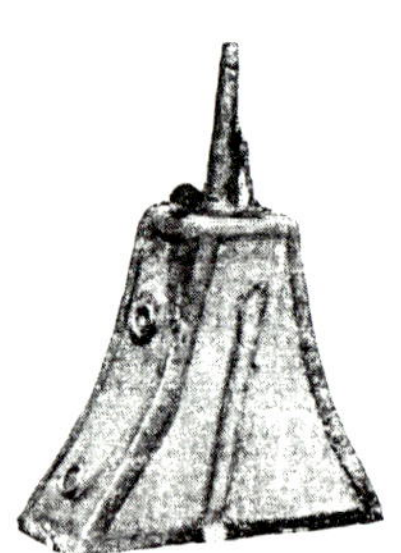

POWDER-HORN FROM SEDGEMOOR

WESTON-SUPER-MARE

SEA-BOARD of Mendip is an arbitrary term here applied to that portion of the Mendip Country which is bordered by the Bristol Channel, or is within a short distance of the coast. It is true that, of the parishes included in this district, there are only five which are now maritime: the parishes of Wick St. Lawrence, Kewstoke, Weston-super-Mare, Uphill, and Brean. But there is no parish throughout the whole area which does not include a part of the great alluvial plain which, at a period far remote, was covered by the waters of the Severn Sea. Remote as that period is, and before the dawn of history, it was while man was in the Mendip Country. Rows of mouldering fishing-stakes, the crumbling hull of a primitive canoe, and even an ancient iron anchor, have been found deep beneath the soil at points far inland from the present tide-line.

Three small headlands, mere flaws upon the English coast-line, stretch westward from the shore of Somerset into the brown waters of the Bristol Channel. These headlands, the little promontories of Brean Down, Sand Point, and Worlebury Hill, are the last spurs of Mendip; while, farther out, half-way across the broad estuary of the Severn, are the Holms, the outlying fragments of the range. Two of these headlands are left for the most part to the birds, and to the sheep that graze upon their bare and treeless slopes. Their louder sounds of life are the shrill cry of the kestrel, the plaintive call of the curlew, or the clamour of a troop of daws. In the cliffs of one of them even the raven still finds sanctuary, and on the grassy steeps of both the shieldrake breeds among the rabbit-burrows.

But round the third of these small promontories—though a hundred years ago it was, to judge from the description given of it by the historian of Somerset, barer even than the others—are the sounds of traffic, and the stir and bustle of a town. "This mountain," wrote Collinson, in describing Worlebury Hill, "is an immense rock of limestone, with but very little herbage intermixed; yet here and there a solitary sheep is seen pasturing on its naked, barren ridge, which, being elevated far above the surrounding country, and overlooking the long tract of the Severn Sea, is buffeted by every blast." Collinson was, it is true, speaking more particularly of the part above the village of Worle, which, although cultivation creeps each year still farther up the slope, is even now comparatively treeless; but the description would, in his time, apply to all the hill. At its western end the Worlebury of to-day is crowned with woodland; and clustering along its southern and western slopes, and reaching far out over the moorland lying at its feet, is the growing watering-place of Weston-super-Mare.

It is a town without a history. The Norsemen left their mark close at hand, in the names of the Holms, of Uphill, of Wick St. Lawrence, and perhaps also in that of the little island of Birnbeck. On the heights that overlook the town are the ruined ramparts of a fortress that was, it is believed, stormed by the Romans in the first century of the Christian era. A few miles away there still stands the Priory of Woodspring, founded in the stormy days of King John. But Weston itself is wholly modern. Even its church was entirely rebuilt so recently as 1824; and although there may be traces of ancient workmanship in the Pigott mansion in the Grove Park, it is doubtful if, with the exception of the existing fragment of Leeves's Cottage, there is a building in the town which has been standing for a hundred years. From a little fishing village with a mere handful of houses, Weston has grown, in the course of a single century, to be a favourite seaside resort, whose residents exceed those of Frome and Wells together, and which has a floating population of visitors that, during the summer months, increases the number of its inhabitants by some thousands.

A few years ago there were old men still living who well remembered its day of small things: when there was no post-office, and no delivery of letters; when not only beer but bread had to be fetched from Worle; when the laying of the foundation-stone of its first hotel was an event of such magnitude in the eyes of the villagers that a company of the West Mendip militia fired volleys from their flint-lock muskets to celebrate the occasion. Those were the days when smugglers watched and waited for the red glow of the signal-fires by Uphill Church, or on Worlebury Hill, or on St. Thomas's headland, that should warn them which landing-place to run for, and when many a keg of brandy that had never paid the king's dues was hidden under a pathway that crossed the sand-hills where Regent Street now stands. Once, it is said, a French lugger ran into the bay at high water, and began to put her cargo of spirit-kegs over the side, buoying them to wait for boats from the shore. But the tide went down before the work was finished. When morning broke the sea was half a mile away. The hapless craft was high and dry, with her precious casks strewn round her on the mud.

Several Somerset manors called "Westone," are described in Domesday Book. But, although Collinson held the contrary view, it is the opinion of more modern antiquaries that Weston-super-Mare is not alluded to in the Survey, and that the hamlet was, in Norman times, included in the then more important Manor of Ashcombe, of which Domesday Book gives the following details:—

"*Herluin holds from the Bishop (of Coutances) Aisecombe. Brictric held it in the time of King Edward, and paid Danegeld for three hides and a half. There is land for five plough-teams. In the demesne there are two plough-teams, and seven serfs and six villeins, and five boors with three plough-teams. There are forty acres of meadow, and three acres of coppice, and a hundred acres of pasture. It was worth and is worth a hundred shillings.*"[1]

According to Collinson, the two manors of Weston and Ashcombe were, in the reign of Henry III., held by William Arthur of Clapton. His descendants had possession until the beginning of the sixteenth century, when the property passed by marriage to the Winters. From an old book of Parish Accounts, lately examined by Mr. Ernest E. Baker, it appears that Edward Gorges, through his marriage with Grace, daughter of William Winter, was Lord of the Manor in 1694. In 1696 the estate was bought by John Pigott, ancestor of the present owner.

In the registers of the Dean and Chapter of Wells, the name of the place appears in 1221 as Weston. In 1234 it is Weston prope Worle, that is to say,

[1] A hide averaged about 240 acres, but varied according to the quality of the land.

A plough-team corresponded to about 120 acres.

Serfs were mere slaves, the personal property of the landlord, but not belonging to the manor.

Villeins were the highest of the classes which had no sort of freedom; but they had land and chattels of their own.

Boors were probably the highest class of farm-labourers employed on the estate.—Eyton, "Domesday Studies."

Weston, near Worle. In Bishop Drokensford's register the name is given in 1311 as Weston juxta Mare, or Weston-on-the-Sea. And lastly, in the register of Ralph of Shrewsbury, in 1348, we have the name in its present form. One other variation may perhaps be thought worthy of notice, though it may have been merely based upon a misreading. In one of Speed's maps, dated 1610, the village is marked Weston on the More, or, as we should write it, Weston-on-the-Moor; not an inappropriate designation, when we consider that the fishermen's huts of the original hamlet stood on the edge of a moor that reaches from the sea-shore to the hills beyond Yatton. The word Weston is one of those place-names of whose origin and meaning there can be no doubt. The Anglo-Saxon *tun* or *ton* signified a single homestead; and this usage is still retained in Scotland, where even a solitary farm-house is called a *toun*. More than 300 towns and villages in this country are named after points of the compass, and of Weston there are fifty-five examples.[1]

The modern parish extends from the Sanatorium at the end of the sea front, on the south, to Kewstoke on the north. Its limit on the eastern side is the boundary of the wood, though the village of Milton, which is part of the parish of Kewstoke, has lately been included within the area controlled

[1] Isaac Taylor, "Words and Places," "Names and their Histories."

WESTON-SUPER-MARE, FROM WORLEBURY CAMP

by the Weston-super-Mare Urban District Council. The highest ground on Worlebury Hill, occupied by the high-pressure reservoir, near which is the cairn of stones called Peak Winnard, is 357 feet above the sea; while there are parts of the moor on the south side of the town that are less than twenty feet above high-water mark. Ashcombe Manor, of which the little fishing village of Weston was once an insignificant member, has, in the lapse of ages, changed its relative position, and is now a suburb of the flourishing watering-place of Weston-super-Mare.

For its rapid rise into favour Weston is largely indebted to the late Dr. Fox, the eminent physician of Brislington, who, seeing how well the place was suited for a health-resort, had much to do with the early improvements of the town. His high opinion has been confirmed by the experience of two generations; and what is now one of the prettiest of watering-places has also the reputation of being one of the healthiest in the United Kingdom. Few towns are more picturesquely situated than the part of Weston that climbs the side of Worlebury Hill; and, especially in early summer, the foliage of its abundant trees and the colours of its laburnums and scarlet hawthorns add greatly to its beauty. Above the houses are the woods, towards whose western end there show at intervals among the trees the grey stones of Worlebury Camp. Along the margin of the bay a broad sweep of sand runs far down the shore to the banks of the river Axe. At the farther side of the bay is the long headland of Brean Down, now separated by a wide interval from the hill to whose bare summit clings, like a storm-driven sea-bird, the ruined Church of St. Nicholas. Inland are the low levels of the moor, and beyond them rise the green slopes of the heart of Mendip. It is but a tawny sea that comes swiftly in across the level sands; and they are dreary mud-flats that the ebbing tide leaves bare. But the air that blows in from the open Atlantic gathers up from these broad banks a pleasant odour of the sea; and no sunsets are more beautiful than those which are reflected in their smooth and monotonous expanse.

Collinson has very little to say about the parish of Weston, whose entire population probably numbered then—the last decade of the eighteenth century—about a hundred and fifty souls. The only things he mentions are the Church of St. John the Baptist, and a remarkable ebbing and flowing well, empty at high tide, but full at low water. This well was known for many years after Collinson's time, and was formerly to be seen at the eastern end of the garden of Glentworth; but it is now concealed by masonry. A similar well still exists on the Flat Holm. The first real glimpse we get of Weston is in a letter from Mrs. Piozzi, better known as Mrs. Thrale, the lady to whom Dr. Johnson wrote his "Letters from the Hebrides." This letter, which Mr. Ernest E. Baker has recently printed in his new edition of the old Weston Guide Book of 1822, shows that, although the village was in a decidedly primitive condition, it was already becoming popular:—

"WESTON-SUPER-MARE,
"*27th August* 1819.

"I feel delighted, Dear Sir, that you have not forgotten me; some ladies that I met upon the Sands last night said Sir James Fellowes had mentioned my name at fashionable Bognor. This little place is neither gay nor fashionable, yet full as an Egg, insipid as the White on't, and dear as an Egg o' Penny. I enquir'd for Books, there were but two in the Town was the reply—a Bible and a Paradise Lost. . . . They were the best, however. No Market . . . but I don't care about that.

"When Miss Burney asked Omiah the Savage if he should like to go back to Otaheite? Yes, Miss, said he. . . . No mutton there, no Coach, no Dish of Tea, no pretty Miss Horneck, good Air, good Sea, and very good Dog: I happy at Otaheite. My Taste and his are similar. . . . The breezes here are most salubrious; no land nearer than North America, when we look down the Channel: and 'tis said that Sebastian Cabot used to stand where I sit now and meditate his future Discoveries of Newfoundland. Who would be living at Bath now? The Bottom of the Town a Stewpot, the top a Girdiron, and London in a State of Defence or Preparation for Attack or some strange Situation, while poor little Weston is free from Alarms on Juvenals Principle *Cantabit vacuus coram Latrone Viator.* I offer'd a cheque on Hammersley at the Hotel here. . . . Yes, Madam, by all means, says the Landlady: but, pray, who is the Gentleman does he reside in Bath? or is he a Bristol Merchant? . . . Our Banker little dream'd that such Questions could be asked concerning him; and, indeed it reminded me of the Character of Congreve, who, when spoken to of Epictetus enquired whether he was really a French Cook, or only one who wrote out particular Receipts.

". . . We have swarms of Babies here, and some bathe goodhumouredly enough while others scream and shriek as if they were going to Execution. . . .

"I am going on a Water Party next Monday with a very agreeable Young Man, Mr. Rogers. There are few People here that I know, one Lady, however, challenged me as an Acquaintance of her Brothers—just 70 years ago, when he was a little boy at Weston School and used to come home for Holydays with Sir Robert Salusbury Cotton Father of this Lord Combermere to our House in Jermyn Street, now part of Blake's Hotel.

"Adieu, Dear Sir—portez-vous bien: present me to Lady Fellowes, and tell your children they have an humble and attached Servant in "H. L. PIOZZI.

"Sir JAMES FELLOWES,
Bognor Rocks, Sussex."

The officials of the head office in London can find no record of the population of Weston in 1801, the year when the first regular census was taken in this country. Probably the parish, like some others, sent up no return. But in 1811 the inhabitants numbered 163. It is interesting to trace the increase of the population. We are perhaps accustomed to think that the growth of the town has been most rapid of recent years. But during the first half of last century its rate of increase was much faster than it has been in more modern times.

The following table gives the results of the census since a record was kept :—

1811 . . .	163	1861 . .	8033
1821 . . .	738	1871 . .	10,565
1831 . . .	1310	1881 . .	12,872
1841 . . .	2103	1891 . .	15,529
1851 . . .	4033	1901 . .	19,060

Small and insignificant as the place remained for long after that time, the birth of Weston-super-Mare may fairly be reckoned from the year 1808. For it was then that many of the old fishermen's huts, or Auster Tenements as they were called, were, together with their plots of land, sold by the Pigott family—subject to perpetual ground-rents—to Mr. Richard Parsley of Weston, and Mr. William Cox of Brockley. Two years later, in 1810, these two gentlemen obtained a special Act of Parliament under which the waste lands over which the village Common Rights extended, were enclosed. The Commissioner appointed under the Act, after setting out highways, bridleways, and footways which should be common to the public, decided upon two sites from which the new freeholders were ever after to obtain stone for building, and gravel for maintaining the roads. The words of the award are as follows :—

"I do set out, allot, and award the two several plots or parcels of land next hereinafter described as and for stone and gravel pits to be used as well for the repairs of the roads within the said parish, as by the owners or occupiers of the several and respective allotments in the said moors, commons, and waste lands hereinafter set out and awarded in respect of their old Auster or Antient Tenements hereinafter described, and their tenants for their own necessary use (other than and except for that of making lime)."

The Commissioner then proceeded to define the two quarry sites in South Road and in Ashcombe Road, the first of which has provided building stone for almost the entire town, besides metal for making and maintaining nearly all the roads throughout the township. It will be seen, therefore, that these quarries are not the property of the Urban District Council. But that body has the right of taking stone and gravel therefrom for the purposes before named, in common with all other persons who possess any old Auster Tenements or parts of such Tenements. And since the land formerly belonging to these Tenements has been to so great an extent divided and sold for building sites, nearly all owners of property in the town claim rights in Weston Quarry.

From an old map, dated 1806, published in the "New Guide" of 1822, we may form some idea of the condition of Weston before the commencement of the changes which were inaugurated in 1808. The village was bounded on the south by Watersill Road, which followed the line of the present Locking Road and Regent Street to the beach. From this road ran the main thoroughfare of the village, "The Street," as it was called, which took the line now occupied by Union Street and High Street. On or near The Street was the chief part of the village, comprising twelve buildings in all. At the beginning of West Lane, now West Street, were two more cottages; and on the beach at the other end stood the house of the Rev. William Leeves (part of which still survives under the name of Reed's Dairy) with a cottage behind it. Beyond this point no houses are shown, and no roads are marked; though, some distance farther on appears a rough track leading from Knightstone—then and long afterwards really an island—in the direction of Kewstoke. The only other road which is named in the map is the Bristol Road, which was united with The Street by a sharper and more awkward corner than that which characterises the top of the High Street of to-day. A path across the fields, nearly corresponding with Lower Church Road, led to the parish church, near which stood the old Rectory and the Grove Mansion, with a couple of cottages or lodges. Twelve other cottages, or about thirty in all, made up the entire village.

The cottage called Reed's Dairy, near the angle formed by the two main parts of the Sea Front, is part of the house built in 1791 by the Rev. William Leeves for his use during the summer; and is one of the very few remaining relics of Old Weston. Leeves began his career as an officer in the Life

Guards, but he ultimately took Holy Orders, and became Rector of Wrington. He held the Living for nearly half a century, dying in 1828, in the eightieth year of his age. It was he who, in 1771 or 1772, composed the familiar and beautiful air of "Auld Robin Gray," the ballad which had been written a short time before by Lady Anne Lindsay, daughter of the Earl of Balcarres.

An early improvement, dating probably from or near 1808, was the erection by Messrs. Cox and Parsley of what was then looked upon as a very large and profitless inn, called "The Hotel," and now known familiarly as "The Royal." On the same site had stood an old farmhouse, which was burnt down on Whitsunday 1792. "Many years elapsed," to quote the words of Brown's "New Guide," now half a century old, "before any custom was obtained for this house, except upon very extraordinary occasions, when it was usual for a bellman to announce that beer was to be had at the hotel in the evening."

The original Waterloo House at the corner of the Boulevard was built in the year of the great battle; but in 1860 it was partly pulled down in making the Boulevard. The South Parade, however, which was built in 1819, has probably changed but little in the years that have intervened.

A hundred years ago Knightstone was still an island at every high tide; and in the early years of last century the Cardiff coal-smacks, after discharging their cargoes, used frequently on their way back to sail between the rock and the mainland. The Guide-Book of 1822 speaks of it as "joined to the village by a bank of pebbles thrown up by the sea;" and it adds that "the unwary stranger has frequently been detained some hours here, but a boat is now always in attendance." We learn from the same source that "A Reading-room, Hot and Cold Baths, and a Lodging-House have been erected there by a spirited individual who purchased the island for that purpose." This purchaser was the Rev. Thomas Pruen, who also built a small pier and constructed a low causeway uniting the island with the shore. It was at that time that, in preparing the foundations of a new bath-house, those "human bones of a gigantic size" were found, which Rutter says that he saw and examined, and which, as he considered, "in some measure confirmed" the tradition that the spot had taken its name from having been the burial-place of a Roman knight, who had been stationed either at Uphill or in the camp on Worlebury Hill—a tradition, however, which has no other evidence to support it.

Some twenty years after Mr. Pruen's time the Knightstone property was bought by Dr. Fox of Brislington. At an outlay variously estimated at from £16,000 to £20,000 he erected bath-houses, made the causeway which now joins Knightstone to the shore, built the present wharf, and provided moorings for boats. Until the construction of the Birnbeck pier in 1867 Dr. Fox's wharf was the only place where vessels of any sort could call. The property now belongs to the town, but for shipping purposes it is included in the port of Bristol. No dues are levied, except for registration. So much coal is now brought into Weston by way of the Severn Tunnel that comparatively few colliers put in to Knightstone pier.

A graphic picture of the state of Weston-super-Mare as it was eighty years ago, and of the limited nature of its means of communication with the outer world, may be found in the pages of the Guide of 1822. By that time there was a second hotel—"a comfortable house . . . in the village" —and many lodging-houses offered entertainment to visitors. A schoolroom for a hundred children had lately been built; and there were also a "seminary for young gentlemen," and two establishments "for the education of young ladies." There were then two doctors, one of whom lived in the village itself. "Perhaps no sea bathing-place," says the old Guide, "presents greater allurements to those who seek for health, or a retreat from the bustle of business or the fatigues of fashion, than Weston. Every necessary and convenience of life can be procured in abundance, and the people are civil and obliging." Popular ideas of what are the necessaries and conveniences of life have advanced somewhat since those days. Weston may fairly be considered to have kept pace with the increasing requirements of the altered times. "The people" are probably still more "civil and obliging" than they were. And the town has certainly more attractions to offer to its visitors than the one billiard-table, two pleasure-boats, and three bathing-machines of eighty years ago.

In 1822 Weston was "a penny post from Bristol." Those who are tempted to complain of the irregularities and the infrequent deliveries of the modern post-office may be interested in knowing that, eighty years since, the letters were "regularly brought by a letter-carrier from Churchill every evening from May to November;" and from December to April they were delivered "every Monday, Wednesday, and Friday morning." Twenty years before the opening of the Bristol and Exeter Railway the Bristol coach left Weston every morning at eight, starting again at four and getting back at seven in the evening. Another coach started from Bristol at the same hour—eight o'clock in the morning—and left Weston again at six every evening. A third coach left Bath at noon—on Sunday, Tuesday, and Thursday in each week—arriving in Weston "about five." In addition to the coaches, "Harse's Caravan" travelled to Bristol every Tuesday and Friday, and "Richard West's Cart" performed the same journey on Mondays and Thursdays.

In 1826 was built the old Esplanade—a sea-wall

and asphalted walk without a parapet—which ran from Knightstone to the end of Regent Street. Before that time a beach of shingle skirted the bay, and inside this was an earthen dyke kept in repair by holders of Auster Tenements. The Esplanade was succeeded in 1887 by the present Sea Front—a fine piece of work, with seats and shelters, extending all the way from the pier to the Sanatorium, a distance of nearly two miles. During its construction its fronting wall, which had been left temporarily unsupported, was, on October 17, 1883, thrown down throughout its entire length by an unusually high tide, coming in before a strong south-westerly gale. About two years after the completion of the old Esplanade, in 1828 or 1829, a road was made from Weston to Uphill. Before that time the only way between the two places was along the sands. In the same way the only communication between Weston and Kewstoke until 1848, when the Lord of the Manor cut the beautiful road along the seaward base of the hill, was by the lane leading over Worlebury, beyond the eastern end of the wood. The wood itself, which adds so much to the beauty of the town, was planted in 1823 on what was then a bare and treeless hill. It is said that at first all the young trees died, either because of the exposed nature of the situation, or because of unskilful treatment, and that it was not until the fourth attempt that the plantation was successful. The wood was a game-preserve until about the year 1855, since which time it has been freely thrown open to the public. It is occasionally closed in order to prevent the establishment of a permanent right-of-way. The last time was about twelve years ago.

It is said that the old Bristol and Exeter Company, long since merged in the Great Western, originally intended that their railway should run direct through Weston-super-Mare, then a little town of more than two thousand inhabitants, and fast coming into notice as a health-resort. But the strenuous opposition of the townspeople induced the directors to divert the line to the open moor, at a distance of about a mile from Weston. For the first ten years after the completion of the railway in 1841 trains were drawn by horses along a short branch line from the junction—whose site is now marked by an elevated water-tank—to the first Weston terminus, which stood not far from the Railway Hotel on what is now called the Alexandra Parade, but which was long known as Old Station Square. Those who remember the discomforts and inconveniences of that most disagreeable of junctions know how dearly the people of Weston paid for their short-sighted policy. In 1866 there was opened a much improved station, also a terminus, now given up to goods traffic. This was in use until 1884, when the completion of the new loop-line gave the town for the first time a good service of trains. A light-railway or steam tramroad, first projected in 1885, connects Weston with Clevedon; and steamboats from Cardiff, Bristol, and other ports, call frequently at Birnbeck pier.

In the same year in which the railway was opened, the first Gas-Works were started, and in 1841 there were forty-two public lamps, and about fifty private consumers.[1] The price of gas was then 10s. 6d. per thousand feet; in 1853 it had fallen to 6s. 6d. New works were built in 1852, and incorporated by Act of Parliament in 1855. The price was then 6s. a thousand feet; the prescribed quality was 10 candle-power, and the gas supplied had an illuminating power of from 9 to 10 candles. The present price of gas in Weston is 3s. 2d. per thousand feet, with discounts, which in some cases reduce the price to 2s. 7d. The prescribed candle-power now is 15 candles, and the gas supplied is from 17 to 17¼ candle-power. The number of street lamps is 554.

The Weston Water-Works, established by a company in 1853, were, in 1878, purchased by the town for £65,000. The pumping-station and the powerful spring which supplies all the water are at the foot of the hill at Ashcombe, to the east of the town. The main or low-service reservoir is below the Bristol Road, near the corner of Arundell Road; and immediately above it, in the woods at the top of the hill, is the small high-service tank for supplying water to the upper parts of Weston.

[1] Brown's "New Guide to Weston-super-Mare," 1853.

Until twelve years ago some of the houses in the Shrubbery had a private water supply of their own, and they still use the tower which was part of the original system. About the year 1847, before the formation of the Weston Water-Works Company, the late Miss Sophia Rooke sank a well for the use of her residence, Villa Rosa, and of other houses on her estate, at the same time putting up pumping machinery, and building a tower to serve as a small reservoir. And as Miss Rooke sold building sites from time to time, she agreed to provide the houses which should be built thereon with a limited quantity of water daily, at a fixed cost. This arrangement lasted for more than forty years. But in 1890, in consequence of repeated complaints of the shortness of the supply, it was agreed that the local authorities should purchase, for about £500, the site of the Shrubbery Well, together with the tower and the machinery, and should lay on the town water to the tower tank, which was already connected with all the houses. The water of the well is no longer used, but it was found, on analysis, to be almost exactly the same as that which comes from the Ashcombe spring.

Repeated analyses have shown that Weston water is excellent for drinking purposes. But its great hardness renders it less suited for the almost as important purpose of washing; and when boiled it leaves a heavy deposit of solid matter which rapidly chokes up boilers and hot-water pipes. The following is a copy of the latest expert report upon the water:—

"ANALYSIS OF WESTON WATER FROM THE TOWN PUMPING STATION AT ASHCOMBE, TAKEN BY MESSRS. J. BELL AND R. BANNISTER, DATED JUNE 1885.

"The samples referred to have been analysed with the following results:—

	No. I.	No. II.	No. III.
Ammonia—			
Free (parts per million)	.032	.022	.046
Albd. " "	.056	.040	.030
Total	.088	.062	.076
Specific gravity	1.00088	1.00084	1.00086
Chlorine, grains per gallon	19.8	20.9	20.9
Calculated as common salt	32.6	34.4	34.4
Oxygen consumed in one hour	.004	.005	.004
Total Solids	73.9	74 2	81.6
Loss on ignition	17.3	10.9	24.5
Hardness—			
Temporary	16.5°	15.7°	16.2°
Permanent	18.0°	18.9°	18.3°
Total	34.5°	34.6°	34.5°
Nitrogen as nitrates . . .	Nil.	Nil.	Nil.

"The waters are all odourless and tasteless. Nos. 1 and 2 contain a small quantity of finely divided and flocculent matter in suspension, and No. 3 is clear and bright. The above results show that the three samples of water are practically alike in composition, and can only be objected to on two grounds, viz. :—

1. The large amount of chlorine they contain, and
2. Their hardness.

"The chlorine is, however, derived from a salt deposit through which the spring passes, or from salt water. It can therefore be safely used for drinking and other domestic purposes, but it is not so suitable as water practically free from chlorine.

"The hardness detracts from the merits of the water for detergent purposes on account of the large quantity of soap which will be required for washing. In other respects the waters cannot be objected to, as before stated, and there will be no risk in using them for drinking and domestic purposes.

"(Signed) J. BELL, Ph.D., F.A.S.
R. BANNISTER, F.T.C., T.C.S.

"SOMERSET HOUSE, 5*th June* 1885."

Weston may be said to have become a town in 1842, by virtue of the Weston-super-Mare Improvement Act of that year, and it was long governed by a Board of eighteen "Improvement Commissioners." Their authority, however, originally extended to only about half the parish, in consequence of objections on the part of some landowners to the levying of town rates, which then amounted to 9d. in the pound. Knightstone was within the prescribed limits; but the Board so far yielded to the opposition of the owner of the island as to allow him to pay no more than one-fourth of the rates to which his land was lawfully liable. The borrowing powers of the town, limited by the Act of 1842 to £5000, were raised, by another Local Improvement Act passed in 1851, to £7000, when the limits of the township were further extended. In 1859 the community adopted the Local Government Act of the previous year, in which were incorporated several Public Health Acts; and the Commissioners became in consequence the local Board of Health, as well as being a body of Improvement Commissioners. Since that time the limit of the town's borrowing powers has depended upon the amount of its assessment to the poor rates; so that, as such assessment increases, so do its borrowing powers increase, to the extent of two years of assessable value. According to the last Improvement Act, the local district rates must not exceed 3s. 6d. in the pound, without the consent of the ratepayers. In 1894 the local governing authority was vested in the Urban District Council.

The most important and conspicuous public building in Weston is the Town Hall, which stands at the corner of Oxford Street and the Walliscote Road. Originally erected in 1856 by a private individual, it was bought and given to the town by Archdeacon Law, who was twice Rector of Weston, first from 1834 to 1838, and again from 1840 to 1862. But in 1898 it was greatly altered and improved by the Urban District Council. The building contains a large room for public meetings, and accommodation both for the Council and the County Court. The latter authority includes in its jurisdiction the parishes of Weston-super-Mare, Kewstoke, Wick St. Lawrence, Puxton, Worle, Locking, Hutton, Bleadon, Uphill, Brean, Brent Knoll, East Brent, Lympsham, Berrow, and Burnham.

Attached to the Town Hall is the station of the Volunteer Fire Brigade, a body originally started in 1846, but remodelled in 1879. During the half-century of its existence the brigade, which consists now of twenty members, well equipped with a steamer, two manual fire-engines, and two fire-escapes, has done good service for the town. It has, moreover, distinguished itself at public competitions with other brigades, especially at Exeter, where on one occasion the Weston men took the first place, and at the Alexandra Palace, where they were second in all England.

Two beneficent institutions, whose value to the community it would be hard to overestimate, are the District Hospital in Alfred Street and the West of England Sanatorium at the Uphill end of the Sea Front. The Hospital was first opened in 1847, but has at various times been much improved and enlarged, especially in 1865, when a new building was opened. And in 1887, the Jubilee of Queen Victoria, the women of Weston added a children's ward as a memorial of the late Rev. William Hunt. In 1866, when the Hospital had been started nearly twenty years, there were seven beds; the number of in-patients for the year was 24, and of out-patients, 923. In 1900, after more than half a century of useful work, there were 35 beds, and the number of in-patients for the year was 299. The out-patients, on the other hand, were fewer than they had been fifty years before, and amounted to only 641. But this apparent diminution was due to the establishment, in 1886, of the Provident Dispensary. Before that time the Hospital out-patients had averaged more than 2000 a year for ten years. And so far from the number of out-patients having fallen off, the resident medical officer of the dispensary reported that in 1900 he had paid 5266 visits to patients in their own homes, and had attended to more than 10,000 cases in the out-patient department. Patients are admitted to the Hospital not only from Weston and the immediate district, but from many other towns and villages. In 1900, Bristol sent more cases than any other place except Weston-super-Mare itself. The institution has a small income from invested property, and there is also a source of revenue in Patients' fees and in the surplus from the dispensary. But for its large annual outlay of more than £2000 the Hospital is mainly dependent on subscriptions and collections.

The West of England Sanatorium, a conspicuous building at the southern extremity of the Sea Front, stands close to the beach, in its own ground of three acres. Through the exertions of the late R. A. Kinglake, it was first started, in 1868, as a small cottage hospital, which provided four beds for the benefit of persons residing in any part of the British Islands, and who, while recovering from disease or accidents, were in need of sea-air and sea-bathing. It soon became very popular; and in 1871 the foundation-stone of the present building was laid by the Earl of Carnarvon, the president for the year. Improvements and extensions have continued from that time until the present, and the Sanatorium can now accommodate 100 patients. The usefulness of the institution may be estimated from the fact that during 1901, 2125 patients were admitted, while many applications were refused for want of room. As might be expected, Somerset sends more patients to the Sanatorium than any other three counties in England. The next in order are Worcester, Gloucester, Wiltshire, and Devon.

The inmates pay 18s. a week, which covers all expenses. Those admitted through the recommendation of life governors, subscribers, or benefit societies, or through the aid of church or other collections, pay only 5s. a week from April 1 to the end of September, and half-a-crown weekly for the rest of the year. "Patients must be well and strong enough to take their own meals at the common table, to dress themselves, and to attend to their own wants."[1]

The authorities do not receive persons suffering from fits, cancer, advanced consumption, diseases requiring active medical or surgical treatment, contagious or infectious diseases of any kind, or persons coming from houses where infectious or contagious disease exists. The Sanatorium has a regular income of nearly £700 a year from endowment and invested funds; but its heavy annual outlay of more than £3000 is met by subscriptions and donations, by collections, and by the payments of inmates.

In addition to the District Hospital there is a small Isolation or Fever Hospital, with a steam disinfector attached to it, on the Uphill Drove. And in the Clifton Road the Bristol Medical Mission have established a Children's Convalescent Home. Two very useful institutions are the District Nursing Association, founded in 1892, in affiliation with the Queen Victoria Jubilee Institute for Nurses, and the Weston-super-Mare Charity Organisation Society, established in 1894, with the twofold object of relieving cases of real distress, and of discouraging professional begging of every description.

The original Weston Museum was built by public subscription in 1862 in memory of Prince Albert,

[1] Rules of the institution.

and stood at the back of Emmanuel Church. But in 1900 the natural history collections, antiquities, and other curiosities were removed to the new Free Library and Museum building in the Boulevard. One main object of this building was to provide suitable accommodation for the valuable collection of books, many of them relating to Somersetshire, which Mr. F. A. Wood, of Chew Magna, had promised to bequeath to the town. The old Free Library, consisting of about 4000 volumes, was formerly kept in the Pigott Mansion in the Grove Park. The most important features of the museum are a large case containing some of the relics from the pits on Worlebury, chiefly those discovered by Messrs Dymond and Tompkins; a collection of fossils arranged in nine cases; bones from caves at Uphill and Bleadon; a fine collection of foreign and British shells; and a case of about eighty stuffed birds said to have been shot in the neighbourhood. There are also many interesting remains of primitive man—skulls, pottery, &c., which have been found from time to time in or near the town, and a few models of remarkable fish which have been caught off the coast, including those of a Swordfish, and a Fishing-frog or Sea-angler. The South Kensington authorities have lent to the Weston Museum a very interesting collection of works of art, the objects in which will be periodically changed.

Two weekly newspapers are published in the town. The older of the two, the *Weston Mercury*, whose offices are in the Boulevard, was established in 1843, under the name of the *Westonian*, as a monthly periodical of eight pages. It was long a Liberal paper, but since the Home Rule split it has taken the opposite side. The *Weston Gazette*, printed at the Mendip Press in Wadham Street, was founded in 1845. It also appeared monthly, and cost three-pence a copy. Like the *Mercury* it has changed its politics, and is now a staunch supporter of the Liberal Party.

The School of Science and Art, formerly held in rooms at the Church Institute, was in 1894 transferred to new premises in the Lower Church Road. The schools, which are in connection with South Kensington, and are also assisted by the County Council, are well equipped with all necessary apparatus required for the various classes. In 1901 there were 82 art students, 144 science students, and a wood-carving class numbering 18 members.

The Auxiliary Forces are represented at Weston-super-Mare by detachments of volunteer artillery, engineers, infantry, and cavalry. The latter are part of a regiment which has been in existence for more than a century; and the old 13th Foot, now Prince Albert's Somerset Light Infantry, of which the Rifles form part of the 3rd Volunteer Battalion, has distinguished itself on many a hard-won field.

The Weston-super-Mare contingent of the North Somerset Imperial Yeomanry, forms part of the

North Marsh Troop, and numbers about thirty men. Several of the troopers, together with others who then joined the regiment, volunteered for service in South Africa, where they had the distinguished honour of forming part of Lord Roberts's body-guard, and were with him all the time. They saw no fighting, and all returned safe.

Originally enrolled in 1797 under the title of the Selwood Volunteers, the corps was, in the following year, turned into a cavalry regiment; and, in 1814, the year before the battle of Waterloo, it received the name it bore until the date of the South African War, of the North Somerset Yeomanry Cavalry. Like similar corps, its duty was to hold itself ready to defend king and country in case of invasion or in any other emergency. It was first called out in 1810, and marched to Bath, when a disturbance was feared on account of the embodying of the local militia. On various other occasions, the last of which was in 1885, the regiment has been called out in consequence of election troubles. And in 1831, after the suppression of the memorable Bristol Riots, it received high praise from both military and civil authorities for "its valuable and efficient services in preserving the lives and properties of the citizens and in restoring tranquillity."

Before the Boer War the uniform of the North Somerset Yeomanry was blue with white facings, and the head-dress was a helmet and plume. The arms were a sabre and a Martini-Henry carbine, both attached to the saddle, so that a trooper accidentally dismounted was defenceless. Two years ago mounted infantry drill was adopted. The carbine was exchanged for the long Lee-Enfield, which, with its butt resting in a shallow bucket, is attached to the rider by a strap, so that if a man happens to fall, his rifle comes with him. Recruits of 1902 wear khaki, with "slouch" hats. In 1903 the old blue and white uniform and the heavy brass helmet are to be finally given up. More welcome changes are the grant of five pounds a year to each trooper towards the keep of his horse, and the serving out of more ammunition. Before going under canvas, which they do for about a fortnight every year, each man fires 100 rounds at the rifle-range in Sand Bay, belonging to the artillery; and 100 more while in camp. The last camp was at Kingsdown, near Box, where the hilly country is well adapted for scouting work and for outpost duty. The Weston contingent have squad drill one night every week, in a field near the Ashcombe Manor-House, and two mounted drills each year before going under canvas.

The "F" Company of the 1st Devon and Somerset Royal Engineers was founded at Weston in 1869, and is now nearly double its nominal strength, consisting of about 170 men. The uniform is scarlet with dark-blue facings, and almost exactly corresponds to that of the regular Royal Engineers. The volunteers have white cord and silver lacing, while with the army men the cord is yellow, and the lacing is of gold. A considerable number of the men volunteered for South Africa, but only two very small detachments were allowed to join. The first of these saw a good deal of fighting, and some of them were taken prisoners. All, however, returned safely. The second detachment remained on active service until the close of the war.

The first Weston Rifle Corps was, like so many others in the country, established rather more than fifty years ago, at a time when there was much talk of a French invasion. At a large and enthusiastic public meeting held in the Town Hall, on November 3, 1859, under the presidency of Mr R. A. Kinglake, it was proposed by Mr T. T. Knyfton, D.L., that a rifle corps should be formed, and the proposal was seconded by Captain Law. Names were then called for. "Some fifty or sixty people from the body of the hall rushed forward to the platform, amid the cheers of the hundreds present, in order to sign their names as volunteers."[1] Captain Law was elected commanding officer, and the meeting then dispersed, with cheers for the Queen.

The corps which was thus constituted was long called the 6th Somerset Rifle Volunteers, and in 1860 consisted of three officers and seventy men. A year later, the ladies of Weston presented the force with a silver bugle. The corps is now known as "B" Company of the 3rd Volunteer Battalion

[1] *Weston Mercury*.

of Prince Albert's Somerset Light Infantry. The whole battalion, whose headquarters are in Weston-super-Mare, is made up of nine companies, with a total strength of 29 officers, 57 non-commissioned officers, and 818 rank and file. To each of the three chief battalion staff officers, Colonel W. E. Perham, V.D., Lieut.-Colonel C. E. Whitting, V.D., and Lieut.-Colonel A. J. Goodford, V.D., has been awarded, as the letters after their names imply, the Volunteer Decoration for long service with the force.

"B" Company, the strongest of the whole nine, includes 2 officers, 8 non-commissioned officers, and 136 rank and file. The original weapon of 1859 was, of course, the old muzzle-loading Enfield rifle. This was changed for the Snider, the converted Enfield, the first British military breechloader. The Snider gave way to the Martini-Henry, which in its turn has been lately superseded by the Lee-Metford. The range was for many years at Uphill. But a man who was about to fire at the target there having accidentally discharged his rifle, and the bullet having gone over the hill and through the window of a house on the other side of the Sanatorium, the Uphill range was condemned. "B" Company have at present no targets of their own, and are obliged to use those belonging to the artillery volunteers, which are situated in Sand Bay, on the other side of the town. The uniform of the battalion is the original rifle grey, and the only important change has been that the old képi has given place to the military helmet.

For service in South Africa, the battalion furnished a contingent consisting of 1 officer, 2 non-commissioned officers, and 38 rank and file. They saw a good deal of fighting. Thirty-one of them received the medal with three clasps, six gained two clasps, and one had it with a single clasp. Four men died while on service and two more at sea. Out of the whole contingent thirty-three got safely back to England.

In 1860 the 2nd Somerset Artillery Corps was formed at Weston, and a battery for their use was built among the sand-hills. The force had a brief existence. The regimental records, with the exception of a muster roll which still hangs in the officers' room, have been destroyed, and it is difficult to say exactly what happened. But it appears that in 1863 the authorities attempted to call out the artillery volunteers in view of an anticipated riot; that many of the men refused to obey their officers, and that the corps was in consequence disbanded. Their uniforms were for a long time stored in the Town Hall, but became moth-eaten, and were ultimately burnt. The sole remaining relics of this short-lived body are the muster roll already alluded to, and a silver trumpet bearing this inscription:—

VIXI · LIBER · ET · MORIAR

PRESENTED BY THE LADIES OF WESTON-SUPER-MARE AND ITS NEIGHBOURHOOD TO THE 2ND SOMERSET ARTILLERY VOLUNTEERS, DECEMBER 1860.

The Somerset Artillery were succeeded in Weston

by a detachment of the 1st Gloucestershire Royal Garrison Artillery Volunteers, of which there are now in the town two companies, the 11th and 12th. The two Weston companies are armed with four 40-pounder rifled breech-loading guns, which have a calibre of 4.75 inches, with a muzzle-velocity of 1160 feet per second. The practice battery is at Uphill, where there are platforms for two guns, and a magazine for stores and ammunition. From this point there is frequent practice at floating barrel-targets, moored out at sea at ranges varying from 2000 to 3500 yards; and the companies go through an annual training at Fort Staddon, Plymouth. The force also practise with the Martini-Enfield carbine at targets up to 1000 yards, at their range in Sand Bay. The uniform is blue, with scarlet facings, and with a scarlet busby-bag. The badge, in addition to the Royal Arms and Supporters, is a gun, between the mottoes *Ubique* and *Quo fas et gloria ducunt.* All the officers and nearly all the non-commissioned officers and men of the two companies, which are together 150 strong, volunteered for service in South Africa, but garrison artillery were not required. A few of the men, however, went to the front.

The climate of Weston-super-Mare is mild and equable, but very bracing, and its meteorogical statistics compare favourably with those of more noted health resorts. In the following table[1] are given

[1] From Bayard's "English Climatology."

details of temperature and rainfall at ten well-known places, during a period of ten years :—

	Tempera-ture at 9 A.M.	Average Mini-mum.	Average Maxi-mum.	Average Tempera-ture.	Inches of Rain.	Days on which Rain Fell.
	Degs.	Degs.	Degs.	Degs.		
Scarborough . .	48	42	52	47	27.5	197
Buxton . . .	45	38	52	45	49.3	196
Cheltenham . .	48	40	55	48	27.5	190
London . . .	49	42	56	49	26.2	165
Brighton . .	51	44	56	50	28.7	159
Ventnor . . .	51	45	56	51	28.1	164
Llandudno . .	50	44	54	49	28.1	176
Babbacombe . .	51	44	56	50	33.9	189
Falmouth . .	50	46	55	51	43.5	204
Weston-super-Mare	50	44	55	50	28.9	178

The number of hours of bright sunshine recorded in Weston during the year 1901 was 1631¼.

The death-rate of the town is remarkably low, a point which is all the more significant when it is remembered that not only do many people come there in search of health, but that not a few invalids come to the place as to a haven in which to end their days. A few figures are here given for the sake of comparison.

Death-rate in—

Dublin . . .	27.5	London . . .	18.8
Manchester . .	24.1	Brighton . .	17
Birmingham . .	21.5	Weston-super-Mare	13.99

In addition to the two large public parks, the Grove, eight acres in extent, purchased from the Lord of the Manor by the Urban District Council, and Clarence Park, measuring sixteen acres, presented to the town in 1883 by Mrs. Finden Davies, in memory of her husband, there are in Weston several small enclosures of a somewhat similar character. Ellenborough Park, on the Walliscote Road, and Eastfield Park, on the Bristol Road, are reserved for the use of residents in their immediate neighbourhood; while the Prince Consort Gardens, three acres in extent, not far from the pier, and now the property of the town, are open to the public. The Recreation Grounds, near the railway station, opened by a private company in 1885, cover fifteen acres, and include a cycling track, spaces for cricket and football, and grand stands for spectators. The Golf Links, which are really in Uphill parish, are close to the shore, beyond the Sanatorium.

The mild and equable, and yet invigorating climate, which has made Weston so popular as a health resort, has led to the establishment of so many schools that these are now a characteristic feature of the town. Three of the oldest establishments, though not one of them occupies the building in which it was first started, are the schools now known as the College, Southside House, and Brynmelyn. Weston College was originally built by Mr. Jonathan Elwell in 1859, and the school was for many years carried on in the house afterwards bought by the proprietors of the Grand Atlantic Hotel. Southside House is the descendant of the

Girls' School, so long and ably conducted by the Misses Ravis and Smith. Brynmelyn is the lineal successor of the Friends' School for Boys, established in the 'fifties by the late Till Adam Smith, at 2 Victoria Villas, removed by him to 1 Atlantic Terrace—premises now occupied by St. Peter's School —and continued after his death by the brothers Sharp. When the Sharps' school was given up in 1881, a Friends' school was re-established at Brynmelyn.

It was on the lawn in front of this school that, on the day after the great storm of March 16, 1887, the boys made a colossal Snow Statue of Queen Victoria. A photograph of the statue, together with the following brief address, was sent to Her Majesty :—

"O Gracious Lady, if our feeble skill
In sculptor's art have caught the likeness ill,
Our glad young hearts with loyal wishes glow,
Who framed its outline in the yielding snow.
Nor know we truer type than this alone,
Of that pure life that pulses round thy throne.
And if this figure vanish in the sun,
Ere windy March his blustering course has run,
Our hearts, more true, thine image still shall hold,
When youth is past, when manhood's fire is cold;
Shall keep thy memory free, until the last,
From mists that gather round a fading past.
And loyal sons in coming years shall tell
Of that Good Queen their fathers loved so well.

"THE BOYS OF BRYNMELYN."

A few days later the young artists received this reply :—

"WINDSOR CASTLE,

"*March* 26, 1887.

"Sir Henry Ponsonby has had much pleasure in laying before the Queen the Photograph of the Snow Statue, which has been forwarded to Her Majesty by the Boys of Brynmelyn.

"Her Majesty was much pleased with it, and with the loyal expressions contained in their address to the Queen."

In the "New Guide" of 1822 is an allusion to "A school-room for a hundred children, with a house annexed for the master and mistress," which had been recently built at the sole expense of the Rev. Stiverd Jenkins, the officiating minister of the parish church. This was succeeded in 1846 by the National School, erected chiefly at the expense of that benefactor to the town, the Ven. Archdeacon Law. Accommodation was provided for 160 boys and 160 girls, but the actual numbers even in 1872 were only 110 boys and 100 girls. In the following year, however, the state of the school improved, and the attendance averaged 205 boys and 224 girls.

In 1894 the boys' department was transferred to the School Board, and three years later moved into new premises, the Central Board School for Boys. At this moment there are 382 boys on the register. The Central Board School for Girls, with accommodation for 184 scholars, was founded in 1897.

There are 119 girls now on the roll. The Central School for Infants, originally founded in 1862, was taken over from Emmanuel Church in 1894 with the National School, and housed in its new buildings in 1898. At the present time there are in it 63 infants.

The British School was founded in 1851, but no regular records appear to have been kept for the first twenty years of its existence. The Government inspector reported in 1866 that the school was at a very low ebb. The attendance then was between 50 and 60. There was some improvement in the five years that followed, and in 1871 the average attendance was 147. In 1874, however, the numbers had again fallen, and the managers were seriously thinking of closing the school. That, however, was the last of the lean years. From that time to the present the career of the school has been one of almost unvarying prosperity. In 1885 the buildings were greatly enlarged, and the average attendance during the past ten years has been about 300, including 65 to 70 infants.

A conspicuous object from Weston sands is the tall iron beacon, erected in 1885 to mark the shore end of a submarine telegraph which in that year was laid down by the cable-ship *Faraday* between Weston-super-Mare and Waterville, which is on Ballinskelligs Bay, at the south-west corner of the County Kerry. This cable has two cores, worked independently, on the duplex system; that is to say, two messages can be sent through each core in opposite directions at the same time. It has occasionally been interrupted from various causes—once from the piercing by teredos of the gutta-percha sheathing of the cores. To guard against similar mishaps the core of the second cable, laid between Weston and Waterville in 1901 by the ship *Silvertown*, is covered throughout its entire length with brass tape.

From their station on Ballinskelligs Bay the Commercial Company have four submarine cables to Canso, in Nova Scotia, three of them direct, and one going round by the Azores. From Canso there are two submarine lines to New York, and one to Rockport, Massachusetts. A German cable to New York, also by way of the Azores, is worked in connection with the company's lines. Another cable unites Waterville with Havre, on the north coast of France.

From the Weston office there are two land-lines to London, and also what is called an "Omnibus" line, taking in Bristol, Liverpool, Edinburgh, Glasgow, Dundee, &c. The object of laying cables to Ireland from Weston, instead of from some point farther west, was to make the land-lines as short as possible, and thus to reduce the chances of interruption by breakage, through snow or heavy winds. More than once, during rough weather, the Weston route has been the only one open between London and New York. The instruments in Richmond

Street, which are all automatic in their action, were until lately worked by two-fluid bichromate of potash batteries. But these have been replaced by the much cleaner and more satisfactory system of accumulators charged from the newly laid electric light mains.

On the 21st of May 1901, just sixty years after the first gas lamps were lit in Weston, the Weston-super-Mare and District Electric Supply Company began its first public supply of Electric Light. There had, however, been a previous attempt in the same direction. Some years ago there was a temporary installation, but for some reason it was of short duration. The plant employed by the existing company, at their works on the Locking Road, consists of Brush multiplex continuous-current dynamos, with Hart accumulators, driven by Raworth universal engines. The current is distributed by means of underground cables. The charge to consumers is on the Maximum Demand system ; and for the first 100 hours per quarter, whether for lighting, or for heating, or for power, is at the rate of 7d. per unit of maximum demand. A Board of Trade unit is the quantity of electricity sufficient to supply thirty-three ten-candle power lamps for one hour. The average price to the consumer is officially stated at from 4½d. to 5d. per unit for light, and 3½d. for power.

The recently started Tramway, which is worked on the overhead trolley system, is promoted by the same company, who provide the power from the buildings from which they supply the light. In the same way they provide electricity for the Commercial Cable Company, who were formerly dependent on batteries for their current.

The most important of recent improvements in Weston are the Board School premises in the Walliscote Road, and the Infant School in the Locking Road, opened in 1900; the new Post-Office on the site of Verandah House, so long a conspicuous object from High Street and the Sea Front, finished in 1899; the new Market House in High Street, opened in 1900, on the site of the original building which was erected in 1827; the Pavilion and other new buildings on Knightstone, which is now the property of the town; the installation of the Electric Light in 1901; and the starting of Electric Trams by the same company on the 5th of May in the following year.

When Rutter wrote his "Delineations of Somerset," in 1829, Weston-super-Mare contained only a single church, and he makes no mention of any dissenting place of worship. The "New Guide" of seven years before, however, alludes to a Methodist Chapel "in the village, open every Sunday and Wednesday evening at six o'clock." The Independent Chapel in High Street, which has since been converted into a shop, was built in 1830, but no other church or chapel seems to have been built until some years after the opening of the railway. The town is now divided into four parishes, with four principal and three subsidiary churches, and there are chapels or other places of worship belonging to most of the chief religious denominations.

Old Parish Church of Weston-super-Mare, 1823.

The Parish Church of Weston, dedicated to St. John the Baptist, was, with the exception of the chancel, entirely rebuilt in 1824, chiefly at the expense of John Hugh Smyth Pigott and of his brother, the Rector, the Rev. Wadham Pigott, who was then the Lord of the Manor. In 1837, the chancel was rebuilt by the Rector, the Ven. Archdeacon Law, and it was in the same year that Bishop Law presented the great east window. In 1844, the north aisle was built, and four additional stained glass windows were put up by Archdeacon Law, who was then Rector for the second time. The latest alterations in the structure of the building were carried out in 1890 by the late Rector, the Rev. Arthur Salmon, who built the new south aisle.

The date of the original foundation is unknown, but in the Registers of the Dean and Chapter of Wells, it is recorded that in 1221 the Advowson of the Church of Weston was granted to Bishop Jocelin. Another entry, in 1234, records an ordinance of this bishop that, out of the revenue of the Church of Weston prope Worle, one hundred pounds of wax should be paid annually to the treasurer of Wells Church—viz., fifty pounds at the Passion of St. Andrew and fifty pounds at the Translation of the same saint, the wax to be burnt close to the altar of the glorious Virgin at all houses in which the divine office is celebrated by day and by night.

In 1256, the Church of Weston was appropriated to the Convent of Bath, and there is a later record showing that the Abbey confirmed the grant of appropriation.

In 1246, the payment of a hundred pounds of wax was included among the assets of the Church of Wells in the list of church property made out by Bishop Roger, Jocelin's successor. This hundred pounds of wax was no slight burden. One hive would yield about a pound of wax, so that it would need a hundred hives to produce the full amount, which would mean the taking of perhaps a ton of honey. Entries in the Wells Records show that the payments were not kept up without pressure. In 1277, the Rector of Weston, Guy de Schevingdon, was sued before the official of the bishop by the treasurer for arrears of wax, and was ordered to pay up thirty pounds before the Feast of St. Gregory, thirty pounds in Lent, and forty pounds before the Translation of St. Andrew; and he was further directed to continue the half-yearly payments of fifty pounds on the appointed days. A later entry shows that the difficulty of collecting the tax lasted at least into the next century. In 1349, John the Rector was sued by the treasurer for arrears, and ordered, on threat of sequestration, to pay up fifty pounds of wax within fifteen days. The Dean of Axbridge, the Rector of Uphill, and the Vicars of Kewstoke and Worle were appointed a commission to carry out the order.

Little or nothing further is known of the history of the Parish Church. State papers of the reign of Queen Elizabeth record that in 1586 the Rector of Weston-super-Mare contributed £3, 2s. 6d. towards the expenses of the preparations that even then were being made in Somerset to resist the expected descent on British shores of the Spanish Armada.[1]

The present Rectory was built by the Rev. Arthur Salmon in place of the old residence near the church. The old house is marked on the map

[1] Green, "Somerset and the Armada."

of Weston in 1806, but we learn from the "New Guide" that in 1822 the officiating minister of the parish lived at Locking.

There is slight but clear evidence that the original Parish Church of Weston was Norman. When the chancel, which had been left untouched in 1824 when all the rest of the edifice was pulled down, was rebuilt in 1837, there was found beneath it part of a very small Norman window. This significant fragment, which is now in the Weston Museum, is ornamented with two rows of rather shallow carving, the inner row showing tooth-pattern, and the outer row zigzag. The font, too, though it has been re-worked, is probably Norman. "It was," says Rutter, "for a long time neglected, and suffered to lie exposed in the contiguous paddock. But," he continues, "the present Rector (the Rev. Francis Blackburne) has had it cleaned and restored to its proper place in the church."

The church, which was destroyed in 1824, had been much altered, if not entirely rebuilt, in Perpendicular times. Some idea of what the edifice was like in 1823, may be gathered from old prints, though we must not place too great reliance upon the draughtsman's rendering of architectural details. Pictures taken shortly before 1823 usually show three similar three-light, square-headed windows in the south side of the building, and a fourth window of two lights to the west of the porch. The former appeared to be late Tudor, or Perpendicular of a debased character. It has been suggested that the window west of the porch dates from the fourteenth century; but there is extant an earlier drawing by Mr. George Bennett, of Rolstone, dated September 12, 1804, which shows several points of difference. There was then no clock. The tower-head had six pinnacles instead of four. The tracery of the tower-windows is not the same; and in the place where the two-light window appears in drawings of some years later, there is a very tall and narrow lancet-shaped window, of the simplest character, without tracery or ornament, and filled with small diamond-shaped, leaded panes. In another drawing two similar windows are shown in the north side of the building. Mr. Bennett visited the church again on the 6th of June 1823, and he specially mentions among various changes, that the building was now "lighted by a tawdry mock-Gothic window on the south side." He adds that the old church was taken down in February 1824, and the foundation-stone of the new one was laid on the 2nd of March immediately following.[1]

[1] Mr. George Bennett, of Rolstone, near Banwell, was a gentleman of keen antiquarian tastes, whose researches are several times alluded to by Rutter. In two books of manuscript, which his granddaughter, Miss Say, has most kindly allowed the writer to examine, he collected many most interesting notes, chiefly on antiquities, relating principally to Banwell and its neighbourhood, but extending to a number of other towns and villages in Somerset. The notes begin in 1804, and continue until near the time of their writer's death in 1834. Many very curious and interesting things have since then been lost sight of, of which there is apparently no other record than Mr. Bennett's notes.

Parts of some of the old windows can still be seen. One is in the sunk fence near the vestry. Others are built into the walls of houses in the narrow street at the south end of Oriel Terrace. And over the door leading from the old Rectory garden into the churchyard are two finely carved heads, which no doubt came out of the old church; one of a queen and one of a monk. Two of the old corbels may be seen in Worle, built into the posts of a gate by the roadside.

The chief feature of the interior of the church is the noble east window, the gift of Bishop Law, containing glass of various periods, some of it very ancient. At the foot of the window is a double row of scenes from Scripture history, six of them taken from the life of Christ and four from the life of David. The coloured glass used in these pictures is of remarkable beauty, and to judge from the treatment of the subjects it may be as old as the thirteenth century. In the scene where David is rescuing a lamb, the lion is spotted like a leopard, after the manner common to the heraldry of the Plantagenet period. Again, in David's duel with Goliath, the Philistine champion is clad in chain-armour, and his shield and helmet are such as were used by Norman knights not later than the thirteenth century. On the Great Seal of Henry I. is a similar helmet; and in a thirteenth-century drawing of the murder of Thomas à Becket, reproduced in Hewitt's "Ancient Armour," two of the knights carry shields like that of Goliath in this window.

The only ancient monument in the church is a slab in the chancel floor, bearing a nearly obliterated figure and a deeply cut cross, with a book on one side of it and an hour-glass on the other. Among modern memorials of the dead is the last work of Chantrey, a beautiful bas-relief representing the head of Lady Smyth of Ashton Court. And not far from it is a fine marble figure by Weeks, the great sculptor's favourite pupil. On the chancel wall is a marble tablet in memory of Colonel Rogers, who, in 1819, lost his life in consequence of his brave but vain attempt to rescue the two sons of Sir Charles Elton, of Clevedon Court, who, having been cut off by the rising tide, were drowned in trying to wade across from Birnbeck. On a slab near the reading-desk is a quaint epitaph in memory of Edgar Willan, son of a former Rector of the parish :—

"Of two brothers born together,
Cruel Death was so unkind
As to bring the eldest hither,
And the younger leave behind.
May George live long,
Edgar dy'd young,
For born he was
To Master Sam. Willan, Rectour
Of this place, of Jane his wife,
Sepr. 5, 1680, and buryed Feb.
the eleventh, 1686. The 9th
did put an end to all his pain,
And sent him into everlasting gain."

It was this "Master Sam. Willan" who had such trouble about collecting his tithes. In "Persecution Expos'd," published in 1715, relating the sufferings of Quakers in the West of England, is this passage :—

> "Edmund Chappel of Worle (imprison'd before by Sam Willan, Priest of Weston and Kewstoke; but after several years imprisonment discharg'd on a misnomer of Edward for Edmund :) yet the said Priest being never weary of persecution, imprison'd him again on the old account for Tythes the 7th of the 12th month 1683. Telling the said Edmund once in discourse about Tythes, when he could not answer the said Edmund that he would answer him with a gaol. Which now he did."

The old parish Lock-up, possibly the one in which the unfortunate man was imprisoned for "several years," stood, until 1853, on part of the ground now occupied by Weston Lodge, near the beginning of the Bristol Road.

Old books describing the Parish Church refer to the Pigott Manorial Pew. This pew, originally brought from Brockley, was removed from the church in 1880, and placed in the Grove, then the residence of the Lord of the Manor.

One of the oldest possessions of the church is the silver communion chalice, which bears on its cover the date 1573. The date is significant. In the previous year the Dean and Chapter of Wells decreed, "That the plate that beforetime were used to superstition, shalbe defaced, and of the greatest challaice shalbe made a fayer Communion cuppe with as much convenient speed as may be before the ffeaste of Easter, and of the lesser challaice another by the tyme before limited." The mandate was very generally obeyed. In some cases it had been anticipated. And it is rare to find a Somersetshire chalice of a date much earlier than the one preserved in Weston Parish Church.

The second of the six bells that hang in the tower is very old, as may be gathered from its inscription, the single word MARIA, in antique lettering. The rest of the bells are modern. The following are the devices on the whole peal :—

1. IEFFERIES & PRICE. BRISTOL 1842.
2. Maria.
3. } The same as 1.
4. }
5. MAY . THE . CHURCH . OF . ENGLAND . FLOURISH AND . ITS . ENEMIES . DECREASE. RECAST BY W. IEFFERIES 1831.
6. The same as 1, 3, and 4.[1]

Built into the north wall of the chancel is an ancient and remarkable piece of sculpture, formerly in the south porch of the church that was rebuilt in 1824. It represents four principal figures. One, seated in the centre, bears on his knees a human body, and to right and left are two battered, headless effigies. These figures may represent the Father, supporting the body of the crucified Saviour,

[1] Ellacombe, "Church Bells of Somerset."

with St. John and the Virgin standing by. Two small figures higher up in the composition may be intended for angels. Somewhat similar groups, now built into the porches of Ubley and of Bleadon, are usually regarded as the heads of ancient crosses, remains of which, in each case, stand near the church. And this stone may once have formed the top of the cross which stands in Weston churchyard, near the south porch. This cross was considered by Dr. Pooley to be thirteenth-century work, and therefore probably contemporary with the church of Bishop Jocelin's time. The base of it is gone, but the socket remains, and the broken shaft, still about five feet high. In a field near where Ellenborough Crescent now stands, there was formerly another cross, the "White Cross," which gave its name to the estate. The base of it only was still to be seen in Rutter's time, but even this has now disappeared. It was probably named in honour of Saint Whyte, Sancta Candida, an early Roman martyr, who, it is believed, has given her name to White Stanton, Whitchurch, and White Lackington.

The Parish Records of Weston are brief, and are not of great antiquity. The first date in the old Registers is 1668, but it is clear that the book is only a copy of some more ancient volume. The work has, moreover, been carelessly done, and there are whole years for which there is no record whatever. The first entry, dated February 4,

1668, refers to the Rev. Samuel Willan; and it is remarkable that for the twelve years following there is only a single entry besides those connected with the family of that gentleman, who was Rector of Weston from 1667 to his death in 1689. Few notes of interest occur in the Registers. As in the other sea-board parishes, the authorities were sometimes called upon to dispose of bodies which the tide had left upon the shore. Among the burials is this entry:—

"1796, August 18th. A sailor unknown, washed up by the sea."

The custom of the time was that unclaimed bodies found thus upon the shore should be buried in the sand, just above high-water mark. A few years later it was enacted by Parliament (48 Geo. III., c. 75) that:—

"Where dead bodies are cast on shore from the seas, the churchwardens or overseers of the Parish, or in extra parochial places, the constable or head-borough, are to remove the bodies to some convenient place, and there cause them to be buried in the churchyard. . . . Their expenses in so doing are to be repaid by the treasurer of the county. . . . The minister, parish clerk, and sexton are to perform their respective duties at this as at other funerals, receiving such fees as are paid to them for funerals made at the expense of the Parish."[1]

The oldest book of parish accounts is that of the Overseers, begun in 1685. The first entry records

[1] Phillimore's "Ecclesiastical Law."

the levying of a rate "after ye proportion of 16d ye pound for ye relief of ye Poor." Five years later, a rate was levied "after ye proportion of 1s. 6d. ye pound for ye relief of ye poor maimed Souldiers Hospital and other necessarys." All the parishes in the district contributed to the support of this hospital which, as is shown by an entry in the Kewstoke accounts, was at Woodspring, probably in the Priory. Many of the entries relate, as we should expect, to the relief of the poor. Members of the family of Backwell seem frequently to have appealed to the parish for help. On one occasion we read :—

Sent Joan Backwell by Will Lucky, Nov. ye 6th, when her arme was broke . . . 000 05 00

Presented Mr. Leman a peck of samphire for setting Joan Backwell's arme . . . 000 01 06

Samphire is no longer used for pickle, as was the case a century ago; and it is probable that no Weston surgeon of our time would consider a peck of it a sufficient fee for the setting of a broken arm. In Joan Backwell's days it was to be found on Birnbeck, and it still grows freely, unpicked and unregarded, on Brean Down and Sand Point.

In 1722 is an allusion to relief of another kind :—

Item pd. for 2 yeards of sarge and one ell of collord linning for Elizabeth Backwell to bodie her gown 00 04 06

Item pd. for one ell of shagg to macke Elizth. Backwell a mantel 00 01 04

A member of the family died in 1731, and the entire expenses, not only of her funeral, but of the accompanying feast, were borne by the parish :—

Pd. for a shroude for Mary Backwell .	00 08 08
Pd. for a coffing	00 09 00
Pd. Robert Loude for a quarter barrel of syder	00 07 00
Pd. Thomas May for bread . . .	00 02 00
Pd. for 14 pound of cheese . . .	00 03 02½
Pd. for a quartern of tobaca and too peniworth of pipes	00 00 06
Pd. for ringing the bell and diging the grave	00 03 00

There has lately been presented to the Free Library by J. P. Capell, Esq., an old volume of Weston Parish Records, containing the Churchwardens' Accounts from 1694 to 1819, and the Church Rates for nearly the same period. The entries in this ancient book are most interesting, and throw not a little light on the condition of Weston and its surroundings in days when it was the most insignificant of fishing villages.

Among interesting local allusions are the references to payments made by Weston, in common with all the villages of the district, towards the maintenance of a hospital at Woodspring for wounded soldiers, which has been already alluded to. No records have yet been found which actually connect this hospital with the Priory, but it is at least probable that the old monastic buildings were thus made use of. That there was a hospital at Woodspring within seventy years after the canons were dispossessed is clear from an entry in the Puxton Parish Records:—

1604. Spent at severall times when I carried in the Hospitall money . . . 00 01 00

No records have been found of such payments later than 1734, so that we may perhaps conclude that the Woodspring Hospital was discontinued after that year. There are two such entries in the Weston accounts under the year 1694:—

Paid ye first payment of ye Hospital . 00 03 10
Paid ye second payment of ye Hospital . 00 03 10

In a statute of Queen Elizabeth (viii. cap. 15), entitled "An Act for the Preservation of Grayne," various kinds of "noysome fowls and vermin" are mentioned, and rewards are offered for their destruction:—

"Old Crowes, Chawghes, Pyes or Rookes to be paid for at the rate of three a penny, evrie syxe young crowes a penny, everie syxe Eggs unbroken a penny; everie twelve stares heades a penny; every heade of Martyn, Hawkes, Fursekytte, Moldkytte, Busarde, Schage, Carmerant or Ringtayle two pence; everie Iron or Osprayes head fower pence. For the heade of everie Byrde which is called the Kyngs Fyssher one penny. For the heade of everie Fox or Gray twelve pence; and for the heade of everie Fitchewe, Pole Catte, Wesell, Stote, Fayre, Bade, or Wilde-catte one penny: For the heade of everie Otter or hedge-hogge two pence: For the heades of everie three Rattes or twelve Myse one penny: for the heades of everie Moldwarp or Wante one halfpenny."

The "vermin" for whose destruction rewards were most frequently paid in this district were hedgehogs, polecats, foxes, and "grays," that is to say, badgers. The otter, too, was often killed on the moorland streams. In the Weston record occur such items as these:—

Item paid John More and William Masy for to poulcats heds	00 00 08
Paid William Masy for a poule cat . .	00 00 04
It. Paid for cilling one hedggodg . .	00 00 04
It. Paid for killing one foxk . . .	00 01 00
Pd. Thomas Oakly for killing a gray . .	00 01 00

In the year 1728 sixty-four hedgehogs were killed, presumably within the parish bounds, and were paid for by the churchwardens at the rate of fourpence apiece. In 1745 Mr. John Pigott, the principal landowner, protested against certain items in the accounts. One of his remarks runs: "I know no law for ye allowance of 2 pence for Hedgehog and as they seem by this allowance rather to increase I don't consent any longer to this custom of payment."

Many entries refer to the relief of tramps, especially of those pretending to be sailors—turnpike sailors, as they were called. The Weston accounts, like those of all parishes in the district, contain many such notes as these:—

Gave to poore wemen which was undun by fire	00 01 00
Gave a pore wooman that was tacken by the french	00 00 06
Gave a poore man which Beged for his father in Turkey	00 02 00
Gave severall poore seamen	00 00 06
Gave a poore man which was wounded .	00 00 06

The most numerous entries are those relating to the repair and maintenance of the church :—

Pd. Robert Liveridg for six load of stones .	00 06 00
Pd. Robert Liveridg for haling of 3 load of morter	00 02 06
Pd. James Haiden for mending ye bells and ironwork	00 08 00
Gave to ye bel carpenters to drink . .	00 01 00
Paid for glaseing the church windous .	00 03 00
Item for to sacks of lime to whitelime the church	00 02 04
It. Paid for cleaning the Church when he was whit limed	00 01 00
For waishing the serples at Whitsentide and cleaning the flagon and boule	00 02 06
Paid for to Silke tossels for the pulpit coochin	00 05 06
Pd. Nicholas Ricketts for going to Banwell to by a tree of oacke to mend ye church .	00 10 00

How many readers of history remember the attempt which the Old Pretender made in 1708 to invade England? How he put to sea from Dunkirk with 5000 men, and how his fleet was scattered by Admiral Byng—the same man that was afterwards tried by court-martial, and shot on the quarter-deck of his own ship for failing to relieve Minorca? Yet here, in this old book, we have the entry, picturesque, if slightly ungrammatical :—

> 1708. Item for a boock of thans that ye pretenders not landing in Scotland . . 00 00 06

In 1701 is this curious note :—

> Gave too ye paritor for a paper too pray for the qune . . . . co 01 00

What Queen? Queen Mary, the wife of William III., had been dead some years, and Queen Anne had not yet ascended the throne. Another entry in the accounts is :—

> For a boock of prayer for the unian beetween the Scots and the Englinsh . . . 00 00 06

In 1713 the Weston bells were rung to celebrate the signing of the Treaty of Utrecht, after the great victories of the Duke of Marlborough :—

> Gave ye ringers ye day of proclimation of peace 00 05 00

And when Queen Anne died, in 1714, the village was prompt to welcome to the English throne the first of the four Georges :—

> Paid for a Book of prayers ye fust of August 00 01 00

In the chapter on the Mendip Country has been briefly traced the history of the terrible pestilence called the Black Death, which in 1348 and 1349 is believed to have carried off half the population of England. The list of institutions to the Rectory of Weston-super-Mare, preserved in the Bishop's Registers at Wells, shows that, in all probability, two of the incumbents fell victims to the plague:—

1341. Rog. de Pykeslegh.
1348. Joh. Powey.
1349. Joh. de Otterhampton.[1]

Emmanuel Church in Oxford Street, whose fine square tower, 112 feet high, is one of the landmarks of the town, was built in 1847, on a site given for the purpose by Mr. Richard Parsley, already alluded to as one of the chief promoters of early improvements of Weston. There are several memorial windows in the church. One in the north aisle was put up in 1887 to commemorate the Jubilee of Queen Victoria. The present organ, first used in 1873, took the place of one said to have originally belonged to King George III., and which had once stood in the parish church.

Christ Church in Montpelier, whose spire is so prominent an object on approaching Weston from the Bristol side, and can also be plainly seen from places ten miles to the eastward, was built in 1855.

Another spire is that of Trinity Church, built in 1861, and dividing the two wings of Atlantic Terrace. Among the numerous memorial windows

[1] The Rev. F. W. Weaver, "Somerset Incumbents."

in Trinity is one in the north aisle filled with fragments of stained glass of the fourteenth, fifteenth, and sixteenth centuries. Each of these three churches contains only a single bell.

St. Saviour's Church in the Locking Road, still far from being finished, and St. Paul's Church in the Walliscote Road, belong to Emmanuel parish. All Saints' Church, between the Bristol Road and the Queen's Road, recently rebuilt of stone, and consecrated in 1902, is connected with the Parish Church of St. John. Of places of worship belonging to other denominations two were built in 1846—the Wesleyan Chapel in Regent Street, and the Friends' Meeting-House in Oxford Street. The site for the latter was presented by Mr. Richard Parsley, who, as already observed, gave the ground on which Emmanuel Church was built. No other chapel is yet fifty years old. The burial-grounds attached to several of the Weston churches and chapels are now all closed, and interments are permitted only in the cemetery in the Bristol Road, to the east of the town. Here, in 1856, were built two mortuary chapels, one for services of the Church of England, and one for the use of dissenters.

The most interesting feature of Weston-super-Mare, at least to the archæologist, is the ancient British stronghold, the grey lines of whose ruined ramparts show plainly through the trees that crown the western end of Worlebury. The defences of the camp, which enclose a space rather more than five hundred yards long, and, except in the centre where it is wider, not quite a hundred yards broad, and measuring ten acres and a quarter, are now ruinous, and are mere heaps of loose stones. But it has been shown, by clearing away some of the rubbish, that these fortifications were originally walls, faced with dry masonry, none of which has been dressed, or shows any sort of tool-mark; that they were in most places about six feet thick at the top, and that they varied in height from five to fifteen feet. The stones are small. "The largest are about eighteen inches in diameter, and as much as a man can well lift; while vast numbers are not more than two or three inches across. Perhaps the average size may be about five inches."[1] The outer wall was strengthened by a buttress, from four to eight feet thick, reaching to within five feet from the top, and running the entire length of the works. In some places there were three such buttresses, greatly increasing the thickness of the wall, and having the effect of a series of terraces.

Except for a short distance towards the eastern and western ends, the northern side of the camp, which is much steeper than the others, was undefended, except by outworks at the foot of the cliffs. From the eastern extremity of the cliffs ran a massive wall of unmortared masonry, curving round to the south, and continued along the southern and western sides, meeting the cliffs again at the seaward end of the camp, with gaps for two entrances; the main one, thirteen feet wide, at the south-east angle of the

[1] C. W. Dymond, F.S.A., "Worlebury."

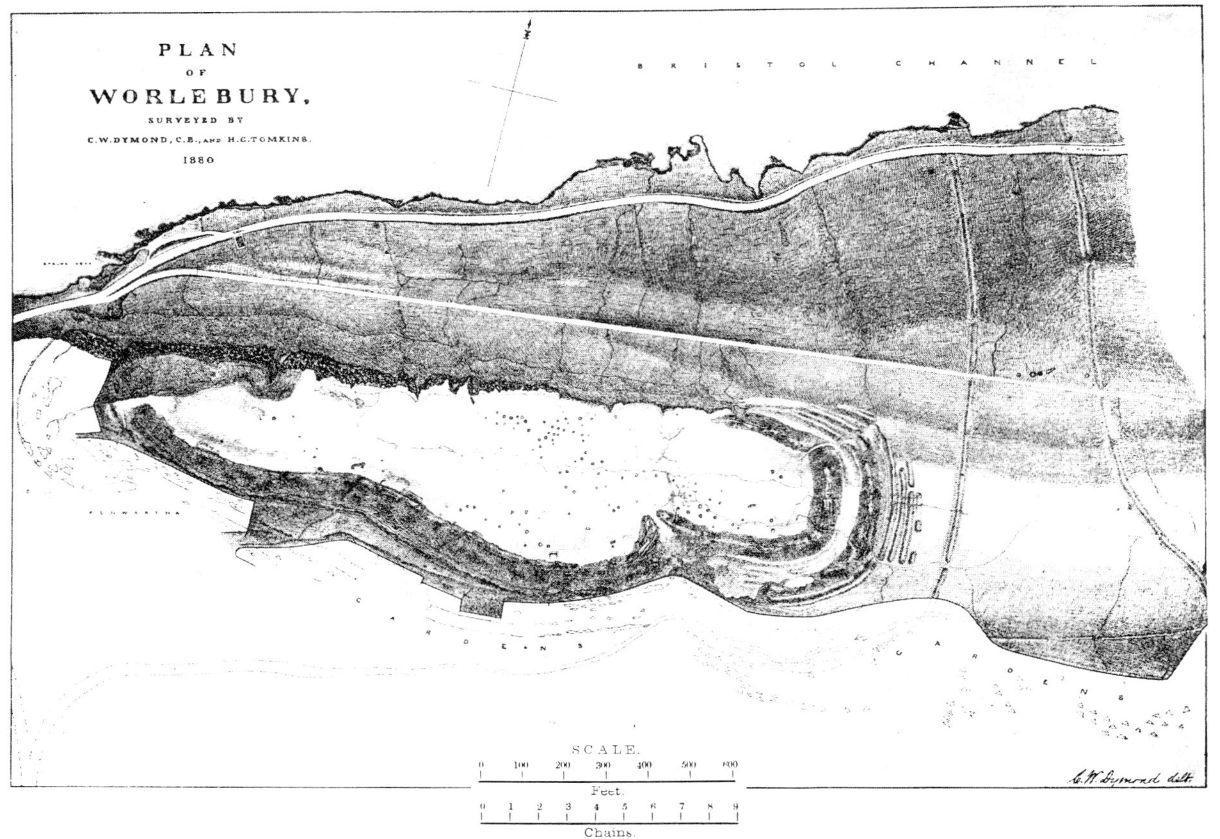
PLAN
OF
WORLEBURY,
SURVEYED BY
C. W. DYMOND, C.E., AND H. C. TOMKINS.
1880
BRISTOL CHANNEL
PENWARTHA
GARDENS
GARDENS
SCALE.
0 100 200 300 400 500 600
Feet.
0 1 2 3 4 5 6 7 8 9
Chains.
C. W. Dymond delt.

fortifications, where the walls curve inward, and another at the western end. There was a third entrance, eleven feet wide, close to the cliffs. This and the main gateway were practicable for chariots. At the eastern end of the camp, which was the one most exposed to attack, is a second great wall, fifty feet or more from the first, with a ditch in the intervening space, deeply cut at the extremities, but disappearing at the top of the hill, and ending at the main entrance at the south-east. From the northern end of this wall a ditch with a low breastwork ran to the edge of the cliff; and from the other extremity of it a ditch was carried along the whole southern side of the encampment. In addition to this ditch and breastwork there were two more earthworks at the north-eastern corner; and at the eastern end there were three, making at that point four in all. One of these was continued for a short distance towards the south. On the southern and western sides there were also a number of outworks, consisting partly of ditches and partly also of triangular patches of loose stones, the use of which is not known, but which have been called "slingers' platforms." In Rutter's time, in the early years of last century, many more works, which have now almost or altogether disappeared, could still be traced. That writer says:—

"The ground to the west, at the brow of the hill, above Devonshire Cottage (now Cairo Lodge), is covered with evident vestiges of extensive earthworks, one of which is a somewhat irregular figure, approaching to the form of a parallelogram, from which there was a broad and gradual descent to the beach. Another embanked enclosure, though small, is in the form of an amphitheatre, and at the western extremity, beyond Claremont, is a tumulus, surrounded by a low ditch, curiously excavated from the sides of the shallow channel in which it is excavated."

About thirty yards beyond the most easterly defences of the camp was a stone rampart which went straight down the slope of the hill to the brink of the cliffs above the sea. At a varying distance of from eighty to a hundred yards farther still to the east was another wall, connected with the former by a third rampart at right angles to both, thus making an enclosure which it has been suggested was a cattle-pen, though, as the author of "Worlebury" points out, it is in the position most open to attack. In addition to the three entrances already alluded to, five passages appear to have led up the cliffs on the north side, one of which was an actual tunnel through the rock, but is now blocked up with rubbish. The pathways across the ramparts and a flight of rude stone steps near the middle of the south side are modern. An ancient road, part of which can still be traced in the gardens of Petra Villa and the adjoining houses, passed close to the south-eastern entrance. There was no spring within the camp, and the occupiers of it probably got their water-supply from Spring Cove, at the foot of the cliffs not far from the pier, the site of which was destroyed by a landslip in 1861. At intervals along the inner side of the south wall of the camp are some long patches of stones, now mostly overgrown and concealed. Three which are still visible are twelve to fifteen feet wide and about fifty feet long. These may have been the sites of sentry-stations, or platforms for the piling-up of stones for slinging. But their real use can only be a matter for conjecture.[1]

Inside the camp, chiefly in the centre and towards the eastern end of it, are nearly a hundred shallow pits, which are often spoken of as pit dwellings. They are, however, too small for actual habitation, being seldom more than six feet in diameter, and it seems more likely that they served as places of store for huts which were built over them. These pits, which have been hollowed out of the rock in places where it was loose and easily removed, vary both in size and shape. The largest, which is six feet deep, is triangular, its sides measuring ten feet, nine feet, and six feet; but most are roughly square, and are about six feet across and five feet deep. The sides of one pit, which is rather more than thirty yards north-west of the main entrance, are faced with dry masonry. It may be observed that the only stone-work in the camp in which mortar has been used is a fragment of ivy-covered ruin at the south-east corner, which is probably not really ancient. In one place, to the left of the main entrance of the

[1] C. W. Dymond, F.S.A., "Worlebury."

camp, are three pits so close together that they may well have been covered by a single roof. Several writers have alluded to circular earthen mounds round these pits, which they regarded as the foundations of huts. These mounds, however, the author of "Worlebury Camp" quite failed to trace; nor can any vestige now be found of a circle in the centre of the encampment, mentioned by Rutter, Mr. Warre, and others. Close to the inner side of the southern rampart, at the point where the camp is widest, is a shallow rectangular chamber about seventeen feet long, and varying from slightly more than thirteen feet to a little over fourteen feet across. The northern side is of masonry, rather more than two feet high, and continued for a short distance along the eastern and western ends.

Before the pits were first explored by the Rev. Francis Warre in 1851, they were filled with stones, and appeared only as slight depressions in the ground. On the 18th October 1851, there was found, at the bottom of one of the largest pits, at a depth of rather more than five feet below the surface, and with charred wood lying under it, a nearly perfect human skeleton. The skull was pierced by three sword-cuts, while on the left arm and on the collar-bone were other marks of wounds. Three days later, in the walled pit about thirty yards north-west of the main entrance to the camp, three skeletons were discovered, one of them that of a particularly tall man, whose skull had been cut clean through—"a coward's blow," as Professor Macalister says, "delivered from behind." Under these skeletons were a quantity of pebbles, about half a peck of charred corn—wheat and barley—a few thin plates of lias, and some charred wood. A week later the explorers found another skeleton with a spear-head under it—perhaps the very weapon that gave the man his death-wound before he fell forward into the pit. Here, again, in addition to what appeared to be the burnt roof of the hut, there was found a quantity of wheat and barley, in this case heaped on a board, and with pieces of wood between, as if to keep the two sorts apart.

It was in the following year, in May 1852, that two skeletons were discovered at the bottom of one of the pits, lying in an attitude which seemed to point to their having perished locked in the death-struggle. From first to last the explorers found parts of eighteen skeletons, some of them nearly entire, but about half of them bearing marks of wounds. One skull, now in the museum at Taunton, bears the scars of seven sword-cuts; and another skull had been taken off by a blow which cut right through one of the vertebræ. Among the fragments were parts of the skulls of three women, one of them marked with two wounds. In all cases a layer of dark earth, with remains of thatch and charred wood, was found beneath the human relics. The sides of the pits were marked with fire, the stored corn was charred, and stones at the bottom were even burnt to lime.

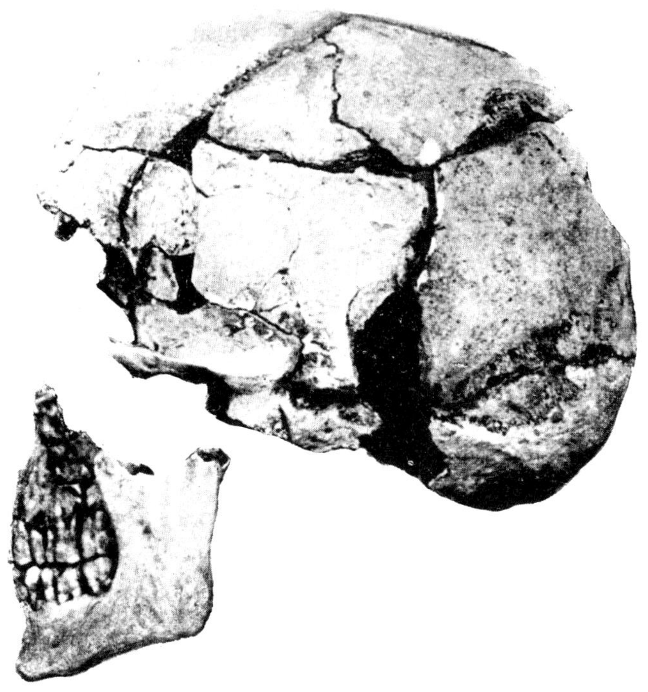

Human Skull marked with Seven Sword-Cuts, from a Pit on Worlebury Camp

In addition to the human remains, the explorers of 1851 and 1852 found in the pits the bones of various quadrupeds and birds, and many limpet-shells; quantities of rude pottery, from which three vessels have been restored, one of them almost entirely; small implements of bone and flint, spindle-whorls, a bead of half-transparent blue glass; a small bronze torque, with a broken ring and other small objects of the same material; a great many round stones that may have been used for slinging; two spiral iron rings that had apparently been carefully put away under a projecting ledge of rock; two iron spear-heads, several iron spikes that may have been either tools or weapons, and many fragments of the same metal. No Roman remains of any kind, unless one of the skeletons was that of a Roman soldier, were found in the pits. Most of these objects were found by Mr. Warre. So thorough, indeed, was his search, that when, in 1881, the whole camp was carefully examined and surveyed by Messrs. Dymond and Tomkins, who reopened about fifty of the pits, "nothing of any significance was discovered."[1]

Professor Macalister of Cambridge, who examined the human remains, says that the skulls are neither Celtic nor Saxon, but that they closely resemble those of the Iberians, "the dark race which still survives in our own western islands, and in the west and north-west of Ireland . . . and I have no hesitation," continues the Professor, "in referring them to that race."

It may be fairly concluded, from the absence of

[1] C. W. Dymond, F.S.A., "Worlebury."

Roman remains in the pits, that they were used by people who had not come under Roman influence. The garrison of the fortress, at the time of the storming, were most likely, as we have seen, Iberian Britons. It is probable that Worlebury Camp was made and used by them; that it was taken by the Romans—Mr. C. W. Dymond suggests by Vespasian, who, while serving in Britain under Aulus Plautius, commanded the Second Legion; that the huts were then set on fire; that the bodies of the slain were thrown into the pits, among the burning thatch and rafters; and that the pits were filled up and not again made use of.

If, as is quite possible, one of the two skeletons above alluded to was that of a Roman soldier, there is no ground for wonder that there should have been nothing distinctive in the appearance of his skull. He may well have been one of the same race as the man with whom he fell fighting. The Roman legions were recruited from many different nations, and the Iberian, that is to say, the Spanish infantry, was among the best in the Imperial army.

But although no Roman remains were found in the pits, many traces of their occupation have, from time to time, been met with inside the ramparts—great quantities of pottery, many glass beads, red and green, brown and blue; fragments of bronze ornaments, and some hundreds of coins. On one occasion more than two hundred Roman coins were found in the surface-soil. Among them were brasses of the Constantine family, of Carausius, Lucilla, and Valerian. Of a much smaller number discovered in 1833 eleven only now remain. But among these are represented no fewer than nine different rulers of the Roman Empire: Tiberius, Nero, Vespasian, Domitian, Hadrian, Marcus Aurelius, Julia Mamæa, Maximinus, and Constantius, thus covering the period from A.D. 18 to A.D. 361.[1] It is also extremely likely that the Saxons, whose frontier was, for a long period, formed by the river Axe, two miles to the southward, should have occupied the camp as an important military station. There is, however, no allusion to Worlebury in the Anglo-Saxon Chronicle, or, indeed, in any ancient writer; and there is no evidence, beyond the relics of battle found in the pits, of any fighting there or in the country round.

The author of "Worlebury" quotes the opinion of "a general officer, experienced in savage warfare . . . that from 7000 to 10,000 barbarians might encamp in a fort the size of Worlebury; while it would afford room for not more than 3000 or 4000 infantry of a modern force."[2]

All the pits connected with human habitation were inside the ramparts of the camp. Outside the enclosure, rather more than a hundred yards east-north-east, and within the "cattle-pen," are several old mine shafts, and there are others at various points on the

[1] C. W. Dymond, F.S.A., "Worlebury."
[2] Ibid.

hill. These are remains of ancient Calamine-workings, of which there were so many in the Mendip Country. The ore was zinc, chiefly the carbonate. Mr. C. W. Dymond, F.S.A., quotes a very interesting allusion to these mines from Norden's description of Middlesex, in which, writing in 1592, of a "copper and brasse myll," near "Istleworth, a place scituate upon the Thamise," the author says: "The oar, or earth wherof it is contryved, is browght out

British Urns from Pits in Worlebury Camp

of Somersetshire from Mendipp, the most from a place called Worley Hill."

The growth of modern Weston has destroyed many traces of primitive inhabitants, in the shape of burial-mounds, cattle-pens, and earthworks. And at various times there have been found, on the southern slope of the hill, especially on the sites of Park Place and of Greenfield Place, at Montpelier, above Church Road, and elsewhere, the remains of ancient interments.[1] In the autumn of 1901,

[1] Jackson's "Visitors' Handbook."

the men employed in making the new road above the Parish Church cut into a chamber, not unlike one of the pits in Worlebury Camp, and which appeared to have been used first as a dwelling and afterwards as a place of burial. On the floor of this chamber were crouched the skeletons of a man and woman, and near them lay the bones of a very little child. On the ground was a hearthstone, and near it were remains of food—bones of the ox, sheep, pig, and horse, all of which had been split as if to extract the marrow. Scattered on the ground were some fragments of coarse pottery, but no tools of any sort. The only things of the nature of weapons were a number of round pebbles, which may have been intended for slinging. The skulls are of the Iberian type, otherwise dolicocephalic or long-headed; and the date of the interment probably coincides with that of the occupation of Worlebury Camp, that is to say, it may be assigned to the commencement of the Christian era, or a century or more preceding it.

Close to the entrance to Birnbeck pier, on the ground now covered by the road, there formerly stood the tumulus described by Rutter, but all trace of it has disappeared. At Ashcombe there was another, which, although much damaged, can still be made out. A third grave-mound, at Castle Batch, beyond Worle, has happily escaped destruction. It is circular, with a hollow in the centre. On the site of the houses numbered 1 and 2 Royal Crescent, the builders found several small enclosures, about twelve feet long and six feet wide, with walls three feet high and eighteen inches thick, and floored with stones, much worn, as if by the feet of animals.[1]

In 1862 the remains of a very ancient boat were found about a quarter of a mile inland from the present high-water mark. And near the Potteries, about a mile from the shore, there was found a curved row of fishing-stakes, such as may yet be seen upon the Weston mud-flats. Still farther inland at Worle, the men who were digging out the foundations of the brewery came upon an old iron anchor, ten feet below the level of the ground.

Rather more than three hundred yards from the foot of the cliff below Worlebury Hill is the little island of Birnbeck, joined to the mainland since 1867 by a light iron pier. So long ago as 1845 a company was formed, called "The Weston-super-Mare Packet Station, Landing Pier, and Slip Company," with the object of uniting Birnbeck with the shore by means of a suspension-bridge, and building out a stone pier on the west side of the island. The attempt failed, because the stonework that was employed offered too much resistance to the waves. Fragments of the masonry still lie on the beach below the present pier. The foundation-stone of the latter was laid in 1864, and the work was finished in three years. Steamers from Cardiff and Bristol, and others bound for Ilfracombe,

[1] C. W. Dymond, F.S.A., "Worlebury."

Clovelly, and various other Channel ports call at the wooden jetties which have been thrown out from Birnbeck.

At Birnbeck is the station of the Weston lifeboat, the *William James Holt.* The first lifeboat was placed here in 1881, and since that time the crew have put out in aid of ships in distress on the Wolves, the dangerous group of rocks between the Flat Holm and the Welsh coast, where the *William and Mary* was lost in 1817; on the Gore Sand off Burnham; on the Hook Sand, north of Clevedon; off Brean Down, and in Sand Bay. Perhaps the most conspicuous service was the rescue of the passengers on board the *Welsh Prince*, a screw steamer belonging to Newport, which, at half-past six in the evening of the 22nd of September 1884, left Weston pier on her way to Bristol. By some means a hawser became foul of the propeller, and the vessel began to drift into Sand Bay. A strong north-west wind was blowing, and there was a rough sea. The ship's anchor would not hold, and she continued to drift towards shore. At eight o'clock the lifeboat was launched, and in twenty minutes had reached the now stranded steamer. Forty passengers were on board, and they were not all brought ashore until long after dark.

Early in the morning of the 2nd of October in the following year, the Weston lifeboat was called out to join the Burnham boat in trying to assist a steam-barge called the *Bulldog*, which, during a west-northwesterly gale and on a very rough sea had gone ashore on the Gore Sand, in Berrow Bay. The distressed ship, however, got safely off, under her own steam, and the services of the lifeboat were not required. Three years later, during a storm on the 22nd of November 1898, the lifeboat went to the assistance of the *Colleen*, a ketch, which was seen to be dragging her anchor in Weston Bay, and which was in great danger of going ashore on the rocks under the high part of Brean Down. On reaching the ketch the coxswain put four men on board and got her safely into Uphill. Much more tragic is the story of the last time that the Weston crew put out. On the last day but one of last century, December 30, 1900, a message was received from Clevedon, saying that a barque was ashore on the Hook Sand, about four miles from that town, and that men could be seen in the rigging. It was Sunday morning, but the men were got together and the boat launched in three-quarters of an hour. She was not long in reaching the wreck, but no sign of life was to be seen on board. Nothing more was ever known of her. All that could be made out was that she was a barque of about 1200 tons. She became a total wreck, and her port, the fate of her crew, her very name alike remain a mystery.

In the course of the present year the Royal National Lifeboat Institution will place upon the Weston station a new Watson sailing lifeboat of the finest type, to be called the *Colonel Stock*, in memory of the husband of the lady who left £5000 to the Institution for the purpose of building and equipping the boat and boathouse. The boathouse and slip are to be at Birnbeck, not to the north of the pier as at present, but on the south side, so that the boat can be taken into deep water at any state of the tide.

Rutter says that in his time a hut for the occasional use of fishermen stood on Birnbeck, which then, as now, was famous in the winter for its sprat-fishery; though we can no longer, as he did, watch "the children of the village . . . gleaning into their baskets" the fish that fell from the nets. The hut was a low, thatched building, kept in repair by a fund raised among the fishermen, and inhabited during the fishing-season by two men called "Gull Yellers," specially selected for their strength of lung, whose duty it was to scare away the gulls from the nets as the tide went down and left the captured fish exposed. The importance of the Weston fisheries has much declined of recent years. Three centuries ago or more, leases of the "Fishing Stalls" were granted by the Lord of the Manor, generally in connection with houses or lands. And to him was always carried the first basket of fish, and the first salmon of the season. In the same way "Fowling Layers," or stations from which birds might be shot while flying to and from the shore, were also granted by lease. The growth of the town has driven away many birds that once frequented the bay. The wild geese that pass fly now far overhead. And the days have long gone by when a fisherman could kill thirty gulls at a single shot, as was done on one occasion by a man concealed within the Birnbeck hut.

For about two hours at low water it is possible to walk across to Birnbeck by a ridge called the Stepway. But the rising tide runs with great force between the island and the shore; and it was here that Sir Charles Elton's two sons, having reached the rock at low water, were cut off by the tide, and were drowned in trying to wade back to shore. It was near the same spot that the Rev. Francis Blackburne, then Rector of the parish, lost his life in June 1829. The story, as told to Mr. Ernest E. Baker by an old fisherman, is that Mr. Blackburne, in spite of many warnings, persisted in sailing too close to the Birnbeck fishing stakes; and that at last one of the stakes ran through the bottom of the boat. "You mind yourself," said the Rector to the man who was with him in the sinking craft; "never mind me." He was swept away by the current and drowned, but his companion swam safe to shore.

The word Birnbeck may be of Scandinavian origin, like the names of the two islands out in the Channel, and of the neighbouring village of Wick St. Lawrence. If so, it may mean "The House on the Point"; the first syllable coming from the Norsk *byr*, "a dwelling," and the second being the *Bec*, so common in the names of headlands along the coast of Normandy. It is, however, possible that the name is connected with the family of Bec, of Eresby in Lincolnshire, who, in the time of Edward I., were the owners of the Steep Holm.[1]

The woods, which now add so much to the beauty of Weston Hill, are of modern growth, having been planted no longer ago than 1823, on what was then a bare and open down. Originally intended for a game-preserve, the woods have for the last fifty years been thrown freely open to the public; and in addition to five principal roads which meet at the top of the hill, near the ancient heap of stones called Peak Winnard, they are traversed in all directions by innumerable footpaths. The Peak Winnard, or Picwinner Cairn, was found by Mr. C. W. Dymond to consist of "loose stones, in the form of a very low bowl-barrow." The stones in the middle having been removed, the ground underneath was excavated to the depth of a foot; but the only ancient objects discovered were "two bits of bone and three limpet-shells." It is said that in old days it was the custom for fishermen going over the hill to the nets at Birnbeck to throw stones on this cairn for luck, saying as they did so—

> "Picwinner, Picwinner!
> Pick me some dinner!"[2]

---

[1] Collinson.

[2] C. W. Dymond, F.S.A., "Worlebury."

The thick foliage of the abundant fir-trees provides food and shelter for many Squirrels, which, though not very often seen by ordinary wayfarers, leave ample traces of their presence in the gnawed cores of fir-cones which they scatter on the ground beneath their haunts. Other four-footed inhabitants of the wood show themselves after their manner to any one who will watch and wait. Many of them are lovers of darkness, and doubtless venture out more boldly under cover of the night. But even in broad daylight, and on well-trodden paths, the quiet loiterer in Weston Wood may meet a Hedgehog shambling along, or see a Stoat sit up on his hind-legs to reconnoitre the intruder, or watch a little party of Weasels rolling over and over, purring like so many kittens, or surprise a Mole crossing the hard path on his way to softer digging-ground. While any one who will sit down in a quiet spot among the thickets and wait in silence for a half-hour or so, may have Wood-mice and Shrews, and Field and Bank Voles playing fearlessly about his feet. A few Rabbits linger still, and occasionally a Fox finds temporary quarters in the wood, even venturing down among the houses on the upper roads.

The Bird-Life of Weston Wood differs but little from that of other parts of the Mendip Country. The resident population are the ordinary woodanders: Sparrow-hawks and Kestrels, Ringdoves, Jays, Magpies, which are particularly numerous, and

Carrion Crows, together with Tits, Goldcrests, Tree-creepers, the Common Finches, with an occasional Hawfinch, the three ordinary Woodpeckers, especially among the scattered timber along the edge of the wood, and many other common species. In the breeding-season come the wood-loving migrants; and among these there is usually a pair of Nightingales, and although so dry a wood is not altogether suited to their habits, these birds might be more abundant were they left in peace.

The rookery in the Grove Park is one of the features of the town, and for a great part of the year the Weston Rooks are joined by others of their race from other colonies, sometimes miles inland. Many Jackdaws, too, have their nests in the neighbourhood, in church-towers, under the roofs of houses, and in crannies of the cliffs of Brean. And these, again, are joined by parties of Daws from Burrington, Blagdon, and even from Cheddar. The assemblies are only for the day. At sunset the visitors start for home, and make their way in bee-lines to their distant haunts among the hills.

In hard weather Bramble Finches sometimes frequent the wood, especially where beech-trees grow; and they have even been known to feed among the sparrows and robins on the window-sill of a house near the Bristol Road. More rarely the hill is visited in winter by little troops of Black Redstarts. They also have ventured at times into the same garden, and it is said that a pair once nested somewhere on Worlebury Hill.[1]

Few birds of any kind are to be seen on the Weston shore in the breeding season. The quiet-coloured little Rock Pipit is perhaps the only permanent resident, making its nest in rocky places near the beach, and seldom, it is believed, going far from the shore. But even as early as July the Dunlin Sandpipers, white and grey birds about the size of starlings—Purres as they are called by the fishermen—begin to come down from their summer haunts on the moors. Throughout the autumn and winter the wide mud-flats are thronged by multitudes of waders. The most abundant are Sandpipers of various kinds, especially Dunlins. And with these are associated Curlews, Oyster-catchers, Whimbrels, Redshanks, and other shore-loving species, among whom may often be seen the tall grey figures of Brockley Herons. In the winter the waters of the bay are sometimes literally darkened by great flocks of ducks, especially Scaup Ducks. In the winter of 1884 there were three such flights, each containing some thousands of birds.

The fishing nets at Birnbeck attract in winter all the common gulls: the Kittiwake, the Black-headed Gull, the Herring Gull, the Lesser Black-headed Gull, and the Common Gull; and these are sometimes joined by rare wanderers. Sabine's Gull, the Little

[1] "Som. Arch. Pro.," vol. xxxix., "A Revised List of the Birds of Somerset."

Gull, the Glaucous Gull, the Ivory Gull, and the Iceland Gull have all been shot at Weston.[1] The Common Tern is sometimes seen on the autumn migration, and an Arctic Tern was shot here in 1842.[2] Gannets, Cormorants, Guillemots, Puffins, Shearwaters, Razorbills—birds that are familiar on the opposite coast—are here but casual visitors, finding little to attract them in water so muddy and near a shore so much frequented. Rarer still on this shore are the Skuas, but both Richardson's Skua and the Pomatorhine Skua have been recorded.[3] Both Leach's Petrel and the Storm Petrel have been driven ashore here in rough weather, and once at least a Fulmar Petrel has been shot.[4] In 1883, after a long-continued gale, a Great Northern Diver was shot in the bay, and in the following year the same fate befell two black swans, which had no doubt escaped from some private water, and may have been looking for a suitable breeding-place. In 1890 a Long-tailed Duck was shot near the Steep Holm by one of the fishermen. The Goosander, the Redbreasted Merganser, the Brent Goose, and the Great Crested Grebe have all been shot at various times.[5] Among the rare waders that have been recorded here are the Collared Pratincole, the Spotted Redshank, the Ruff, the Little Stint, the Sanderling, and the Purple Sandpiper.[6] Though in no sense sea-birds, flocks, both of Twites and Snow

[1] "Som. Arch. Pro.," vol. xxxix., "A Revised List of the Birds of Somerset."
[2] Ibid. [3] Ibid. [4] Ibid. [5] Ibid. [6] Ibid.

Buntings have been seen among the sandhills in the winter.[1] In the great invasion of Sand Grouse in 1888, several of these wanderers were observed near Weston.[2]

Many birds frequent the low-lying country between Worlebury and Hutton. There are a few Dabchicks and Moorhens on the ponds near the railway. And both these broader waters and the narrow moorland ditches are the haunt of Reed Warblers, Sedge Warblers, and Reed Buntings. There is some evidence that the Spotted Crake breeds among these ditches, for few winters pass in which a troop of these shy little birds is not flushed on this moor, apparently the parents and their brood. The Water Rail is a more regular resident. A few years ago one walked in at the door of a house some miles out of Weston-super-Mare, past the servant who was cleaning the steps, and was made a temporary prisoner within. Bitterns are among the occasional visitors, and in 1865 a Little Bittern, a bird of very much greater rarity, was killed on Weston Moor.[3]

A few Peewits breed in these low-lying meadows, and many more appear in the autumn, but their numbers are insignificant in comparison with the vast flights of Starlings which assemble in this district early in the winter. Fifty years ago Star-

[1] "Som. Arch. Pro.," vol. xxxix., "A Revised List of the Birds of Somerset."

[2] Ibid. [3] Ibid.

lings were scarce in the Mendip Country; now, when summer is over, they collect, especially near the sea, in scores of thousands. Some years since, a flock of Starlings appeared in the autumn at Weston-super-Mare, and night after night about sunset they performed beautiful evolutions in the air before retiring to roost in the wood or among the elms of the Grove Park. So vast was this army that sometimes in its flight it extended, not in a long-drawn line, but in a crowded column, the whole two miles of the length of Weston Wood. Conspicuous figures here all through the winter are the Kestrels, for whom, however, the moorland is less a home than a hunting-ground.

Few reptiles are to be found in the immediate neighbourhood of Weston, except Slow-worms, which are common in dry places on the edge of the wood, especially under stones. Neither the Grass-snake nor the little Viviparous Lizard can be called common, while the Viper is now seldom seen near the town, though abundant in some parts of the Mendip Country. The Grass-snake, known by its olive-brown colour, and the black and yellow rings round its neck, is a harmless and beautiful reptile. Not only is its bite not poisonous, but it is very difficult to get the creature to bite at all. Its minute teeth produce less effect than those of a mouse. The length of snakes is often exaggerated. A Grass-snake a yard long is a fine specimen. One was taken in the New Forest which measured five feet eight inches; but the longest ever seen by the writer, who has handled a hundred or more, was one which he caught at Brockley Combe in 1865, and which was three feet nine inches long.

The Viper or Adder is much smaller. Out of 117 specimens the longest was only twenty-seven inches, while the average is not more than from twenty to twenty-two inches. The ground-colour of the Viper's skin varies from dull white to rich brown. Along its back is a broad, rather irregular, zigzag stripe of black, very conspicuous, except just at the time when the creature is about to change its skin, which it does by pulling the old one entirely inside out, even to the covering of its eyes. On its head is a not very conspicuous dark mark, like the letter V, or it might pass for A if looked at the other way up—V for Viper, A for Adder. The Viper is provided with two poison-fangs—two long, very sharp, slightly curved, and hollow teeth, one on each side of the upper jaw. Connected with the root of each is a gland from which poison runs down into the wound, which is very small, and at first hurts no more than a slight pin-prick. In a short time, however, a dull pain sets in, gradually growing in intensity until it feels like a bad wasp's sting, while the neighbourhood of the wound swells and becomes discoloured. It is usual to recommend the outward application of olive oil or some kind of fat—viper-catchers use the fat of the creature itself—and weak ammonia taken internally. The most efficacious remedy yet discovered for snake-bites, however, appears to be the subcutaneous injection of permanganate of potash—a ten per cent. solution or even stronger. A Viper's bite is sometimes very painful, but is very rarely fatal to human beings. Sheep not infrequently die from its effects, and in the summer of 1901 a cow was killed near Winscombe by the bite of a Viper. Grass-snakes are fond of low-lying meadows and of the neighbourhood of water, perhaps because their food consists largely of frogs. Vipers, on the other hand, which live more on mice, frequent, as a rule, higher and drier ground, and are especially fond of basking among stones under a sunny hedgerow. Both snakes, however, are to be found in woods.

The Slow-worm, which is not a snake but a lizard without legs, is the commonest reptile in the district. A skiagraph taken of a large Slow-worm caught by the writer showed not even the rudiments of legs in the skeleton, only a slight thickening of the vertebral column at the point where the forelegs would have been. The Slow-worm is a perfectly harmless and very pretty little creature, whose one drawback is its habit of dropping its tail when startled or suddenly picked up. This habit, seen also in the less common little Viviparous Lizard, is believed to be intended to divert the attention of a pursuing bird or beast, who turns aside to seize the wriggling tail, while the self-mutilated reptile glides away unnoticed.

The Batrachians of the district are the Frog and the Toad and three Newts—the Triton, the Smooth Newt, and the Palmated Newt. The latter may be distinguished by the filament at the end of its tail, and by having its hind-feet webbed, which the common Smooth Newt has not.

For the sake of anglers, coarse-fish have been introduced into some of the ponds in the neighbourhood, particularly those near the railway. But as there are no natural pools and very little running water, the variety of indigenous fish is small. Both the common Three-spined Stickleback and the smaller and darker Nine-spined Stickleback are abundant in the rhines. The male of the first-named species distinguishes himself by assuming brilliant colours in the spring-time, and also by making a nest in which his mate may lay her eggs. The work of building occupies about six hours; and then, for three weeks or more, the male Stickleback keeps watch over the nest and its contents, attacking all fish or insects who chance to come too near, and using his sharp spines as very effective weapons of offence. Another small fish, found particularly in the slow-moving waters of the Weston Rhine, is the Loach, a species distinguished by having several small tentacles hanging from its mouth.

Quite as widely distributed as the Stickleback is the Eel. It was long supposed that there were several kinds of fresh-water eel. It is now known, however, that there is only one species. The male is known by his blunt head, and the female by her sharply pointed nose and by her greater size. The largest male eel on record measured only 1 foot $7\frac{1}{5}$ inches, while females have been known to reach 3 feet 3 inches, or even more. As a rule the males stay in the brackish water, near the mouths of rivers running into the sea, while the females ascend the streams. They are sometimes found, however, in water not connected with the sea, for they are quite able to travel over grass, and even to cross high-roads. When they have reached maturity, which is probably not until they are some years old, eels all go down to the sea. And from the sea they never return. There they pair, there they spawn, and there they die. Early in the year, from February to May, young eels, often called Elvers, and believed to be about six months old, ascend the streams in swarms. In the Parret they are caught in great numbers, salted, and made into cakes.

Unlike the Eel, the Flounder is found only in waters connected with the sea. "Of all the British flat-fishes," says Mr. Cunningham, "this species is the least marine in its distribution. It belongs essentially to estuaries, ascending into fresh water in many rivers where there are no natural or artificial barriers to obstruct its passage. It is common, and in most estuaries abundant, and there is no estuary in the British Islands where it does not occur. However, I know of no instance where it is found in fresh water cut off from connection with the sea, unless artificially introduced; it can live in fresh water . . . but cannot propagate in it."[1] In the spring the Flounders all go down to the sea, where they shed their spawn, which floats on the surface. In about seven days the young appear, and for nearly another week have no mouth at all, being supported by the unexhausted yolk of the egg. They swim upright, like the majority of fishes, and like most other fishes they have one eye on each side of the head. After a time, however, and while the infant Flounder is still less than half an inch long, its left eye begins to move, and travels by degrees to the same side as the other eye. In the Turbot and some other species it is the right eye that changes its place. There is a species found in the open Atlantic, though not on our coasts, in which the right eye actually goes through the head. The fish have been watched while the change was taking place.

There is nothing specially remarkable in the Insect Life of the district, though the ditches of the moor are crowded with interesting forms, and although Worlebury Hill and Weston Wood have provided good hunting-ground for many generations of youthful entomologists. About forty species of butterflies have been at various times taken in the neighbourhood. Perhaps the rarest of these are the Comma, the Purple Hairstreak, the Marbled White, and the Black-veined White. The last-named, however, has not been recorded for some years. Of

[1] Cunningham, "British Marketable Marine Fishes."

moths, the number of species is, of course, much greater. Among the most striking of those seen every season are the Death's Head, Lime, and Humming-Bird Hawk-Moths. The Convolvulus and the small Elephant Hawk-Moths are less frequently taken. One moth, the Clouded Magpie, rare in some other parts of England, is very abundant in the wood.

A large proportion of the very numerous Land and Fresh-water Shells of the Mendip Country are to be found within a short distance of the town, in the wood, on the open hill, among the sandhills by the shore, or in the ditches of the low-lying moors. The smallest British land shell, *Carychium minimum*, a species of no great rarity, but one that, on account of its extreme minuteness, is probably often overlooked, is, especially in some years, very plentiful under stones in damp places among the trees. Its size may be estimated from the fact that it took 105 specimens to cover a threepenny-piece, and that all these together weighed, when dead, exactly half a grain.

Fresh-water shells of many kinds abound in the moorland ditches. In the ponds, and also in the Weston Rhine, are to be found the large Swan Mussel, *Anodonta cygnæa;* while in the last-named water two other mussels, *Unio tumidus* and *Unio Pictorum*, have been naturalised. One of the prettiest water-shells of the district is *Planorbis nautileus*, a small, flat, coil-shaped creature, very like a diminutive Nautilus, and needing a magnifying glass to reveal its beauty properly. *Limnæa truncatula*, a small, thin, long-shaped spiral shell, particularly abundant in the ditches towards Kewstoke, is the "host" of one stage of the Liver-Fluke, the destructive internal parasite that causes the deadly disease called "fluke," which is so fatal to sheep in wet meadows.

The Flowers which grow in Weston Wood are for the most part such ordinary species as one would expect to find in so newly established a plantation. Primroses have become so rare that the name of Primrose Valley is now altogether a misnomer. But the wild Hyacinths remain. And few woodland sights could well be more beautiful than the mist of Bluebells which, year after year, gathers among the thickets on the south slope of the hill. Within sight of Worlebury Camp, however, are to be found some of the rarest plants, not of the district merely, but of Britain. The Steep Holm is the only habitat in these islands of the wild Peony, for instance. And on the same rock still grows the almost equally rare Great Round-headed Garlic. Brean Down, again, is one of the two English stations for the White Rock Rose. One very rare plant, the insignificant little *Trinia,* found in only two other districts in the British Islands, grows on the hill itself, though more particularly outside the limits of the wood. Other scarce flowers of the hill are the Willow Lettuce, the White Mullein, the rare *Eryngium campestre* (one of the sea-hollies), a rare cress (*Cerastium pumilum*), and the Broad-Leaved Sea-Lavender. *Aster Linosyris*, which formerly grew on Birnbeck, has been exterminated, and is to be seen now only in collections of dried plants. The Scurvy-Grass, whose shining leaves are so conspicuous on the rocky slope above the sea, has been recorded for only one other spot in Somerset. If, as tradition declares, this plant first appeared here after the exploration of Worlebury Camp in 1851, it can only have been because the seeds, carried perhaps on the feet of birds, either from some garden, or even from the distant cliffs of Cheddar whose daws so often visit Weston, found congenial soil in the fresh earth of the newly opened pits. They did not come out of the pits. Botanists have long abandoned the once popular and certainly very picturesque idea that seeds can retain their vitality for hundreds, or as has even been said, for thousands of years. A striking flower of the wood is the Red Valerian, or Good Neighbours, which still grows, as it did in Rutter's time, among the stones of the old encampment, where it attracts hosts of honey-loving insects. The Fœtid Iris, which still grows among the trees, is probably, like the Valerian and the evil-smelling Hound's-Tongue, a survival from the days when Worlebury was an open hill. The seeds of the graceful and sweet-scented Spurge

Laurel, on the other hand, have no doubt been brought here by birds since the wood was planted.

The common ferns of Weston Hill are Bracken, Male Fern, Lady Fern, Hart's-Tongue, and three Shield-Ferns, *aculeatum*, *angulare*, and *dilatata*, which grow in the woods. *Asplenium adiantum-nigrum* is found, but sparingly. In the walls below the wood grow Ceterach, Common Spleenwort, and Wall Rue, with Common Polypody, which occurs also in rocky places round the hill. Outside the wood, and towards Kewstoke, Adder's-Tongue has been found. There is also a little Sea-Spleenwort in the cliffs. Both *Blechnum spicant* and *Cystopteris fragilis* have been reported, but the writer has not seen specimens.

At Weston - super - Mare the ordinary rise of spring tides is 37 feet; but at the equinox the rise is 39 or 40 feet. At Portishead, where occur the highest tides in the Bristol Channel, and, with one solitary exception, the highest tides in the world, the ordinary rise is 42 feet, and the equinoctial rise 45 feet. This is equalled at the eastern entrance of the Straits of Magellan, but only exceeded in the Basin of Minas, in the Bay of Fundy, between Nova Scotia and New Brunswick, where the ordinary spring rise is 50 feet.[1]

At low tide the sand and the mud-flats that fringe the greater part of the Mendip Sea-board dry off for about a mile. Beyond the line of

[1] Hydrographic Department, Admiralty.

low-water the whole area between the Steep Holm and the shore, with the exception of a few small patches rarely exceeding ten fathoms, is very shallow, and as a rule not more than five or six fathoms deep. In one of the deeper patches, nearly parallel with Weston sands, at a point half-way between Worlebury and Brean Down, and two miles and a half north-west of the Sea Front, is a sounding of twenty fathoms, the greatest depth between Barry Dock and the port of Bristol. Two miles south of Barry is another small patch of twenty fathoms. These two are the deepest soundings in the Bristol Channel for nearly forty miles from the mouth of the Avon. The navigation of the channel is a good deal obstructed by rocks and shoals, and to add to the difficulties, "changes in depths and in the position of banks are constantly occurring."[1]

Within sight of Weston the channel is marked by three principal lights. The lighthouse on the Flat Holm, fully described in the chapter on the Islands, shows a light of what is termed the group-flashing order, visible for twenty-one seconds, occulted for three seconds, again visible for three seconds, and again occulted for three seconds, making up altogether a cycle of half a minute. Two lightships can also be seen from the pier and from parts of the Sea Front. The "English and Welsh Grounds" light-vessel is anchored at

[1] Admiralty Chart, corrected to 1902.

the tail of a shoal called "The Bridge," seven miles farther up the channel than the Flat Holm, and about five and a half miles due north of Birnbeck. This ship shows a light that revolves once in thirty seconds, and during fog it gives two blasts on a powerful siren, repeated after an interval of two minutes. Breaksea Point lightship, which is seven miles from the Flat Holm in the other direction, down channel, shows a similar light, but revolving once in a quarter of a minute. In thick weather a fog-horn is blown at intervals of fifteen seconds. The fixed light on Cardiff Flats can, on clear nights, just be seen from the Sea Front at Weston.

There is comparatively little to attract the naturalist in the brown waters of the Weston shore. The water is too muddy, and perhaps also too fresh, for much Marine Life to flourish in it. No Star-Fish or Sea-Urchins, no Sea-Mice, no Jelly-fish even, and very few beautiful Zoophytes, are here left stranded by the ebbing tide. Only the commonest Seaweeds are, as a rule, to be found along this shore, and even the Shells are, with few exceptions, small and unattractive.

The most prominent feature of Marine Life among the rocks near the pier is the abundance of Sea-Anemones, which no doubt find the strong currents between Birnbeck and the mainland most convenient carriers of food. Attached to the rocks are great numbers of the common red species, which, unattractive as they are when the tide has left them, are most beautiful objects when their tentacles are expanded in clear sea water. Buried in the sand in open spaces among the stones are other Anemones, of much larger dimensions, but paler in colour, though relieved with beautiful markings. The ordinary Crustaceans of the shore are Shrimps, sometimes caught in considerable quantities; small Green or Shore Crabs; Hermit Crabs, inhabiting shells of the whelk, *Purpura*, or even of the periwinkle; Sandhoppers, small shrimp-like creatures which frequent the heaps of dry seaweed near high-tide mark; and Sea Slaters, like great woodlice, which creep about among the rocks, mostly towards evening. Acorn Barnacles whiten the rocks in some places with their little limpet-like shells; and about seven years ago, a large piece of timber came ashore in Glentworth Bay after a storm, completely covered with very fine Goose Barnacles, the curious creatures within whose mussel-like shells it was once supposed that geese were formed. Gerarde, the herbalist, who wrote in 1597, not only described and figured the Barnacle-Goose-Tree with its strange "fruit," but declared that he himself had seen the young bird come gradually out of the shell, until it hung only by the bill. "In short space after," he goes on, "it commeth to full maturitie, and falleth into the sea, when it gathereth feathers and groweth to a fowle bigger than a Mallard and lesser than a Goose, hauing blacke legs and bill and beake, and feathers blacke and white spotted in such a manner as is our Magpie, which the people of Lancashire call by no other name than a Tree-Goose: which place therof and all those parts adjoining doe so much abound therewith that one of the best is bought for threepence. For the truth wherof, if any doubt, may it please them to repair unto me, and I shall satisfie them by the testimony of good witnesses."

The commonest and most conspicuous Sea-Shells to be found on Weston sands are the small bivalves, some pink, some yellow, others prettily banded with white and pink, or white and orange, according to the species, which, especially near the mouth of the river Axe, whiten the beach by thousands, but all dead. The living molluscs are only to be obtained by dredging, or at very low tide. These shells belong chiefly, if not entirely, to the genus *Tellina*, of which, though there is so much variety of colour, due chiefly to age, there are here probably only two species. Much the most abundant is *Tellina Balthica*, with which may sometimes be found a few specimens of the slighter *Tellina tenuis*. Equally common, but much less conspicuous because of their extreme minuteness, are the tiny little spiral shells belonging to the two genera *Hydrobia* and *Rissoa*. They are so small that the different varieties cannot be distinguished without the aid of a magnifying glass. Great numbers of these little molluscs may be found dead in hollows in the sand. But they may also be seen alive along the edge of the tide, and may easily be traced by the lines which they make in crawling on the wet sand in search of food.

The commonest shells among the rocks, near the pier or at Brean Down or Sand Point, are the Limpet, the *Purpura*, three kinds of Periwinkles, and the Whelk, though the latter is much more often found dead than alive. If a limpet be detached from its hold there will often be found underneath it an oval scar or groove, to which the creature has been closely fitted. It is believed that this mark, which seems to serve as a sort of mooring if not as a home for its owner, is made partly by the long-continued friction of the sharp edge of the shell, and partly also by the extremely tenacious secretion which helps the animal to cling so firmly to the rock. The experiments of Dr. Hamilton[1] seem to prove that a limpet retains its hold less by suction or atmospheric pressure, than by means of this sticky secretion, which to some extent preserves its adhesive power even after the creature itself is dead. A live limpet has been known to take so firm a grip of the rock that a force of sixty-two pounds was required to move it.[2] And Dr. Hamilton found that it took twenty-five pounds to lift even a limpet that had been killed by the injection of corrosive sublimate. Twenty-four hours after death a force of nine pounds and a half was still required to detach the

[1] "Natural Science," vol. i. June 1892.
[2] Warne's "Imperial Natural History."

creature from its hold. When the tide has just left them limpets leave their resting-places, and wander away in search of food, afterwards returning to their own particular scars or moorings. Professor C. Lloyd Morgan has watched a limpet crawl as much as twenty-two inches from its home, and has found another individual even three feet from a scar in which its shell fitted perfectly. On returning home a limpet may be observed to feel the spot carefully with its tentacles, turning itself if necessary so as to get into just the right position.[1]

The Limpet, like the Periwinkle, is a vegetarian; but the Whelk, and the much smaller but somewhat similar *Purpura lapillus*, are carnivorous in their habits, feeding on almost any kind of animal food. The *Purpura* is specially addicted to attacking the common Mussel, boring a hole in its victim's shell by means of its rasp-like lingula or radial ribbon, and then scooping out the helpless animal within.

Two other creatures, not in the least like shells, but belonging to the Mollusca, are the Cuttle-fish, or Squid, and the Chiton, both of which occur along the Mendip sea-board. Cuttle-fish are rarely seen alive, except when taken in the fishing-nets; but very large cuttle "bones" are sometimes washed up after heavy weather, especially under the southern side of Brean Down. Chitons, which resemble strongly-built woodlice, have a jointed shell com-

[1] "Animal Behaviour," pp. 156–57.

posed of eight sections, and can roll themselves up like the familiar Pill Woodlice. They live under stones or in crevices in the rocks, much as Slaters or Sea-Woodlice do. But they have no legs, and are no quicker in their movements than snails.

The water of the Bristol Channel, muddy as it is, sometimes shows a slight amount of phosphorescence, chiefly owing, probably, to the presence in it of great numbers of a minute Rotifer, *Noctiluca milliaris*, a round, transparent organism, about a fiftieth of an inch in diameter. In the summer of 1849, these small creatures, which are never, it is said, found far from land, were particularly abundant in Weston Bay, and formed the subject of a paper read that year before the British Association at Birmingham, by Dr. J. H. Pring, of Weston-super-Mare. So striking was the phenomenon, especially in the month of August, that the whole surface of the bay was suffused with "silvery light, which caused the dark headland of Brean Down on the opposite side . . . . to appear as if laved by liquid silver." On the beach the waves came in like "masses of liquid fire;" and particularly beautiful effects were seen in the water under the lee of Knightstone, between the rock and the vessels which were moored to it.[1]

The Sea-Weeds of this coast were noted by Miss Isabella Gifford, who collected marine algæ along the shore from Portishead to Minehead. Her col-

[1] Brown's "New Guide," 1853.

lection is in the museum at Taunton, but it is not known which of them were found near Weston. Miss Gifford names thirty-seven native species, and adds that a good many more are occasionally drifted in after rough weather. A great many Diatoms from the mud-flats and the shore were identified by Dr. Pooley, who found altogether about 110 species of these minute plants in the neighbourhood of Weston.

The Fish of Bridgwater Bay have been carefully studied; but the Weston records are scanty and unscientific. Perhaps the only fish that can here be seen in their native element are a few tiny little Gobies in the rock-pools. The fish most commonly taken in the nets near shore are Sprats and Whiting, but great quantities of Herrings are sometimes caught off the Holms. A good many Dabs, Cod, Eels, and Congers are also taken by the Weston fishermen. A Cod weighing 37 pounds, believed to be the largest ever taken in this part of the channel, was caught by an Uphill man. About the year 1800 there was to be seen over the door of a fisherman's cottage in Weston, the representation of a large flat-fish of some kind that had been caught in the bay, and that measured 26 inches in length and 15½ inches in breadth.[1] Sword-fish have been seen alive off Weston, and their dead bodies have occasionally been washed ashore upon the sands. The "sword" of one of these, together with a model of its body,

[1] Mr. Bennett's Manuscript.

is preserved in the museum. The Sword-fish, which is one of the boldest and most savage of sea-monsters, uses its weapon to kill cod and other fish on which it preys, employing it, apparently, as a sort of harpoon. There are many cases on record in which one of these creatures had driven its sword through the bottom of a vessel, which it had perhaps mistaken for a whale. In the British Museum is a piece of timber from the hull of an East Indiaman, and sticking in it is part of the tusk of a Sword-fish, which penetrated 22 inches through the ship's side. About the year 1830, a man who was bathing in the Severn was run through and killed by a Sword-fish, which was immediately afterwards caught, so that there was no doubt about its identification. A large and very remarkable species sometimes taken on this coast is the repulsive-looking monster variously known as the Angler, Fiddler, Fishing-Frog, or Sea-Devil. This is a great fish, shaped something like a gigantic tadpole, and sometimes exceeding six feet in length, with a huge head, and with a mouth which, when wide open, would take in an object more than a foot square.[1] It inhabits shallow water, where it is concealed from view partly by its power of changing its colour to suit its environment, and partly by a curious growth upon its head which gives it much the appearance of a piece of weed-covered rock. The Fishing-Frog gets

[1] A specimen caught on the 18th July 1902, by a Ramsgate boat, weighed just over 3 cwt.—*Field.*

its name from a series of long slender spines which take the place of the dorsal fin, the first of them ending in a double membrane and suggestive of a fishing-rod with a bait dangling from the end of it. It has been said that the creature waves this membrane as a lure to entice other fish within its reach. "It is true that anything moving will attract the attention of fishes that hunt by sight. But another and perhaps more important use of the tentacle is indicated by some experiments made during the Irish survey by Mr. Lane, and mentioned in Mr. Holt's report ("Scientific Proc. Royal Dublin Society," vol. vii., part 4, p. 459). Mr. Lane found that when he touched the top of the erected tentacle with a stick the fish at once snapped with his jaws, so as to catch exactly that part of the stick which had touched his tentacle. This was repeated many times, until the fish was exhausted. It is evident that this automatic and precise mechanism of sensitive nerve and jaw-muscles must be most effective in the capture of the Angler's prey. It is a spring trap of the most certain action, always set, and never betraying its nature. Any fishes swimming near the ground are liable to touch the tentacle of an Angler, which cannot be distinguished from the most innocent and insignificant frond of weed or stem of zoophyte, and to touch it is certain and immediate death."[1] The very rare Snipe Fish, a

[1] Cunningham, "Marketable Marine Fishes of the British Islands."

small species with a curiously developed mouth, like the beak of a bird, has been taken near Uphill.

Three species of Marine Mammals have occurred off Weston. Both Grampuses and Porpoises are occasionally seen, and their dead bodies are sometimes washed up on the beach. On the 7th of November 1860, a small Bottle-nosed Whale, about eighteen feet long, was stranded near Knightstone. It was alive when it came ashore, but it soon died. Its dead body was exhibited for several days, and its complete skeleton now hangs in the Weston Museum.

Except for a fringe of Dolomitic Conglomerate—an ancient sea-beach, in which very few fossils are known to occur—found along its southern base, and for a short distance on the north-east, Worlebury Hill is composed entirely of Carboniferous Limestone, a coral rock containing many animal remains. Bivalve shells are very numerous, especially those of the genera *Spirifer* and *Productus*. The most striking species is the large double-shell called *Productus giganteus*. Another very common fossil is *Productus Martini*, of which large numbers are sometimes found lying together as if their tenants had all perished simultaneously. The fossil shells of two cuttle-fish, *Euomphalus* and *Bellerophon*, are not uncommon. The former resembles an Ammonite, while the latter is more like the modern Nautilus, which, indeed, is one of its relatives. Among the common Corals are the horn-shaped *Cyathophyllum*, the thread-like *Madrepore*, and the irregular *Lithostrotion*. Honeycomb Coral and Encrinites, both so abundant in the limestone of the central Mendips, are here comparatively scarce. Among the rarer fossils are Trilobites—small three-lobed Crustaceans, and palatal teeth of coral-crushing fish.

On Worlebury Hill, west of the encampment, there are beds of Volcanic Ash, and on the beach near Birnbeck are masses of Igneous Rock. These deposits were formerly regarded as intrusive, and were spoken of as Trap. But it is the opinion of modern geologists that these lava streams are of very remote antiquity, and that they are probably coeval with the strata among which they rest. In the face of the low cliffs near the pier may be traced the remains of a raised sea-beach, first distinctly seen after a landslip which occurred during a great storm in February 1861. On some of the masses of sand which were then thrown on the beach, cemented together by the lime from ancient sea-shells, and partly perhaps by drippings from the rock above, could be seen ripple-marks, the pits of raindrops and the footprints of birds; and in the sand itself were the bones and teeth of the horse, ox, and other animals. The low-lying moors which stretch away from the foot of Worlebury are Alluvial, and are no doubt chiefly the deposit of the Severn and the Severn Sea. Sand is found near the surface a long way from the present tide-line. Wherever the soil in them has been deeply excavated, as at the Potteries, and on the site of the Gas-Works, there have been discovered, underneath a layer of peat of varying thickness, traces of an ancient forest, with the trunks of yew, oak, and alder trees; and with these there have been also found the bones of deer and various animals.

KEWSTOKE

THE parish of Kewstoke, which adjoins Weston-super-Mare on the north, is bounded on two sides by the sea, and except for the promontory of Sand Point and part of Worlebury itself, including the village of Milton, lies very low, forming part of the great Severn plain which occupies so much of Somerset. The ancient manors of Woodspring, Kewstoke, and Milton, now included in this parish, are thus described in Domesday Book :—

"*William [De Faleise] himself holds Worspring. By consent of King William Serlo de Burci gave it to him with his daughter. Euroac held it in the time of King Edward, and paid Danegeld for six hides and one virgate of land. There is land for twelve plough-teams. In the demesne* (hiatus). *There thirteen villeins and six boors have six plough-teams. There are ten acres of pasture and ten acres of copsewood. Always worth a hundred shillings.*"

"*Gilbert FitzTurold holds from the King Chiwestoch, and Osbern from him. Edric held it in the time of King Edward, and paid Danegeld for one hide and a half. There is land for two plough-teams which are in the demesne; and two slaves and two boors, and twenty acres of pasture, and ten acres of copsewood. Formerly worth twenty shillings, now thirty shillings.*" The Exeter

Kewstoke Church

Domesday adds that at Kewstoke there were five wild brood-mares, *indomitae equae*, and fifteen goats.

"*Anschitil himself holds Mideltone. Osward held it in the time of King Edward, and paid Danegeld for one hide. There is land for one plough-team, which is there, with one villein and two serfs. There are six acres of meadow and two acres of copsewood, and twenty acres of pasture. Formerly and still worth fifteen shillings.*" [1]

About two hundred years after the survey was taken, the Domesday name "Chiwestoch" had assumed nearly its modern form. In a document of the first year of Edward I. it is recorded that the six daughters of Geffrey Vassell held half a knight's fee in Kewstoch.[2] There is a tradition in the neighbourhood that Kewstoke was named after St. Kew, a hermit, who is said to have lived in a cell of which the ruins are still pointed out in the ravine climbed by a long flight of stone steps near the church and known as the Pass of St. Kew. Another theory is that the name is derived from the Celtic *Kewch*, "a boat." The sea at one time certainly came close up to where the houses now stand, and what looks like a landing-place may still be made out near the church, so that the "Place of Boats" may once have been a not inappropriate name for the village. If,

[1] A hide of land was a variable quantity, but is believed to have averaged 240 acres. A plough-team corresponded to half that amount. Serfs were the absolute property of the lord of the manor, and could be sold like cattle. Boors were the highest class of farm-labourers employed on the estate. Villeins belonged to the vill or manor, but they had land and chattels of their own.—Eyton, "Domesday Studies."

[2] Collinson.

however, Mr. Eyton is right in identifying Kewstoke with Chiwestoch, neither explanation seems adequate. Mr. Isaac Taylor derives "Chev," in Cheviot, Chevening, Chevington, and other words, from the Celtic *Cefn*, "a ridge." It is possible that "Chiw" in the old Norman name may be from the same root, and that Kewstoke may mean "the Village on the Ridge."

The Church of St. Paul is chiefly of Perpendicular date, but the building bears evidence of many alterations, and there are remains even of Norman work in it. Some of the windows are Decorated, and some are Perpendicular; but the greater part of the church is of Perpendicular character. Little is known of its history, but in the records of the ecclesiastical taxation of England and Wales, made by order of Pope Nicholas IV. about 1291, "Ecclia de Kystok" is valued at £5, 6s. 8d. It was then the property of the neighbouring priory of Woodspring.[1] The date of its most noteworthy feature, the sole relic of the original building, the fine Norman doorway inside the porch, is probably between 1125 and 1150. The beautiful stone pulpit partly let into the north wall is late Perpendicular work, perhaps of about 1500, while the window near it is older, probably of the fourteenth century. The chancel window, of two lights cinquefoiled, is also Decorated. The old stained glass in the south transept is said to have been

[1] Collinson.

brought from Woodspaing. There is a clerestory, a rather unusual feature in Mendip churches, and the doors of the old rood-loft still remain. No trace can now be found of the "mutilated effigy of a female," which in Collinson's time was to be seen in the floor. The four comparatively modern bells are thus inscribed:—

1. ANNO DOMINI 1637.
2. MR. IOSEPH SHEPPARD. CH. WARDEN, T. BILBIE, 1748.
3. V. A. CH.W.: 1734. T.B.
4. ANNO DOMINI 1637.[1]

The Parish Registers of Kewstoke begin with the entry of a baptism in 1667, but the entries for the first six years have evidently been copied from a still earlier record. An interesting point is the occurrence, at the very commencement of the Register, of names which are still represented in the district, such as Young, "Shippard," Day, and "Bisday." In 1678, in order to damage the linen trade and to encourage the manufacture of woollen fabrics, there was passed an Act of Parliament requiring that all burials were to be in woollen, under a penalty of five pounds. The fourth entry in the Kewstoke Register for that year runs thus:—

"Georgius filius Georgii Counsell. Sept. 4th. Affidavit was brought mee by George Counsell senr Sept 10th under ye hand of Jo Prows of Compton B'p Esqr and under ye hands and seales of Mastr

[1] Ellacombe, "The Church Bells of Somerset."

Norman Doorway, Kewstoke Church

Hobbs and John Layle Esq he made oath yt his son George was buryed in nothing of Linning." The remaining nine entries for the year end with the words, "In nil nisi Laneis," or "In solis Laneis"; that is to say, "In nothing but woollen," or "In woollen only."

The Account-Books of the churchwardens and overseers which have been preserved since the year 1695, contain many curious entries relating to the relief of the poor, to church repairs, to contributions towards the expenses of the county, to the destruction of "vermin," and other subjects of local interest.

Spelling is seldom a strong point in these old records, but it is certainly strange to find that the churchwardens of different periods have written the name of their own village in no fewer than eight different ways, the variation being almost invariably in the second syllable: Kewstick, Kewstoak, Kewstok, Kewstock, Kustock, Kewstoake, Kewstocke, and Kewstoke.

In addition to notes of relief given to poor parishioners there are many curious entries relating to tramps, each of whom was obliged by law to carry a "Brief," or "Certificate," usually signed by a magistrate, to prove his title to assistance:—

1695. Item given to one travelling man, which had great loss by fire, as by his Brief appeared .	0	3	00
It. given to one John Sympson, which had great loss by salt water, as by his certificate appeared	0	2	00

A number of entries in 1695 allude to sailors who claimed to have suffered as French prisoners :—

It. given to 24 seamen, which had been taken by ye French, as by their certificates appeared . 0 2 00

It was likely enough. Five years before, after his victory over the English and Dutch fleets, Tourville had swept the Channel unopposed. His galleys had anchored in Torbay, and had burnt the village of Teignmouth. Since then he had indeed been beaten at La Hogue. But the very year before this entry had witnessed the disastrous attack on Brest by the English fleet under the Earl of Berkeley, when Talmash, in command of a hundred boats full of soldiers, tried to land in face of tremendous odds, and got his last hurt from the battery still called the "Englishman's Death"; when more than a thousand poor fellows perished, and when for days afterwards, the sea "continued to throw up pierced and shattered corpses on the beach of Brittany."[1]

One of the most curious of such entries is this :—

1702. It. gave unto 7 poor ship carpenters that had their bones broken at Bristoll . . 0 1 0

It was not an excessive sum to divide among so many, but he was surely a credulous warden who believed the story. More than forty years afterwards it was decided that, in future, any churchwarden

[1] Macaulay.

who relieved any beggar or vagrant whatsoever, must do so at his own expense.

From 1698 to 1732 (when it was agreed "that no poulcatte nor hedgehodge shall be payd for the yeare ensueing"), many rewards were given for the destruction of "vermin." Among the slain in those years were seventy-three polecats and three martens. The former are now very rarely seen in the Mendip Country, and the latter have long been extinct.

Between 1745 and 1756 a severe Cattle Plague raged in Western Europe and in England, destroying, it is said, about three millions of cattle. It reached Somerset, as may be seen from entries in the Churchwardens' Accounts of the time. In the Kewstoke books are several allusions to it:—

1747.	Item pd. for 3 Boock for ye distemper upon ye cattell	00 03 00
	For to books for distempered cattell	00 03 00
1748.	Pd. for another book about the cattell	00 01 06

Perhaps the most interesting entries in the whole set of books are two which relate to Woodspring. There has always been a tradition in the district, as already remarked, that after the expulsion of the Friars, the Priory was used for a time as a hospital. There are many allusions in the Churchwardens' Accounts of neighbouring parishes to contributions to some hospital, which is further described, in some cases, as for "Maimed Soldiers"; but there appeared to be no evidence to connect this institution with the Priory. Mr. Ernest E. Baker, however, found in the Kewstoke records these two entries, which, though they do not name the Priory, go far to support the tradition :—

1722. It. year allowance for Woodspring Hospitall	0	05	0
1725. It. year's allowance for Woodspring Hospitall	0	05	0

The payments have not been traced later than the year 1734, when it is supposed that the hospital was given up.

In 1748 was re-cast the most modern of the church bells. The work was done, as the inscription on the bell records, by T. Bilbie, of Chew Stoke. In the Accounts are these entries :—

1748. Pd. for casting the second bell .	5	12	0
And for adding 71½lb. of mettall, 1s. per pound	3	11	6
Item paid for casting the ould brasses, 23 at 6d		11	6

It would be interesting to know the true significance of the last line. It does not seem to have been an allowance made by the bell-founder, or it might be taken to mean that the ancient memorial brasses of the church were, with that other "mettall," thrown by vandal hands into the melting-pot.

Kewstoke parish was in 1348 visited by the

The Becket Reliquary: Front of the Capital

Black Death, whose history is briefly given in the chapter on the Mendip Country. Joh. Price, who was Vicar in 1336, probably died in the Plague Year, and was succeeded by Mich. de. Greynton.[1]

The most interesting point connected with Kewstoke, a point of interest not to the county only but to all England, is a discovery which was made in this church in 1849. In that year, in the course of some repairs to the north wall, the masons removed a piece of Caen stone, a material not used elsewhere in the building. On the front of the stone, which resembles the head of a column, there is carved a battered effigy, apparently the half-length figure of a veiled woman. At the back, where it was embedded in the wall, is a hollow, an arched cavity about eight inches high, closed by an oaken panel. In this hollow was found a small cylindrical, dark-coloured wooden vessel, three inches in diameter, and but slightly more in height, and containing at the bottom a layer of some dark substance, pronounced, after careful microscopical examination, to be the remains of blood.

After the murder of Thomas à Becket, on the 29th of December 1170, small vessels filled with what was called "Canterbury Water," that is to say, water containing a minute quantity of the martyr's blood, were sold to visitors to his shrine. Most marvellous are the tales related by the monkish chroniclers of the time as to the virtues of this

[1] Weaver, "Somerset Incumbents."

wonderful water. By its use, sight, hearing, speech, reason, and even life were restored. A few drops of it swallowed or administered externally sufficed to cure the most desperate diseases. Benedict, sometime Prior of Christchurch, Canterbury, and afterwards Abbot of Peterborough, who professed to have witnessed some of the miracles which he describes, relates how a man, on his way home after visiting Becket's shrine, was belated at Rochester. In vain he sought shelter for the night. At door after door he was refused admittance. At last, "for the sake of the Blessed Martyr," he was taken in. In the night the town caught fire. When the citizens were fleeing, panic-stricken, "the pilgrim, whose faith was more fervent than the material flame, remaining boldly on the roof, called for a spear, or something long. A fork [hayfork, perhaps] was handed up to him; then, taking from his neck the Reliquary [containing 'Canterbury Water'], . . . he fastened it to the fork, held it out towards the fire," and thus kept the flames at bay. For "the fire, as if fearing a contrary element, turned aside." Finally, the whole town was burnt, with the single exception of its one hospitable house.

The precious liquid was at first sold in small wooden vessels, fitted with lids, in which mirrors were sometimes fixed; "specula mulierum," as the monkish chronicler puts it. But as wood was apt to split, flasks of lead or earthenware were used instead. These were hung from the neck, as in the

THE BECKET RELIQUARY: BACK OF THE CAPITAL

Showing cavity with oaken door, and cup supposed to have contained blood of Thomas à Becket.

case of the pilgrim in the Rochester episode, and came to be regarded, like the palm-branch of Jerusalem or the scallop-shell of Compostella, as an emblem of the pilgrimage to Canterbury. It was not an uncommon practice, in old days, to place in a martyr's tomb a small vessel filled with his blood. Many such have been discovered in the Catacombs. In the Kircher Museum at Rome there is an agate cup, containing the remains of blood, which was found in the Catacombs of St. Calixtus. It is a bold guess, but still a guess that has much to support it, that this little wooden cup, which was thus found built up in the wall of Kewstoke Church, is one of the very Reliquaries which were dispersed through the country after Becket's martyrdom; that it once held no less precious a relic than "Canterbury Water"—in short, that the dark layer at the bottom is what passed, seven centuries ago, for the blood of the Blessed St. Thomas himself.

Of the history of this little wooden cup nothing is known; but if it really was one of the highly prized Reliquaries of a credulous age, it is quite possible that it was among the most cherished possessions of Woodspring Priory—whose grey tower shows out against the low green hill behind it, a mile and a half to the northward—an establishment one of whose patron saints was St. Thomas à Becket himself. And when, after the Dissolution of the Monasteries, the little company of Woodspring Friars turned their backs upon the Priory, it is likely enough that they should cherish hopes that they might one day return, and that they built this Reliquary into the wall of Kewstoke Church to wait for the better times that for them were never to return.

Near the church, descending a little hollow in the side of Worlebury, sometimes called the Pass of St. Kew, rather more than a mile from the old encampment, is an ancient stairway, roughly built of unhewn stones, known as the Monk's Steps. In a level place at the top of the steps, of which there are rather more than two hundred, is a chamber, about nineteen feet long and twelve feet broad, with sides faced with well-built masonry, and almost entirely below the ground. This chamber is commonly regarded in the district as the cell of a hermit, the traditional St. Kew, the builder of the steps, from whom the village itself has been said to take its name.

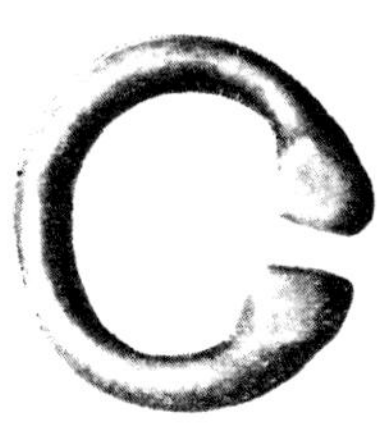

Silver Fibula from the Monk's Steps

From this Cell of St. Kew, the real use and origin of which are quite unknown, many curious things have been recovered, "ranging from early British to late mediæval dates." Among these are a Saxon knife, a fifteenth-century spur, a sword-hilt of the time of the Great Civil War, and a quantity of coarse and primitive pottery.[1] Above the steps was found a

[1] C. W. Dymond, F.S.A., "Worlebury."

The Monk's Steps, Kewstoke

small silver fibula or brooch, like an Arab ring, of a pattern said to be still in use in Egypt and Palestine. It is a slight link of evidence, but this little silver ring suggests the possibility that Phœnician traders came to the mining country of Mendip, either for lead or for zinc for the making of bronze.

There is no evidence of the existence here of St. Kew or any other hermit. And the Monk's Steps are more likely to have been the old church way to Kewstoke from Milton on the other side of the hill. Another theory, that they formed the way down from Worlebury Camp to the landing-place below the church is supported by the fact that the pass appears to have been artificially narrowed by rude masonry, as if for purposes of defence.

At the meeting of the Somersetshire Archæological Society held at Weston-super-Mare in 1851, there were exhibited three Roman cameos, on which were engraved portraits of Nero, Claudius, and Germanicus, which had been found at Kewstoke.

Along the western side of the parish stretches the broad beach of Sand Bay, fringed with grey shingle, and with picturesque and grass-grown sand-hills; while the ebbing-tide leaves bare a vast and monotonous expanse of mud, whose sombre levels form in winter time a feeding-ground for a multitude of birds. The seaward side of the sand-hills, which the gales of centuries have heaped over an old sea-wall, are thickly covered with Marram, a tall sedge whose spreading roots keep the sand from drifting, and so help to form for the low-lying meadows inland a further defence against the tide. In 1607, when, by the breaking of the sea-wall near Burnham, a hundred square miles of the northern part of Somersetshire were flooded to the depth of eleven or twelve feet, as we learn from a Black-Letter Chap-Book of the time,[1] Kewstoke was among the parishes that suffered.

In the greater solitude of Sand Bay the sea-birds that in the winter throng the mud-flats of the coast of Somerset, find a more congenial haunt than on the other side of Worlebury Hill. Perhaps no sea-fowl actually breed on this part of the shore, except a few Ringed Plovers, which lay their eggs among the shingle, and the Sheldrakes that make their nests in the rabbit burrows on the slopes of Sand Point. But all through the autumn and winter, and until late on into the spring, the mud-flats that stretch out from Kewstoke sands are frequented by crowds of Gulls and Waders. The Gulls are plain to see against the quiet colouring of their feeding-ground. Conspicuous too, especially in flight, is the black and white plumage of the Oyster-catcher, and his musical cry is here as familiar a sound of the sea as the plaintive whistle of the Curlew. But the Curlew himself is more difficult to discover as he stalks solemnly along. Nor does the eye find it easy to

[1] "Som. Arch. Pro.," vol. xxiv.

distinguish the graceful figure of the Redshank, or the smaller shapes of the multitudinous Sandpipers. The most abundant of these are the Dunlins, which in hard weather assemble here in thousands, and which, as they sweep along the sands or across the mud-flats, delight the eye of the observer with their marvellous evolutions; now as they fly, flashing in a myriad points of silver, now as they wheel all lost to view against the sober-tinted ground with which their feathers harmonise so well. Great flocks of Scaup Ducks, sometimes numbering many thousands, collect on the bay in winter, and at the same season the mouth of the Wick River, and the wider estuary of the Yeo are visited by many Ducks and Waders.

Among the plants of Kewstoke sands are the Broad-leaved Evening Primrose,[1] an established alien from North America, and the common Sea Lavender,[2] while in a hollow near the Point there lately grew a clump of Deadly Nightshade.

Among the many sand-loving land-shells which are to be found about the roots of the Marram and other plants, are great numbers of the little horn-shaped *Bulimus acutus*, a species never found far from the sea. On the same shore has been taken a rare Tiger Beetle, *Cicindela maritima*, an insect which comes out only in the sunshine, and then but for an hour or two in the middle of the day.

The loose stones of the shingle contain many carboniferous fossils, especially corals, Madrepore

[1] *Œnothera biennis.* [2] *Statice Limonium.*

M

and *Cyathophyllum*. The latter is abundant in the limestone rock at the foot of Middle Hope.

Sand Point is the name usually given to the seaward end of a low limestone ridge called Middle Hope, at the northern side of Kewstoke parish. The whole ridge, which in two places just reaches an altitude of a hundred feet above the sea, is nearly two miles long. But the part that forms the limit of Sand Bay, reckoning from the sand-hills to the end of the picturesque and rugged promontory stretching out into the Channel, measures less than a mile. There is good grazing-ground on the grassy slopes above Woodspring Priory; but on the narrower height to the westward, except for the Hawks that have their eyries in the low cliffs about its base, and for the Sheldrakes that make their nests in the rabbit-burrows higher up, there is little life at any time. The plants to be found there are the ordinary species of this coast—Thrift and Samphire and Sea Lavender. On the down itself grows the rare *Trinia*.

Along the cliffs on the northern side of Sand Point may be traced the remains of a raised sea-beach, of which fragments, consisting mainly of sand and pebbles firmly cemented together by the lime of abundant Limpet and Periwinkle shells, have from time to time been brought down by landslips. On the same shore, though nearer to the Point, is a dyke of Igneous Rock, believed by geologists to be contemporary with the layers of Carboniferous Limestone through which it has been poured.

The hill shows evident signs of human occupation, and there are traces of what was probably a fortified British settlement. Mr. C. W. Dymond, F.S.A., alludes to two sheets of loose stones on the southern side of the down, which are not natural, and which "have evidently been placed where they are for some not very intelligible purpose."[1] They may have formed part of the defences of the settlement, and they may, as has been suggested, have been intended as stations for slingers. "They flank and completely command a long, but not wide, level area, adapted for the concentration of invading troops, at the head of a good landing-place."[2] On one high point is what is often spoken of as the remains of a beacon. But in an old map, "The Coste of England uppon Severne," attributed to the time of Henry VIII., and reproduced in Green's "Somerset and the Armada," there are shown three round towers, each armed with two guns, which formed part of the defences of the county. Of these towers one stood at Uphill, another at Weston, and a third near Woodspring. Of this last it is not impossible that the foundations may yet be discovered among the loose stones on the high ground on Middle Hope. In 1810 there was still standing on the promontory a large mound of earth and stones, called Castle Batch.[3]

Rather more than a mile to the north of Kew-

[1] C. W. Dymond, F.S.A., "Worlebury." [2] Ibid.
[3] Mr. Bennett's Manuscript.

stoke Church, in the shelter of the low green hill that skirts the shore, stand the ruins of Woodspring Priory. Little is known of its history. A letter, bearing date a few years before the sealing of Magna Charta, announcing to the Bishop of the Diocese the writer's intention of founding the Monastery, and the document, signed by the Prior and his handful of companions, acknowledging the supremacy of King Henry VIII., are almost the sole records left of the men who, for rather more than three centuries, lived and died in this grey old house by the sea. In Dugdale's *Monasticon* there is a copy of the letter written in the year 1210 to the Bishop of Bath by William de Curtenai, grandson of De Traci, one of the murderers of Thomas à Becket, saying that the writer intended to found "a monastic house of the order of monks of St. Augustine, to be dedicated to God, the Blessed Mary, and the Blessed Martyr Thomas." The original letter was long preserved in the Cottonian Library in the British Museum. It is remarkable that all four of Becket's murderers—with three of whom De Curtenai was connected—were men of the West Country. De Brito and Fitzurse were landowners in this district, and De Traci and De Moreville were Devonshire men. There is, however, no suggestion in De Curtenai's letter that the founding of the Priory was intended as an expiation for the murder. It was, to use his own words, "for the welfare of the soul of Robert de Curtenai, my

Outer Gate of Woodspring Priory

father . . . and of my mother and myself; also of my wife, my ancestors and descendants." Nor, indeed, have we any evidence that the guilt of murder ever did lie heavy on De Traci's soul; though there is an old tradition that, after a brief reappearance at Court, he spent the remainder of his stormy life in seclusion on his manor near Morthoe, where, in the old churchyard by the sea,

> "Lie all the Tracies, with the wind in their faces."

Nor is there any reason to suppose that he and his companions suffered anything more than temporary disgrace. As Dean Stanley says in his "Memorials of Canterbury," all the murderers were at Court again within two years of Becket's death, and De Traci himself rose to high favour.

The Priory had been originally founded, as we learn from a document dated 1325 (18 Ed. II., part 2, leaf 33)[1] at Dodelyn—possibly Doulting, near Wells—by Geoffrey Gilbewyn. This was, however, probably not many years before the building of Woodspring Priory, since Gilbewyn endowed the new establishment with his manor of Locking. There are indeed records of gifts to the canons by many landowners. De Curtenai himself gave all his lands at Woodspring.[2] Among other gifts were those of William de Cantilupe, who, in 1226, gave to the monks fifty shillings rent and lands in Worle (Close Rolls of 10 Henry III., m. 2); and of Henry

[1] "Som. Arch. Pro.," vol. xxxi. [2] Ibid.

Cary, Vicar of Locking, who, in 1321, gave some Montfort property, a house and 58 acres of land, and a rent of twelve horse-shoes in Sandford (5 Ed. III., pt. 2, m. 30).[1] In 1410 two men, Robert Pobelowe and John Venables, surrendered to the Priory a prospective inheritance of nearly 200 acres of land in Rolleston, Pokerolleston (Puxton), Woodspring, Winscombe, and Worle (Pat. Rolls, 11 Henry IV., pt. 2, m. 21).[2] We may form some idea of the value of the Priory lands from a document (Chapter House, County Bags, Miscell., No. 15),[3] which, though undated, was evidently drawn up soon after the Disestablishment :—

"The rent of the hole demaynes there, beying in the Pryor's handes in parcels, and nowe letten and demysed for xxi yeres at the rent ensuing.

	£	S.	D.
Firste, cxx acres pasture, at viii^{d} the acre	4	0	0
Over cxxviij acres, arable, at iv^{d} the acre	2	2	8
Over xxx acres of wode and waste, at j^{d} the acre	0	2	6
Over xxx acres of mede, at xij^{d} the acre	1	10	0
Over xiij acres, mede, called Elman, lying within the parishe of Worle, at xvj^{d} the acre	0	18	8
Over xiij acres, mede, called Worle mede, lying in Worle aforesaid, at xij^{d} the acre	0	13	0
	£12	16	10"[4]

[1] "Som. Arch. Pro," vol. xxxi. [2] Ibid. [3] Ibid. [4] Ibid.

Woodspring Priory was a small establishment. It is said that the Canons who occupied it were probably never more than ten in number; and there are only eight signatures to the Acknowledgment of Supremacy in 1534. There can be no doubt, however, that the Canons were not the only tenants, and that the whole community, though not really large, must have been more numerous.

The monks belonged to a sub-division of the Augustinians, the Order of St. Victor, who owned only three other religious houses in the country. Dugdale says that they wore a long black cassock, with a white rochet over it, and over that a black cloak and hood. The monks were always shaved, but the Canons wore beards. Collinson gives the following as the list of the Priors:—

> "John, 1266.
>
> "Reginald was Prior in 1317, when he purchased forty acres of land in Woodborough of Henry Loveshate for the use of his monastery.
>
> "Thomas, 1383.
>
> "Thomas de Banewell died 1414.
>
> "Peter Loviare was elected November 18, 1414.
>
> "William Lustre died 1457.
>
> "John Gurman was elected 1458.
>
> "Richard Spryng was prior 1498. He resigned August 30, 1525.
>
> "Roger Tormynton, the last of the Priors, was elected September 24, 1525."

A letter of the year 1534 (S.P. Dom., Henry VIII., v. 6, 126) remarks that the writer was "enformyd by one of my lordes tenauntes there that the Prior of Wulspring shalbe deposed shortly."[1] And the document, of which the following is a translation, still exists in the Augmentation Office (the Office for the Augmentation of Crown Revenues), in which the Prior, Sub-Prior, and six Friars signed their names in acknowledgment that the Pope was a usurper, and that King Henry VIII. alone was the head of the English Church:—

"*Monastery of Worsprynge, in the Diocese of Bath and Wells.*

"SINCE it is not only in accordance with the Christian religion and piety, but also with our Vow of Obedience to our Lord King Henry, the Eighth of that name (to whom alone, after Christ Jesus Our Saviour, we owe all things), that not only should we at all times display towards Christ the same sincere, entire, and lasting devotion of heart, the same faith, respect, honour, worship, and reverence, but also that we should openly and most freely declare to all men (if occasion demand) the reason for this same faith and reverence, how often soever it shall be demanded. KNOW all men to whom this present writing shall come, that we, the Prior and Chapter of Victorine Canons of the Order of St. Augustine of Worspryng, in the diocese of Bath and Wells, with one mouth and voice, and with one heart, by a recent general consent and agreement, do, in this document given under our common seal, in our capitular house, on behalf of ourselves and of each and all of our successors, earnestly declare and testify, and faithfully promise and pledge

[1] "Som. Arch. Pro.," vol. xxxi.

ourselves, that we, the aforesaid Prior and Chapter, and each and all of our successors will always, with reverence and obedience, offer entire, inviolate, sincere, and lasting allegiance to our Lord King Henry VIII., and to Queen Anne, his wife, and to his offspring lawfully begotten and born, and that we will testify these same things to the people, and urge and counsel them, wheresoever place and opportunity may be afforded. ALSO that we hold it proved and established, and that we shall always and for ever so hold it, that the aforesaid Henry our King is Head of the English Church. ALSO that the Bishop of Rome, who in his edicts usurps the name of Pope, and takes upon himself the title of Sovereign Pontiff, should be held in no greater honour than any other bishop in his own diocese. ALSO that none of us, in any sacred observance, held either privately or publickly, shall call the said Bishop of Rome by the name of Pope, or Sovereign Pontiff, but by the name of the Bishop of Rome or of the Church of Rome, and that none of us will pray for him as Pope, but as Bishop of Rome. ALSO that to the aforesaid Lord the King and to his successors will we give allegiance, and that we will keep his laws and decrees, renouncing the laws, decrees, and canons of the Bishop of Rome which are found to be contrary to the Divine Law and the Sacred Scriptures, or contrary to the laws of the King. ALSO that none of us, at any time, in any public or private assembly, will presume to twist anything quoted from the sacred scriptures to any other sense, but that each will proclaim, in a catholic and orthodox manner, Christ and his words and deeds, simply, suitably, and honestly and according to the precept or rule of the sacred scriptures, and of truly catholic and orthodox teachers. ALSO that each of us, in conducting in the customary manner his sermons and prayers, will in future first of all commend to God and to the prayers of the people, the King as Supreme Head of the English Church, then Queen Anne and her offspring, then the Archbishops of Canterbury and of York, with other orders of the Clergy as may appear. ALSO that each and all of us, the aforesaid Prior and Chapter, and our Successors, do firmly bind ourselves, by the sacrament of our conscience and our oath, faithfully and heartily to observe each and all of the things aforesaid. IN TOKEN of which thing we append to this our writing, our common seal, and we have written our names each with his own hand. GIVEN in our Capitular house the twenty-first day of the month of August, in the Year of Christ one thousand five hundred and thirty-four, but in the twenty-fifth of the Reign of our King Henry the Eighth.

"ROGER TORMYNTON, Prior.
"JOHN SERCHE, Sub-Prior.
"Brother ROBERT COKE.
"Brother THOMAS GLASTUNBERY.
"Brother RYCHARD ADAMS.
"Brother JOHN AXBRYGE.
"Brother WILLIAM BRYNT.
"Brother ROBERT EVANS."

Below the signatures is the seal of the Priory, in brown wax. The device is difficult to decipher, but it apparently represents a church built over an archway, under which is what may be the figure of a man.

Two years after the date of this document all the minor monasteries were forfeited to the Crown: "Forasmoche as manifest synne, vicious, carnall and abomynable lyvyng, is dayly usyd and comytted amonges the lytell Abbeys and Pryoryes, whereby they spoyle, destroy, consume, and utterly waste all their goods, and albe it that many visytacons

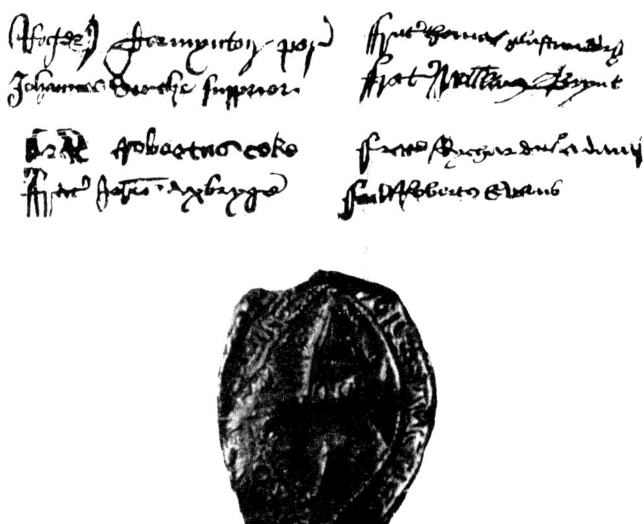

FACSIMILE OF SIGNATURES AND SEAL OF THE PRIORY

hath been had for two hundreth yeres and more, yet with lytell or none amendment." (27 Henry VIII., cap. 28).[1] Woodspring was among the "lytell

[1] "Som. Arch. Pro.," vol. xxxi.

Pryoryes." Its revenues amounted, as we read in Collinson, to £87, 2s. 11d., or some £2000 of our money. The date of the Act of Dissolution was February 4, 1536, but the Priory was not actually suppressed until September of the same year. Three years later, the site of the Abbey, "together with the demesne lands and the manors of Woodspring and Locking," was, by Royal Patent, granted to Sir William St. Loe, who, in 1566, sold the Woodspring property to William Carre. In the reign of James I., it passed out of the Carre family, and it now forms part of the Pigott estate.[1]

At the annual meeting of the Somersetshire Archæological Society, held at Weston-super-Mare, in 1885, Rev. J. W. Hardman, LL.D., of Cadbury, Congresbury, read the following letter, asking for the grant of the Priory lands :—

"RIGHT Worshipful, yn my most humblyst wise I can, I commend me unto your good mastership, thankyng your good mastership ever for the great kyndenes and ffavour shewed unto me always, and when it may please your mastership to call to your good remembrances that ye promysed me to be good master unto me when the tyme came: Sir your mastership shall understond that whereas yet I am not able to doo suche acceptable service unto the kynges highnes my master, as my poore and true hert could, and if I had wherwith to mayntayn it, so it is, pleasith it your mastership to understond,

[1] Collinson.

that when I desyred Mr. Bryan to be so good master unto me as to moshion unto your mastership to help me unto the gift of the priorie of Fynshed, a house of Chanons yn the countee of Northampton, of ye yearly value of lvj^{li} x^{s} xj^{d} ob. yn case it be subpressed, sir your mastership shall understond that sens that tyme my naturall ffather willed me to write to your mastership, and to non others, for to be good master unto me for a house of Chanons, yn Somersett shiere called Worspryng, where my said ffather is ffounder therof and as I do suppose of like value or theraboutes. And if it wold please your mastership to be so good master unto me as to helpe me to Worspryng priorie, I were and wilbe wylst I leve your bedman, and alweys redy to your mastership suche poore service and pleasure as shal become me to doo, whillest I do leve, God wyllyng, who ever have your mastership yn his tuysshon. From Bletherwexe, thus present Palme Sonday, by your own assured to his litle power.

"HUMFFRUY STAFFORD,
Esquyre.

"To the right honorable
Sir THOMAS CROMWELL,
Knyght, Secretorie.
To the Kynges hyghnes d. d. thus."[1]

Although the Woodspring friars were turned out of their Priory, they were not left wholly to shift for themselves. The community was dispersed in 1536; and in 1553 there still "remained in

[1] "Som. Arch. Pro.," vol. xxxi.

charge £1, 6s. 8d. in Fees."[1] Seventeen years after the Dissolution, it is probable that but few of the friars would be still alive; and this sum, about twenty-five pounds of our money, would perhaps relieve at least the pressing wants of the survivors.

We may well suppose that it was at this sorrowful moment that the Kewstoke Reliquary, the little wooden cup which had held the precious "Canterbury Water," and which must have been among the oldest and most cherished possessions of the Monastery, was placed carefully in its carved shrine, shut in with its oaken panel, and built up in the north wall of Kewstoke Church, the wall nearest to the deserted Priory, to wait for the home-coming of the friars. But for them the Abbey doors were closed, never to open more. And here in its dark nook this frail link with the "turbulent priest," who, nearly five hundred years before, had been struck down on the very steps of the altar, remained for three centuries, forgotten and unknown.

There has always been a tradition that after the Dissolution the Priory was used as a hospital. There are entries in the Churchwardens' Accounts of many parishes in the district of contributions to "the hospital," and even of a regular hospital rate, but in only one case is there anything to show where the building stood. This, as already pointed out, is in the parish accounts of Kewstoke, where

[1] Willis, "The History of Abbies," vol. ii. p. 201.

Mr. Ernest E. Baker found two entries which set the question at rest :—

1722. It. year allowance for Woodspring Hospitall 0 05 0
1725. It. year's allowance for Woodspring Hospitall 0 05 0

The payments cannot be traced beyond the year 1734.

For many years the Priory has been occupied as a dwelling-house, and its offices have served as farm-buildings—a fortunate circumstance, otherwise the ancient pile would doubtless have long since shared the fate of the monasteries of Banwell, of Athelney, and of Charterhouse, and have been pulled down for the sake of its materials. Much, indeed, has been thus destroyed. It is clear, from the appearance of the masonry outside the Friars' Hall, from the existence of blocked-up doors and windows in what are now mere boundary walls, and from excavations made some years ago at the east side of the tower, that in its palmy days the Priory was much more spacious than at present. The church, in great part at least, still remains; and its grey tower, on whose belfry floor the daws have heaped for generations their untidy nests, still looks across the level meadows that were grazed in turn by the sleek cattle of Thomas of Banwell, of Peter Loviare, and of Roger Tormynton.

Of the Priory that De Curtenai built but little

now remains. There is, indeed, one stone, a Norman capital, built into the wall at the entrance gate, which is believed to be a relic of the still older Chantry, which was standing here even before De Curtenai's time. But the greater part of what is now left is probably not earlier than the fourteenth century. To that period belong, it is thought by some authorities, the lower part of the tower, the cloister walls, and the walls of the outer enclosure. The upper portion of the tower, and the now detached building called the Refectory or the Friars' Hall, date from early in the fifteenth century; while the nave, the north aisle, and the monastic barn, at some little distance towards the north-west, were probably built late in the fifteenth or early in the sixteenth century.[1] Of these buildings one alone, the barn, still fills its original office. Of the rest the Friars' Hall is now a cart-shed, the nave has been converted into living-rooms, the north aisle is now a cider-cellar, and the tower is tenanted only by the daws.

Excavations in the autumn of 1885, on the east side of the tower, revealed the massy foundations of the choir, and showed that that part of the building must have been more than forty feet long and only slightly less in width than the nave. On the site of the altar there was found a quantity of fourteenth-century pavement, consisting of ornamental tiles bearing the arms of England, France, and the

[1] "Som. Arch. Pro.," vol. xxxi.

Isle of Man. Many fragments of carved stonework, evidently parts of the choir windows, were also discovered, together with leaden coffins and parts of skeletons. Pieces of burnt stone and wood suggested that that end of the church had been destroyed by fire.[1]

The picturesque doorway of the present living-room—once the nave—opens on a grassy space round which once ran the cloisters. Now only the outer walls remain, enclosing the level turf of the cloister-garth, the burial-place of the friars. In the south-west corner is part of the turret-stair that led up to the dormitory, the outline of whose roof is sketched by traces of a gable against the wall of the nave. Opposite to this stair-turret, through the eastern wall of the cloister, was the way to the building now known as the Friars' Hall. In the same wall are two blocked-up arches, and the remains of a fine doorway which may have been the entrance to the Chapter House.

Woodspring Tower, the most striking feature of the Priory, was in the centre of the church; and round the chamber at its base—whose vaulted roof is of beautiful fan tracery, carved in Caen stone—can still be seen four arches, though all but one are built up, and the only way into it now is by the ancient entrance of the choir. It has been said that the tower was at first oblong in its plan, and that the original thirteenth-century work still remains

[1] "Som. Arch. Pro.," vol. xxxi.

encased in the square and symmetrical masonry of two hundred years later. Round the belfry are four tall and graceful Perpendicular windows, with

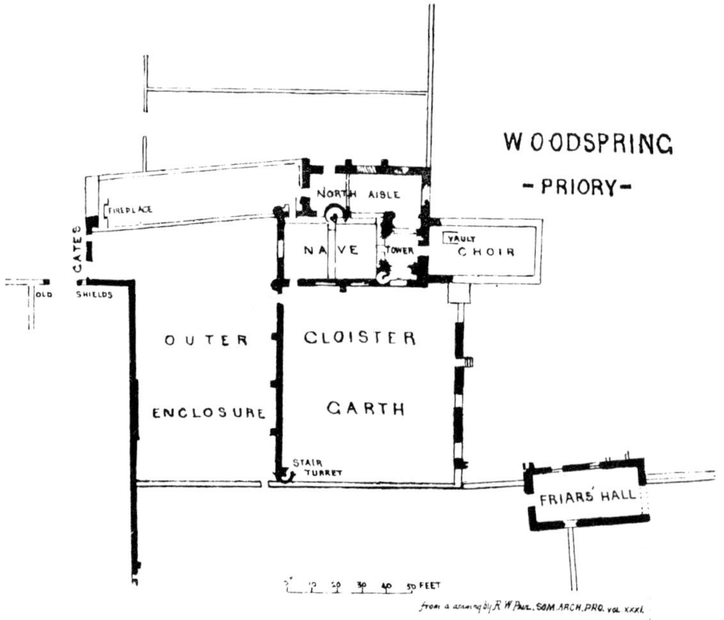

Plan of Woodspring Priory

open carved stonework in the centre. Rutter speaks of the tower having been "originally surmounted by a pierced parapet, with ornamented pinnacles at the angles, and smaller ones in the centre, none of which remain." His drawing, dated

1826, shows neither pinnacles nor parapet. The latter has been restored to its place, but with no pinnacles to relieve its stern and simple outline. On the north side of the Priory is the aisle, now divided for the use of the farm; and half-way up its walled-up windows is the floor of the modern sleeping-rooms. The way to them is by an ancient winding stair, which in old days may have led to a gallery for minstrels, or perhaps to a treasure chamber.

There is little in the interior of the building to suggest that it was ever used as a church. In Collinson's time there was still a chapel on the north side of the nave. In this, he says, "against one of the pillars which support the tower, is a cherub holding a shield, whereon is sculptured a chevron between three bugle horns, and on the opposite wall is another shield sustained in like manner, and charged with a heart between hands and feet pierced with nails, the usual emblems of the crucifixion." The chapel is now merely a part of one of the farm living-rooms, and of the two cherubs no trace remains. But the shields still surmount the tops of the posts of the gate that gives access to the farm precincts.

The west front has suffered severely at the hands of the builder who converted the Priory into a dwelling-house. Only the barest outline is left of the great west window, and of the original doorway under it even less remains. In the gable over the window is a vacant niche. And below, to right and left, are others, each holding a much-mutilated figure. Of these, one is no longer distinguishable, but the less damaged of the two, that on the north side, appears to represent a bishop, and may have been a statue of Thomas à Becket himself. The date, 1701 or 1709, on a stone over the door of the dwelling-house, may perhaps fix the period of the final alterations.

Not quite thirty yards south-east from the tower is the now detached building called the Friars' Hall. It is a well-proportioned room, forty-five feet in length, with lofty walls and an open timber roof. It is lighted by beautiful fifteenth-century windows, whose fine Perpendicular tracery is still perfect. The great doorway on the north, now walled up, was no doubt the original entrance from the Priory. This hall is sometimes spoken of as the Refectory. But it is large for so small a community; nor is it likely that any company of friars, even of the stern Order of St. Victor, would have been content to have a dining-room without a fireplace. It may have been the room in which the Prior gave audience to his tenants and retainers, but its real object can only be matter for conjecture. Part of a winding stair, against the south wall, suggests upper floors and other rooms, all trace of which has vanished. And the outlines of gables over its doorways, together with massy fragments of masonry adjoining it, afford evidence that the

GRANARY DOORWAY, WITH MONK OF THE ORDER OF ST. VICTOR

Friars' Hall formed an integral part of the Priory buildings.

To the north-west of the church is the great Priory Barn, a fine cruciform building, probably of the fifteenth century. There is a battered stone shield, believed to be of that period, on the south-west buttress. Two prominent features of the barn are the flight of stone steps leading to an upper floor, and the archway, now built up, which once, no doubt, gave entrance to the Prior's corn-waggons.

The word "Woodspring" is wholly modern. In Domesday Book the manor is called Worspring. Worspring—or Worspryng—was the name of the Priory from its founding to the date of its dissolution, and in all old records down to comparatively recent times, the word retains this form. In Dugdale's *Monasticon*, 1683, the word is still Worspring. Collinson, a hundred years later, alludes to the Priory as "Worspryng or Woodspring." The first part of the name is probably from the Saxon *Worth*, "a place enclosed." South of the great Priory barn may still be seen the spring that gave its title to the manor, and whose unfailing flow still fills the ponds that, doubtless, in old times furnished fish for the Canons' table.

Three small hamlets in the parish of Kewstoke, each little more than a cluster of houses, are remarkable in having given names to three families of more or less distinction. Sir Hugo de Nyweton, named among the benefactors of Worspring Priory in a Charter of Edward II., dated 1325, took his title from the little village of Newton, at the eastern extremity of the parish. The ancient Manor House, fronted by a noble avenue of elms, is still called Newtons; but it was rebuilt, and for a long time inhabited by the Selwoods, once a family of mark in the district, and repeatedly mentioned in the church records both of Kewstoke and Worle, though in neither place does there remain any monument to their memory. In the Burial Register of Worle it is recorded that, on the 29th of September 1613, "Honer Selwood vid. a gentlewoman well dissended, of the best of the Rodneys, of Rodney Stooke, and late wyfe of Anthony Selwood, was buryed." And in the Churchwardens' Accounts of Kewstoke is this note: "In the year 1739 was gave by John Selwood, Esqre., a sielver flagin to the church for the communion to the church of Kewstoke." Other members of the family of Newton, of the period of the Wars of the Roses and later, were buried in the Newton Chapel in the church at Yatton. In the house known as "Newtons" are three old oak gates, and on the landing is some fine woodwork.

Sir William de Norton, a contemporary of Sir Hugo de Nyweton, and also named in the Charter above alluded to, took his title from the little village of Norton, not far from Kewstoke, on the lower slope of Worlebury Hill; and the farm which stands on the other side of the road from Newtons is called the Manor House.

Towards the north of the parish, on a low knoll of Lias, so slight a rising that it hardly breaks the general level of the moor, is a spot called variously Culm, Colum, Colam, Culham, and Colham Farm. John and Henry Engayne were landholders here in the time of Edward I., and, like Sir Hugo de Nyweton, they both bestowed property on the neighbouring Priory. The former is further distinguished as having been a member of one of the earliest of English Parliaments. The participation of Knights of the Shire "in the deliberative power of Parliament, as well as their regular and continuous attendance," dates only from 1295.[1]

In 1301, King Edward I., then engaged in war with Scotland, laid before Parliament, assembled for the time at Lincoln, a Papal Bull, which had been handed to him by Archbishop Winchelsey at Sweetheart Abbey in Galloway not long before, in which Boniface VIII. claimed Scotland as a fief of Rome, and forbade Edward to molest the Scots.

The Barons, "after discussion and diligent deliberation," unanimously agreed that, as they were bound by oath to maintain the rights of the Crown, they would not suffer the King to comply with the Papal mandate, "even were he to wish it."[2] Among the ninety-seven Barons who, with seven

[1] John Richard Green, "A Short History of the English People."
[2] Stubbs, "Constitutional History of England."

Earls, gave this answer, "for themselves and for the whole community of the land"—the Clergy appear to have kept aloof on this particular occasion—the Lord of this insignificant west-country Manor thus subscribed himself:—

JOHES ENGAYN DNS DE COLUM.,

as may still be seen in a document preserved in the Houses of Parliament at Westminster.[1]

The farm-house at Colham is modern, and contains no traces of former importance. It stands on a slight rising in the moor; and it is possible that in Colham we have another trace of Scandinavian influence, and that the word may, like Cowlam in Yorkshire, which in old documents is spelt Cullum, be a corruption of the ancient Norse *Kulum*, which means, "at the mounds." Norton, like Weston, is named after a point of the compass. There are sixty-five hamlets called Norton in this country. Newton is the commonest of all English village-names, and is one of 129 places bearing the same simple and obvious designation.[2]

[1] The original document is lost. The copy dates only from 1644.

[2] Taylor, "Names and their Histories."

WICK ST. LAWRENCE

WICK ST. LAWRENCE, a moorland parish, no part of which is more than twenty feet above the level of the sea, adjoins Worle and Kewstoke, and, lying between the Wick River and the broad estuary of the Yeo, is bounded on the north by the shallow waters of Woodspring Bay. It includes the three hamlets of Wick, Bourton, and Icelton, but contains altogether only forty houses, with less than two hundred inhabitants, having considerably declined in population since it was described by Rutter eighty years ago. There are many places in Somersetshire called Wick, all of them situated on low ground; and although some, at any rate, probably take their name from the Saxon word *Wic*, "a dwelling," others, like this particular village, which is on the sea-coast, and close to a navigable river, are in all probability derived from the Scandinavian *Wik*, "a creek," a word from which the old Norse Wikings—or, as we usually spell it, Vikings—took their name.

The manor is not mentioned in Domesday Book, being, at the time of the Norman survey, part of

Congresbury, and forming with that parish a distinct pre-Domesday hundred.[1] But a century later, in the reign of Henry II., the property belonged to the family of De Wyke, named after it, no doubt. In 1166, "when the aid was levied for marrying the King's daughter to the Duke of Saxony, Thomas de Wicha is returned as holding two knights' fees in this county, of Robert then Bishop of Bath. To him succeeded John de Wyke, who was living at the time of King John, and had issue another John de Wyke, who was a commander in the army of Edward I. against the Scots." In 1357, the manor of Wyke was granted to one John de Edyndon, by the third John de Wyke, whose mother, Egelina, retained during her life the manor of Yatton.[2] Her effigy, by the side of that of her second husband, lies in the Court de Wyck Chapel in the church at Yatton.

John Leland, King Henry VIII.'s Antiquary, visited Somersetshire twice, in 1540 and 1542. It was apparently in the latter year that he stayed at Sutton Court, near Chew Magna, making excursions through the neighbourhood in search of objects of interest. "From Southetoun onto Wike," he writes, "8. long miles." They must have been very long miles indeed, for, as the crow flies, the two places are fifteen miles apart. The old antiquary's description of the village is brief and uncomplimen-

[1] Eyton, "Domesday Studies."
[2] Collinson.

tary. "Banwelle," he writes, "standith not very holsomly, and Wike worse. The Fennes be almost at hande. Wood meately good aboute them." There is nothing in Wick St. Lawrence to correspond with the "large Maner Place, wherof most Parte was buildyd by Newton chief Judge of Englande," to which Leland alludes. This was no doubt the family seat of Court de Wyck, some miles away, not far from the village of Yatton. In Collinson's time this building was in ruins, and, to judge from his description of it, must have been extremely picturesque. It was, however, entirely pulled down a few years later, and a modern mansion erected near its site. In the reign of Queen Elizabeth, the manors of Congresbury and Wick became the property of John Carr, Alderman of Bristol, who, in 1583, gave both estates to the Mayor and Corporation of that city; and the Bristol Charity Trustees are still Lords of the Manor of both Congresbury and Wick St. Lawrence. Wick Church is still a chapelry of Congresbury, from which it was thus partly separated in 1236 by Bishop Drokensford.

The Church of St. Lawrence, which was restored in 1865, contains little of interest besides its beautifully carved stone pulpit, which is said to have been brought from Woodspring Priory. A staircase in the wall shows where there was once a rood-screen or loft. Among the monuments is a mural tablet in memory of a man who, having lost his way, was overtaken by the tide and drowned. It is thus inscribed :—

"To the memory of James Morss, of this parish, yeoman, who dy'd November ye 25th, 1730, aged 38 years.

Save me O God, the mighty waters role
With near Approaches, even to my soul:
Far from dry ground, mistaken in my course,
I stick in mire, brought hither by my horse.
Thus vain I cry'd to God, who only saves:
In deaths cold pit I lay ore whelm'd with waves."

The Communion Plate consists of a fluted silver chalice, with a cover, both in a good state of preservation, and inscribed:—

LARRENCE
1571
WECKE

There is also a silver paten, marked :—

WEEKE
ST. LAWRENCE
1684

As already noted in the chapter on Weston-super-Mare, the authorities at Wells decreed, in the year 1572 : "That the plate that beforetime were used to superstition shalbe defaced, and of the greatest challaice shalbe made a fayer Communion cuppe, with as much convenient speed as maybe before the ffeaste of Easter, and of the lesser challaice another

Stone Pulpit in Wick St. Lawrence Church

O

by the tyme before limited." The date on the Wick St. Lawrence chalice shows that here, as in some other places, the decree of the Wells Chapter had been anticipated. It may be added that about one-third of the parishes in the diocese possess at least one piece of Elizabethan plate.

The Parish Records, preserved in an old oak chest, consist of the Registers—that of Marriages beginning in 1615, of Baptisms in 1625, and of Burials in 1635; of the Churchwardens' Accounts, which have been regularly kept since 1655; and of the Overseers' Books, beginning in 1797.

The Harkness Memorial Window commemorates "The Providential Delivce from imminent peril" of the Rev. Wm. Harkness, who was being driven in a closed carriage when the horse bolted into a pond. The horse was drowned, but Mr. Harkness escaped unhurt. He afterwards became Vicar of Winscombe, and died in 1863.

None of the five bells is ancient. Three were cast in 1655, one in 1736, and another in 1761. The earlier bells bear curious legends:—

1. I . AM . THE . FIRST . ALTHOUGH . BUT . SMALL IF . I . WILL . BE . HARDE . ABOVE . YOU . ALL IOHN . SHEPEARD . SAMUEL . SHEPHEARD . 1655.
2. I . IN . THIS . PLACE . AM . SECKOND . BELL . I . WILL SHURELY . DOE . MY . PEART . AS . WELL . IOHN SHEPEARD . SAMUEL . SHEPEARD . 1655.
3. MR . IOHN . IONES . CH . WARDEN 1761 . BILBIE FECIT.

4. MR . GEORGE . SHEPPARD . MR . SAMUEL . THOMAS CH . WARDENS . 1736 . I . TAYLOR . THOMAS BILBIE . CAST . MEE . GEORGE . NOTT . PUT . ME UP . GOD . SEND . GOOD . LUCK.
5. I . SOUND . TO . BEED . THE . SICKE . REPENT . IN HOPE . OF . LIFE . WHEN . BREATH . IS . SPENT IOHN . SHEPHARD . AND . SAMUEL . SHEPPEARD CHURCHWARDENS . W 🔔 P . R 🔔 P 1655.

The initials on the last bell are, no doubt, those of two of the Purdues, a famous family of bell-founders who lived at Closworth, near Sherborne.[1]

In 1791 Wick Church was struck by lightning, which greatly damaged the interior of the building, and left a crack in the tower which remained open for more than a hundred years. The incident was regarded as sufficiently important to be mentioned in the *London Chronicle* of January 14, 1791:—

"Last week at Wick St. Lawrence in Somersetshire, a Thunderbolt struck the Weather Cock of the Tower, and very much damaged the Pinnacle, entered the West Window, and took its course into the body of the Church, scorched the Pulpit Cloth, and cracked the Pulpit, which was built with Stone, and very much injured the whole of the Fabric. The damage is estimated at three hundred pounds."

The crack in the masonry was visible until about six years since, when the tower was thoroughly restored.

There were two stone crosses at Wick St. Lawrence. Of one, which stood in the churchyard, only

[1] Ellacombe, "Church Bells of Somerset."

the octagonal base now remains. But in an open space in the village, nearly opposite the church, is a fine example of a late fifteenth-century cross, which was restored by the Rev. Aubrey Townshend. Its delicately fluted, tapering, octagonal shaft rests on a massive square socket with panelled sides, and this again stands on five broad, octagonal steps. The height of the whole is slightly more than fifteen feet.[1]

The building near the church now used as a school was formerly the parsonage house.

Of the two small rivers that form the boundaries of this parish the Wick is an insignificant stream, rising in the pool in the middle of Banwell. The Yeo, which rises in a somewhat similarly situated sheet of water in the village of Compton Martin, is much larger, and was once navigable even beyond Wemberham, near Yatton, where in 1884 were found the ruins of a Roman villa, in which was a long chamber believed to have been a boat-house. The river at this point is tidal, and on both sides of it there are high banks which extend as far as the first weir at the village of Congresbury. The position of the villa, on a site which, were it not for these defences, would be flooded at every high tide, makes it probable that the "sea-walls" of the Yeo were in existence at least as far back as Roman times. From coins which were found among the ruins, it would appear that the house was occupied during

[1] Pooley, "Stone Crosses of Somersetshire."

the second half of the third and the first half of the fourth century. Barges brought coal up the river to Congresbury until the opening of the railway in 1869.

In the upper waters of the Yeo, which are now preserved, and under the control of the Avon and Brue Fishery Commission, fine trout have been taken, and the river also contains some large roach and rudd. In the tidal part of the stream there are a few sea-trout and many flounders, with plenty of eels. Both the latter are taken with the spear. Eels and flounders invariably go down to the sea to spawn, and eels, as is now known, never return.[1]

Otters, for whose destruction rewards were formerly offered by the churchwardens of the district, are still seen on the Yeo, as they are on so many streams in Somerset, and the otter-hounds occasionally meet on the banks of the river.

[1] Cunningham, "Marketable British Marine Fishes."

PUXTON

PUXTON is a small, low-lying, moorland parish adjoining Congresbury, and parted from Hewish by the rhine called the Oldbridge River, a tributary of the Yeo. No part of the parish is more than eighteen feet above the level of the sea, and in the great flood of 1607, which, according to a Black-Letter Chap-Book of the time, covered a hundred square miles of the northern moors of Somerset, Puxton was one of the villages that suffered. It is not mentioned in Domesday Book, being then included in the great manor of Banwell. The two parishes were indeed not divided until 1772, up to which time Puxton was a Chapel-of-Ease to Banwell.[1] Little seems to be known of the early history of the parish. In the Register of Ralph of Shrewsbury, preserved at Wells, is a copy of a letter written by the Bishop in 1333 to the Dean of Axbridge, stating that the visitation to be held at Uphill on the following Saturday will include the "Chapel of Pokerston." In the Patent Rolls of 1410 there is a reference to a gift to Woodspring Priory of some land in "Pokerolleston.[2] According

[1] Collinson.

[2] 11 Henry IV., pt. 2, m. 21. "Som. Arch. Pro.," vol. xxxi.

to Collinson the manor belonged to the St. Loes from the time of Henry VI. to the reign of Elizabeth, when Sir William St. Loe "released his right therein" to Ralph Jennyns of Islington. His son sold the property to Wadham Windham, ancestor of the present Lord of the Manor. It is possible that the Moor Farm, an old building not far from the church, containing some carved stonework, oaken panelling, and moulded and ornamented ceilings, may have been the Manor House. It was in digging a ditch near the Moor Farm that a labourer found, in 1895, a small figure, five and a quarter inches high, either of bronze or copper, of very primitive workmanship, representing our Saviour on the Cross, which belonged originally either to a crucifix or to a piece of church furniture, such as a book of the gospels or a reliquary, and probably dates—on the authority of experts at the British Museum—from the thirteenth century. In the middle of the village are the remains of the ancient parsonage, whose one sign of former importance is a finely built chimney.

The feature of Puxton is its primitive little church, chiefly remarkable for its curious leaning tower, now three feet out of the perpendicular, owing no doubt to the giving way of the peaty soil beneath it. The same cause has led to a similar settlement in the more modern work of the chancel. The Church of St. Saviour was built, it is believed, in the thirteenth century, and although it has been considerably

Puxton Church

altered it still retains some Early English characters, especially in its windows. A good example is the small two-light window between the porch and the tower, which is further remarkable in possessing fittings as if for bars. Over the north door, deeply cut in stone, and surmounted by the arms of the St. Loe family, much spoilt by the chisel of a modern mason, is the date 1557, the year probably of some rebuilding. On the Festival of the Conception, December 8, in the year 1539, the "Church and Cemetery of St. Saviour at Puxton" were consecrated by William Fynch, the first and last Bishop of Taunton.[1]

A notable feature of the interior is a number of old benches of massive oak, hewn out apparently with the axe, quite plain, except for a slight ornamentation along the top. The pulpit, also of wood, is of later and better workmanship, perhaps dating from 1620, and with the usual Jacobean decoration. To the right of it, fixed to the wall, is the old iron frame of a long-vanished hour-glass. The plain circular font may be of the same age as the original church; but its basin rests on what looks like the bowl of a still older font, inverted to serve as a base. The silver communion chalice, whose cover is used as a paten, bears the date 1574. There is also a silver alms dish, six inches across, inscribed: "The Gift of Mary Counsell to the Parish Church of Puxton, Anno Domini 1771."

1 "Som. Arch. Pro.," vol. ix.

Two bells only remain out of the original five. One, which is very old, is inscribed, in antique lettering—

Johannes o Vocabitur

The other bears the inscription—

HENRY HOSKENS CHURCHWARDEN 1680. I P IP

This bell, as we learn from the Churchwardens' Accounts, was re-cast at Bristol in 1680, apparently from two old bells :—

Itm. Pd. for halling of ye Bells to bristol and bring home 01 10 00

. . . .

Itm. Pd. Bell founder as wee Agreed for casting of ye Bell 09 10 00

. . . .

Ye Mottal yt was Left out of the said two Bells was one hundred and five pounds which comes to fower pound seven shillons and nine pence at nyne pence ye pound 04 07 09

In the floor of the church, or let into the wall, are many old tombstones, bearing dates which vary from 1630 to 1666 ; and there are others, doubtless more ancient still, whose inscriptions are no longer legible. The following is one of many memorials to members of the Whippey family :—

MRS. ELIZABETH WHIPPEY WAS BORN IN THE YEAR 1646, AND DIED THE 12TH OF DECEMBER 1683.

" Here do I lye who in the flower of age
Ended the course of earthly pilgrimage.

Nothing is permanent. Swift time doth fly.
Rich, poore, young, old and middle age must dye.
You friends mourn not too much, it is in vaine.
Count that not loss which is my greatest gaine."

The Puxton Church Records consist of the Registers, which go back to the year 1542, and three sets of Accounts, that is to say, those of the Churchwardens, the Overseers of the Poor, and the Overseers of the Dolmoors or Common Lands in this and the adjacent parishes. The old record chest with its ancient locks still attached to it, is preserved in the church. The ancient register is written on vellum, in conformity with the command of Cromwell, Henry VIII.'s Chancellor, in 1536. The first page is headed :—

"The booke or Register of Chrystenings Marriages and Burialls (in) the Parish of Puxton, anno (domini) 1543."

Theregisters of baptisms and burials, however, begin in 1542. Among the baptisms is this curious entry :—

"Dinah, ye daughter of John and Ann Clement, being poore wandering people and as they say inhabbiters of ye Parish of Wootten under hedge in the countie of Gloucester was baptized May 10th, 1640."

Much less definite are these notes of burials :—

"A pore boye named Moses buried ye xiii day of December 1553.

"A pore boye commonly called Dutch Dick buried xi of September 1583.

"A pore boye buried from Henry Paynes house ye 2nd day of September 1586."

Although the entries in the Register are dated as early as 1542, they have all been re-copied from the commencement to the year 1616.

The Churchwardens' Accounts begin, to quote their opening words, in

"the yeare of ye Lorde one thousand-six hundred-sixty and five and in the sixteenth yeare of the Reign of ye sovraigne Lord Charles by the grace of God of England, Scotland, france, and Ireland. deffendr of the ffaith in All Causes—And on all persons As well sacred As Sevill within this his Majesties Realmes And Dominyons."

The entries in these accounts are similar in character to those of other rural parishes, and the majority of them refer to the repairing and care of the church, and to the relief of the poor. There are several allusions in the Accounts both of the Churchwardens and of the Overseers from 1655 to 1734, when the payments ceased, to contributions to a hospital—no doubt the one which is said to have been established at Woodspring Priory, after the dissolution of the monasteries :—

1665. Itm. Paid to the Hospitall and maymed Souldiers at Twelfth tide . . .	00 10 07
1673. I crave allowance for not paying the hospitall rat the time that it was dew at Crismus	0 04

Many poor travellers were relieved by both Churchwardens and Overseers :—

1686. gave to ffifteen poore people yt hath been taken by ye frensh	00 01 06

It must have been long before. There had been no fighting with France since the Secret Treaty of Dover in 1670.

1679. Itm. pd. To Severall poore Travailing people y^{t} came with passes y^{t} Lost Their Estates by ffire and shippwrack . . .	00 04 09
1683. It. pd. to William Shoges and his sonn that came with a pass undon by the Breach of ye Sea in the town of Skidin (?) in Lincolnsh	00 01 00
1688. gave to two poore seamen which was cast away at the homeses (The Holms) . .	00 00 06
1700. Itm. gave to travoling pasons that came with the brif and three Justes of peas hands to him	00 01 06

"To travoling pasons" may be rendered "two tramps"; and the last clause means that their Brief or Licence bore the signatures of three Justices of the Peace.

The charity of the parishioners was not restricted to those asking for aid on the spot :—

1667. Itm. Paid the Apparretor and . . . depputies at Axbridge about the fyer at London	00 01 06
1670. A true and . . . mony is gathered in the pīshe of Puxton by Morgan Williams, Churchwarden for a brife for the redeeming of the captivses in Turkey in November is as followeth : (Then comes a list of 17 subscribers, whose contributions amounted to) .	00 03 03

Many entries refer to the destruction of "vermin." It is interesting to note that the otter and the marten were then found in the district. Otherwise the records are chiefly remarkable for their spelling:—

1667. Itm. ffor distroying of Warments . 00 00 08
1674. It. paide Edm. Lawrance ffor destroying seaven hoadghougs and three poulcuts 00 03 04
1722. It. paid for an Oater . . . 00 01 00
1723. It. pd. for killing a notar . . . 00 01 00
1725. Itm. paid John Dover for a martain . 00 01 00
1726. Item paid David Smith for three Eachgogs 00 06

In 1733 it was agreed that no further rewards should be paid for any "polcat, martin, fox, oter, or grog or badger." "Grog" is no doubt meant for "grey," an old word for a badger. Polecats are seldom if ever seen in our time in the parish of Puxton. The marten—if it is really the marten that is meant, and not the stoat—has long been extinct in the district. But the otter is still seen on the Yeo, and a particularly fine one was lately killed in the parish.

Quaint as is the spelling of some of these entries, that of a century later is not always above reproach:—

1840. June 24. Pd. for a Prayer for the Queen for Her Majesty Providencil Eskepte being shoot at 00 02 06

The entry refers to the attempt, by a youth named

Edward Oxford, to kill the Queen and the Prince Consort, by firing two pistols at them, as they were riding in an open carriage up Constitution Hill, on the 10th of June 1840. Neither the Queen nor her Consort was injured. Oxford was confined for some years in a lunatic asylum, and was liberated in 1868 on condition that he went abroad.

In these Accounts are several allusions to the Cattle Plague which did so much damage in Western Europe and England between 1745 and 1756. The Privy Council commanded that all animals affected should be shot, and their skins destroyed, at the same time granting compensation to their owners:—

1745. Paid for ye Proclamation on ye Death of ye Horn Cattle	00 01 06
1746. Paid for 3 Acts of Parliament concerning ye Sale and Removal of ye fat and leane horned Cattle	00 01 06

In 1738 is the first reference to William Counsell, who died in 1771, and who left ten shillings for a sermon to be preached on the 5th day of January, and ten shillings in bread to the clerk and the second poor, to be equally divided between them on that day for ever. The money to be raised out of the profit arising from a piece of land called East Hayes in this parish.[1] The sermon is still preached, and the bread still divided every year.

[1] Collinson.

The Overseers' Accounts, which begin in 1660, contain many entries relative to the relief of the poor, to their food and clothing, medical treatment and burial. For example:—

	£	S.	D.
1684. Itm. pd. to the potecary for Joseph Avery towards the cure of his legge . . .	00	05	00
1708. It. for going to ye docktor for binwell and for oyle for his head and pills and in money before he undertook ye cure . . .	00	06	05
It. paid for to bottels of Stof for John Binwell	00	03	00

The "docktor" did not, however, perform what he undertook:—

It. paid for burying John Binwell . . .	01	04	06

An extraordinary feature connected with burials by the parish is the amount of money expended on food and drink, especially on the latter, at the time of the funeral:—

1723. It. for a pill, deare, for Francis Lane	00	03	00

"Deare" as the pill was, the patient did not recover, and the next entry runs:—

It. for a Coffing and shroud and ringing ye Bell for Francis Lane	00	16	00
It. for bred chees and buttur and spent at his buriel	00	16	00

Here is a case in which the "bread, cheese, and drink" consumed at the funeral cost more than the coffin, the grave, and the tolling of the bell :—

1710. It. pd. ye Crowners fees . . . 00 14 08
It. pd. for ye Coffin 00 09 00
It. for making ye grave and ringing the Bell 00 04 00
It. bread Cheese and Drink at ye buriall of Robert Amsbury 00 13 03

There is an extraordinary set of entries in 1788, about the death of a poor woman, whose decease was surely hastened by the treatment she received :—

1788. Dec 6. Let Grace Lovel have 13 Quarts of Brandy at 2/ p Qt 01 06 00
Do. 1 Gallon of Wine 00 07 00
Dec. 10 Pd. for a Coffin for Grace Lovel . 00 13 00
Do. for wool 00 03 00
Do. paid towards the funeriel . . . 00 04 00
Pd. Doctor Norman his Bill . . . 02 06 00
Pd. Phebe Ridler for attending Grace Lovel 00 17 00

The official consumption of drink was no small item in the accounts :—

1719. It. pd for ale at the making up of the accts 00 10 00
1744. paid for Licker att the Ester metting . 00 14 00

A few years ago, the parish Poorhouse, a ruinous but ivy-mantled and most picturesque old building, with an outside stair, was still standing in the middle of the village. No funds were available for its repair, and when at length it became quite unsafe for human habitation it was pulled down. This house was originally built with money provided by a special poor-rate, on land for which the Lord of the Manor received a nominal rent of sixpence a year. In 1727 the Overseers of the parish agreed to pay the cost of building "a House for the use of the Poore, which said House is to be built and plac'd on the Lord's Wast" (waste land belonging to the Lord of the Manor). The house was not built then, however; and although the wording of entries in the Parish Records is not clear, it would seem that nothing was actually done for nearly forty years. In 1761 the Churchwardens and Overseers agreed that certain necessitous people should be allowed to go into the Poorhouse "as soon as it is built, and all other Poore Persons that are impotent and Can't pay." In the same passage there is an allusion to "ye Rebuilding the Poore House," so that something may have been done in the interval. In 1867 the payment out of the rates of the sixpence a year to the Lord of the Manor was disallowed by the auditor, and the amount was thereafter paid by a private individual, who allowed two poor families to occupy the building. The last tenants of the house were an old woman and her son, who inhabited it until it was pulled down in 1899, in accordance with a resolution passed at a parish meeting.

In the parish of Puxton, and partly also in the adjoining parishes of Congresbury and Wick St. Lawrence, are two large pieces of land, called the East and West Dolmoors, in which some of the villagers had formerly certain common rights, decided every year by a kind of lottery, held on the Saturday before Midsummer Day.[1] The Dolmoors were in charge of two Overseers, who held office for a year, and appointed their own successors. One of their chief duties was to keep the allotments marked out in "Scroves" and "Sixes," by means of posts, which had to be constantly renewed. On a sheet of paper kept by the Overseers—found in 1883 torn in shreds, and carefully fitted together—are figured and described a number of hieroglyphics, each of which represented an estate or tenant having the right to one or more of the allotments:—

"The Names of the Marks of the Apples that Lays out the two Dolmoors.

"Five Poleaxes, four Crosses, two Dung Pickes, one handreel, one Horne, one Shell, one Oven, one four oxen and a mare, one five pits, one seven pits, one four pits, one three pits Brandierways, one two pits, one hares tail,—perhaps 'Harse' Tail—one Ducks Nest, one Evil (or halter).

"The Names of the Marks of the twelve Apples that lays out the Scroves in the West Moor and the Sixes (?) in the East Moore.

"Two Crosses, two Poleaxes, one four oxen and a mare, one four pits, one two pits, one shell, one Dungpick, one Ducks Nest, one horne, one Evil.

[1] The name Dolmoor is of great antiquity. In a charter of Edward II., dated 1325, it is recorded that Alicia Ofre gave to Woodspring Priory half an acre of meadow in "Estredolmore," and half an acre of meadow in "Westredolmore." [Pat. 18 Edw. II., p. 3, m. 33.]—Dugdale's *Monasticon*.

"The same Apples that Lays out the Scroves in the West moore Lays out the Sixes in the East Moore." (See Diagram on opposite page.)

Early on the morning of the ceremony those who had rights in the Dolmoors assembled in Puxton Church at the sound of the bell, in order to witness the testing of the chain that was kept for the purpose of insuring that the divisional posts were the proper distance apart. The regulation length of the chain is said to have been eighteen yards, measured from the foot of the chancel arch down the middle aisle, to the foot of the arch of the west doorway. Twenty-four apples, on which were cut the "Marks" already alluded to, some of them being, as will have been observed, in duplicate, were then taken in a bag to the moor. There the land was measured out, one acre at a time. As each acre was finished, an apple was drawn from the bag, and whatever mark it bore was cut in the turf of the first allotment, which then belonged for the year to the man whose name corresponded with that particular hieroglyphic.

The company then repaired to some house, in which a room had been hired for the purpose, when, in order to raise funds to pay the expenses connected with the allotments, a part of the Dolmoors, variously called the Out Drift or Out Let, was let for the year by a sort of auction known as "Inch of Candle." A piece of candle an inch high was lit, and silence was proclaimed under a penalty of a

1. Pole ax.
2. Cross.
3. Dung pick.
4. Handreel.
5. Horne.
6. Shell.
7. Oven.
8. Four oxen and a mare.
9. Five Pits.
10. Seven Pits.
11. Four Pits.
12. Three Pits Brandierways.
13. Two Pits.
14. Hares taile.
15. Ducks nest.
16. Evil (halter).

Marks cut on the Dolmoor Apples

shilling. A would-be tenant came forward, made his bid for the Out Drift, and laid down a shilling. Any man who made a higher bid, put down a shilling in his turn, when the first-comer would take his coin back. Each fresh competitor tendered his bid and his shilling, thus releasing the shilling of the man before him. The last bid made before the candle burnt out was taken, and the man who had made it was thereupon declared the tenant of the Out Drift for the ensuing year. The ceremony concluded with a wake or revel, several times alluded to in the Parish Accounts; and a considerable part of the expenses connected with the Dolmoors was for food and drink and tobacco, consumed apparently at this revel.

The following extracts are from the Accounts of the Overseers of the Dolmoors, between 1685 and 1691:—

	£	S.	D.
It. for 4 boushels of malt and grind of it .	0	10	4
It. for a Pound of hops	0	0	9
It. for to backco and pipes	0	1	2
It. for a chees that waied ten pound . .	0	2	10
It. for 2 pound of butor	0	0	9
It. for bred	0	2	0
It. for the yows of the hows	0	5	0
It. Pd. ye Carpenter for hanging ye yat .	0	1	0
It. Pd. for Sharping ye Iron gare . .	0	0	2
It. paid to the markers	0	3	0
It. ffor to Railes	0	1	0
It. for posts and Rails and geting them up	0	7	0

. . . . .

"We hath sould the out drift of Dolmoor this day to Edward Williams for one pound and fifteen shillings." The rent of the Out Drift appears to have varied from £2, 18s. to "attin shillings and sixpence."

In 1779 an attempt was made to allot the Dolmoors in perpetuity. The attempt was unsuccessful, and the land was finally enclosed in 1811, since which time the ceremony and its accompanying revel have been discontinued.[1]

The ecclesiastical parish of Hewish was formed in 1866 out of the parishes of Banwell, Congresbury, Kewstoke, Puxton, Wick St. Lawrence, and Yatton. The church, built in 1866, and dedicated to St. Anne, is rather more than half a mile due north of Puxton Church. Its tower had reached the height of seventy feet, when, owing to the soft and yielding nature of the soil, the foundations gave way. The unfinished tower fell, and has not been rebuilt.

Hewish, or Huish, as it is spelt in other places, is the name of several parishes in Somerset and Devon; as, for instance, Lud-Huish, Huish Champflower, and Huish Episcopi. The word is a corruption of the Anglo-Saxon *hiwisc*, a hide of land.[2]

[1] Mr. George Bennett's Manuscript.

[2] Isaac Taylor, "Names and their Histories."

WORLE

THE parish of Worle extends across the eastern end of Worlebury from a little south of the railway line to within a short distance of the village of Wick St. Lawrence. Although part of it is on the hill, reaching an altitude of two hundred feet above high-water mark, it lies chiefly on the flat, on the edge of the alluvial plain which occupies so much of the western end of the Mendip Country, and which at this point is not quite twenty feet above the level of the sea. Castle Batch, named after a tumulus which stands upon it, is a long ridge of Lower Lias, half in this parish, and half in that of Kewstoke. Between this ridge and the Carboniferous Limestone of Worlebury is a narrow strip of Dolomitic Conglomerate, and a broader belt of Red Marl. But the greater part of the parish is alluvial, with peat—locally known as "Noah's Flood Stuff"—underneath it. The peat is of varying thickness, and contains pieces of wood, perhaps chiefly yew, with hazel-nuts and acorns. Below the peat comes a coarse gravel, with sand and fragments of conglomerate. No doubt the sea once covered all the low-lying country near Worle, and some years ago, in digging foundations for a brewery in the

WORLE WINDMILL

village, an iron anchor was found ten feet below the surface.

The village of Worle, like Frome at the other

end of Mendip, has kept its name unaltered by a single letter since its brief description was set down in Domesday Book. The manor was then the property of Walter of Douai:—

"*Walterius de Dowai holds from the King Worle. Esgar*[1] *held it in the time of King Edward, and paid Danegeld for six hides and a half. There is land for fifteen plough-teams. In the demesne are four plough-teams, and five serfs, and twenty-two villeins, and three boors, with nine plough-teams. There are fifty acres of meadow. Pasture thirteen furlongs long, and two furlongs broad. It was worth ten pounds: now seven pounds.*"[2]

It was suggested by the Rev. J. A. Bennett, that the marked decline in the values of some of the manors in this part of the county, which the survey says took place between the time of Edward the Confessor and the date of the Norman record, was due to ravages committed by one of the sons of

[1] It may be merely a coincidence, but it is a curious fact, that Isgar is still a well-known name among the yeomen of the South Marsh below Worle.

[2] A hide was a somewhat variable quantity, but is supposed to have measured as a rule 240 acres. A plough-team corresponded to half that amount, or 120 acres. Serfs were slaves, the absolute property of the Lord of the Manor, to be bought and sold like cattle. Villeins belonged to the vill or manor, and were the highest of the classes that had no sort of freedom. Boors probably lived near the manor-house, and were the highest class of farm-labourers on the estate.—Eyton, "Domesday Studies."

Harold, who in 1067 suddenly crossed over from Ireland with a fleet of war-ships, sailed up the Avon, and plundered all the neighbourhood. But having failed in an attack on Bristol, the marauders retired "to Somersetshire, where they went up the country."[1] This fall in value, from whatever cause it arose, may be seen in the accounts given in Domesday Book of Worle, Hutton, Berrow, and other places near the coast; and it may also be traced as far inland as Shipham, Cheddar, and Wedmore.[2]

At a later period, Worle was the property of William de Curtenai, the founder of Woodspring Priory, and at his death in the reign of Henry III., the manor passed to his relative, Sir Vitalis Engayne. His sons gave the estate to the Prior and Canons of Woodspring, and it remained in their possession until the dissolution of the monasteries, when it was granted to Sir William St. Loe.[3] At later periods it passed into the families of Wallys and Coker of Dorsetshire, and Wyndham of Norfolk. The principal landowners in the parish at the present time are William Wyndham of Salisbury, and Arthur Hardwick of Worle.

The feature of the village of Worle is the picturesque old Church of St. Martin, which, originally built in the twelfth century, and a good deal

[1] Anglo-Saxon Chronicle.
[2] "Som. Arch. Pro.," vol. xxv. Domesday Book.
[3] Collinson. Dugdale's *Monasticon.*

altered in the time probably of Henry VII., was well restored in 1870. It is referred to in De Curtenai's letter to the Bishop of the diocese, relative to the founding of Woodspring Priory. The low square tower is surmounted by a curiously dwarfed spire, which, owing to a rearrangement of its stonework, has a somewhat disjointed appearance. The south porch has been in great part rebuilt, but round the inner door is the original Norman arch, which possibly dates from about 1125, or from the same time as that in Kewstoke Church on the other side of the hill. The lower part of the tower may be of that period, and the font, a good plain octagon, is no doubt also Norman. In the east wall of the porch is a small window filled with fragments of modern coloured glass, presented to the church at the time of its restoration. The stonework, however, is ancient, older than the porch. There was

DOORWAY OF WORLE CHURCH

formerly a good deal of stained glass in the building. There are old men still living who remember playing with the broken pieces. On the south side of the church, next to the porch, is a fine square-headed window.

The arch of the window at the west end of the north aisle rests on two heads, that on one side almost effaced, but the other representing the head of a woman with a horned head-dress of the time of the Wars of the Roses. There are two other finely carved heads of a king and a queen to right and left of the tower door. Connected by a winding stair with this north aisle is a beautiful octagonal turret. There is a tradition in the village, that in old days smugglers used to carry their kegs up this stair to a hiding-place, which has now disappeared, contrived in the ancient roof of the aisle.

The fine hexagonal stone pulpit is elaborately carved, but its details have been left in a somewhat unfinished condition. It is not, however, in its original position, but was placed where it is when the church was restored. Near it is a small recess, perhaps an ambry. Under the south window of the chancel is a piscina in the window-sill, with a small ambry in the splay of the window-jamb. The water-drain is hidden by a carved leaf. In the chancel is a piscina of simple design, and near it in the north pier of the chancel arch is a narrow, square-headed aperture, which is a squint, or hagioscope.

A hagioscope was an opening in the wall of a church through which those outside—lepers, or other persons forbidden to enter the sacred precincts—might witness the "Elevation of the Host"; or it may have been made so that an attendant could watch for the right moment for ringing the Sanctus Bell which marked the periods of the service. Also in the chancel, to the west of the piscina, are two sedilia—stone seats let into the wall, with finely carved canopies. These were either for priests, or for fugitives who had fled for sanctuary into the church.

The most remarkable possessions of the church are the old "misereres," carved seats which could be turned up, so as to give support to a worshipper while still standing. Only those on the north side of the chancel are original. Those on the south side are copies made when the church was restored. The former are said to have been brought from Woodspring Priory, but the carvings on them, partly because they are on the under sides of the seats, are as fresh and unworn as if they had been finished only a few years since, instead of being, as is quite possible, six centuries old. One of these "misereres" bears a shield, with the letters P.R.S., doubtless for Prior Richard Spryng. Made Prior of Woodspring in 1493, he became Vicar of Worle while still holding that office; and he retained the Living from 1499 to 1516. He resigned his post as Prior in 1525. On the next seat are grapes and vine-leaves, on the third a bud and a leaf, on the fourth a winged dragon, and on the fifth two monks' heads under one cowl.

The organ has a curious history. It is said to have been brought to Worle from a Unitarian Chapel at Blackburn. But it was built at Frankfort-on-the-Maine, and the date of its completion, 1662, is recorded on one of its stops.

The six bells are thus inscribed :—

1. WILLIAM . COCKEY . BELL FOUNDER . W. [Re-cast in 1731.]
2. ED . BILBIE CAST ME · 1723 · · · DAN . STARR . CH . W.
3. No inscription.
4. RICHARD . SHEPHARD . AND . PETER . DAY . CH . W. 1683 . R . P.
5. IOHN . RUDHALL . FECT. ISAAC . PRINTER . CH . W. 1820.
6. MR . IOHN . WATERS . CH . W. 1745 . T . BILBIE.

The initials on the fourth bell are those of one of the Purdues, of Closworth, near Sherborne.

The Communion Plate consists of a modern silver flagon and paten, inscribed: "Presented by T. Castle to the Parish of Worle, 1860"; and of a silver-gilt chalice, with a cover serving as a paten, apparently of the Restoration period. The chalice has, however, no Hall Mark, and some authorities believe it to be of earlier date.

In the churchyard is a small, stumpy gravestone, almost like a fragment of the shaft of a churchyard cross in shape, and on it, in a small panel, is this inscription :—

A MAID IN MOLD
60 YEARS OLD
JOANNA
1644.

The name is almost effaced, and unfortunately the Register contains no entries of burials for 1644. This is apparently the oldest stone in the churchyard.

The Parish Registers of "Burialls, Christeninges, and Weddinges" go back to within ten years of the defeat of the Armada. The oldest volume, which records the period from 1598 to 1703, is written on parchment, and, although it has long lost its cover, it is in a fair state of preservation. One of the first entries contains a name well known in the district :—

"John Prynter, Vicar of Worle, ye 21 March, 1598."

In 1609, under the same heading as the last, is this passage :—

"Note.—Edward Bustle cruelly murthered by consent of his owne wyfe, who, with one Humfry Hawkins, and one other of theyre associates, were executed for the same murther, and hanged in Irons at a place called Shutt Shelfe, neere Axbridge, and the body of the said Bustle barberously used, viz. his throte cutt, his legs cutt of, and divers woundes in his body, and buryed in a stall, was taken up and buryed in the church yard at Worle, March Xth. A good president for wicked people."

Whatever may have been thought of the murderer, no disgrace seems to have attached to his widow, for the next entry but one relates that, on the 11th of the following October, she was married again to a man named Nicholas Pitman.

From 1662 to 1669 there seems to have been no resident Vicar. The entries in the Register are few, and in the whole seven years there is no record of a marriage at Worle. In 1664 is this note:—

"Marriges none that year, they were all maryed at Kewstoke by Mr. Tho. Ham."

There are other records in the book besides those of births, marriages, and deaths. In spaces between the entries have been written at various times notes on quite different subjects. Two of these refer to charitable bequests, which appear to have been long lost sight of. The first is dated 1629, and runs as follows:—

"A sum of money was gyven unto the poore of Worle, by the last will and testament of Lewes (presumably Warren), late of Worle, Yeoman.

"Item.—I give and bequeath to the poore people of Worle, aforesaid, the somme of tenn pounds of lawful Brytish money, to remain in a trust for them for ever. And the yearelye use or intereste thereof to bee distributed amongst them everie Good Fridaie att the church there by the overseers of the said poore for the time beeinge, or by them to bee lett out gratis without interest, in portons not exceedinge fortie shillings a peece, to such of the same poore as can give suffitient securities to repaye itt agayne at the ende of any one yeare, as the said overseers, with the consent of fower other of the chiefeste parishioners theare, in theire discretions shall think fit. Thys will registered the 12th day of Maye, Anno Dmi. 1629."

The second record is less legible, and the date is quite undecipherable :—

"Memorandum.—That the foure and twentieth day of December, Anno , was ent by Worshipful Merchant Adventurers of the cytye of Bristow a pulpitt cloth and a cushion of Jammasey for the pulpitt of the Parrish Church of Worle outt of the wish and benevolence of Mrs. Alice Coles late of the cytie of Bristoll widdowe who gave the rent of the parsonage barne of Worle to be bestowed (?) ad publicos usus by the appointment of herr feoffors for ever."

A curious entry to have found its way into the parish records is this couplet, of which the first two words can no longer be read :—

". . . . . . . in hands and love not to be idell
Sumthing I cann speak but my tongue I will bridell."

Who wrote it? Was it the young bride of some long-forgotten Vicar? The first line is a vow of wifely duty, no doubt; but what about the second? Did the writer mean that she could tell tales if she would; or that although she felt that she, too, possessed the gift of the ministry, she intended thereafter to obey the precept of St. Paul?

The second Register, which was begun in 1712, contains this record of the death of a centenarian :—

"1742. Old Gamma Jennet buried May 19th aged 109 years."

The Churchwardens' Accounts, which date from 1697, are similar in character to those of neighbouring parishes, and contain similar entries relative to the relief of the poor, to church repairs, county expenses, and the destruction of vermin. Here, too, we find the same pleas for help from the many tramps who came before the Wardens :—

1697. Item given to a poore woman undone by fire	00 01 00
Item given unto severall Cornish people that were undone by the breaking in of the sea	0 2 0

Worle, like other Mendip parishes, contributed to the Woodspring Hospital for "Maimed Soldiers" :—

Item paid the Ospital for the year '97. .	00 01 08

The treble bell is not dated. But in the Accounts for 1731–1732 are these allusions to it :—

1731. Item spent when ye treable was toock Down	00 01 00
Item pd. Hugh Flaning for fetching ye Bell from froom	01 01 00
Item spent when ye Treable was onloaded .	co 02 00
Item paid George Nott for Hinging ye treble an boring ye tenor	01 01 00
Item Spent on George Nott when ye worck was done	00 01 00

Item pd. Joseph Starr for Leather for ye third clapper	00 00 04
Item pd. Daniel Hart for ye iron geire for ye tenor	00 05 00
1732. Paid Mr. Cockey for Casting of Bells	43 14 6
Spent at same time	0 1 6

In the Bishops' Register at Wells are some remarkable entries relating to parishes in this district, which suggest that Somerset, like other parts of England, was ravaged by the Black Death. Among the visitations of this terrible pestilence, usually known as the plague—though its symptoms were much worse than that of the Great Plague of 1665 and other years—that of 1348–49, the outbreak of which at Florence suggested the plan of Boccaccio's *Decameron*, was especially severe in England. In London as many as two hundred bodies of those who had died of it were buried daily in the Charterhouse yard. In the Bishops' Register, in the list of institutions to the living of Worle, are these significant entries :—

"1347.	iiij Non. Jan.	Joh. de Stodelegh.
1348.		Joh. le Hayward.
	Id. Jan.	Rob. Geffray.
	ij Non. Feb.	Joh. Marks.
		Will. Harford." [1]

In 1348 the year began in March, and according to our reckoning these dates would refer to 1348 and 1349 respectively. There can be little doubt that

[1] Weaver, "Somerset Incumbents."

so extraordinary an occurrence as the appointment of four Vicars, within so short a space, means that the plague was in the parish. More than that it suggests that one brave priest after another kept his post and ministered to the sick and dying until he himself fell a victim; and that as each in turn went down before the dreadful scourge, another stepped fearlessly into the breach, and laboured and died, and left no sign beyond this brief entry in the Bishops' Book.

In the moor to the south of the village is a windmill, still in regular use. Near the eastern end of the hill there was formerly another, whose broken arms were still to be seen forty years ago. At a later period the old tower was restored and greatly raised in height, and converted into a kind of observatory.

Near the church there stood a monastic barn, which once belonged to Woodspring Priory; and a sketch of part of the old building, which in Rutter's time was in ruins, is one of the most picturesque illustrations in that author's "Delineations of Somerset." The barn has been converted into a school, and retains few traces of its original condition.

When the old barn was made into a school building, the following lines were written on it by Jonathan Ellwell:—

"Where once was heaped the produce of the soil,
The lamp of learning is kept trimmed with oil;
Where vagrant urchins loitering near the door,
Heard sounds suggestive of the threshing-floor,—

There, Charity, delighted, leads our youth
In pleasant paths of knowledge, wisdom, truth,—
There stores of thought succeed the loaded wain,
And no more threshings 'go against the grain.'

"J. E."

To the right of the road leading from Worle to Wick St. Lawrence, on the ridge called Castle Batch, is a large tumulus made apparently of earth, but which has never been disturbed. It is a round, crater-shaped barrow, 160 feet in diameter, and 17 feet high, with a hollow in the centre 75 feet across. It is surrounded by a broad but shallow ditch, from 15 to 25 feet wide, and it has an entrance on the south-west. When the foundations of the New Inn at Worle were being dug out, about the year 1815, there was found an antique bronze stirrup, which still bore traces of gilding, and in 1819, in a quarry in the same parish, there was dug up a very curious and elaborate iron bridle-bit. Many Roman coins have from time to time been found in this parish.

There are people still living in Worle who remember a very old man whose great-grandfather was alive at the time of the battle of Sedgemoor. This man, who was born in 1792, and who, to the end of a long life, is said to have retained his memory unimpaired, used to repeat tales which he said he had heard in his youth from his grandmother, who had been told them by her mother, herself an eye-witness of the events she described, about the battle, and about the cruelties of the soldiers and of Judge Jeffreys. One of the old man's stories described how two fugitives from the battlefield reached Worle, and asked shelter from a

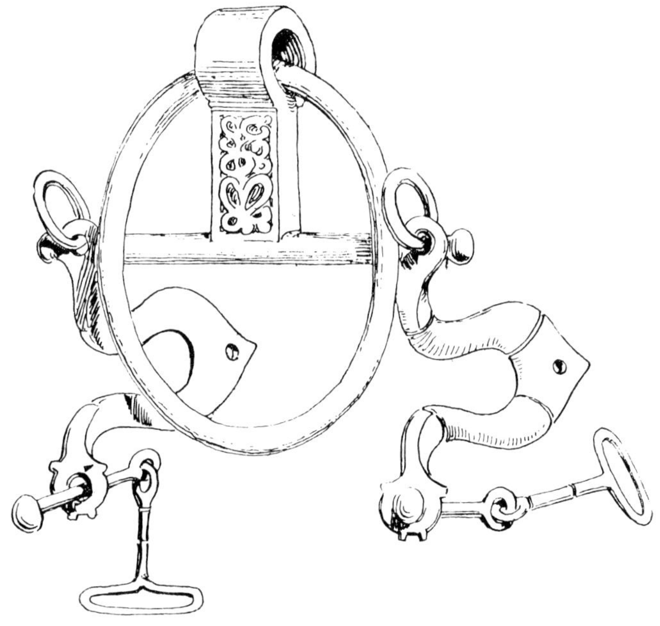

ANCIENT BRIDLE-BIT FOUND AT WORLE

man in the village, usually said to be a man called Starr, and generally known, like his son after him, as "King Starr," from the public-house of which each in turn was landlord, still the "King's Head." On his advice they hid themselves in a hollow in the side of a corn-rick. The villain, however, betrayed them to the dragoons, who dragged them from their hiding-place, and hanged them on an elm-tree near where the New Inn now stands, fixing their heads afterwards upon the church porch. Another of the stories was about the Plumleys, landowners at Worle and Locking, of whom three took part in the rebellion. The two sons fell at Sedgemoor, and the father, though he escaped for a time, and lay in hiding at various places among the hills, was at last taken, and was hanged and quartered.

The natural history of the neighbourhood of Worle differs from that of Weston owing to the absence both of sea and wood. The district is too slightly timbered and too scantily supplied with cover to be the haunt of many birds. The Lesser Spotted Woodpecker, a bird which is probably more common than is often supposed, is sometimes seen near Worle; and, less frequently, the Kingfisher. A pair of Black Redstarts are said to have nested somewhere on Worle Hill, but whether near this village or nearer Weston is not recorded.[1] Both the Black Redstart and the Ring Ouzel are sometimes observed here on migration; the former in the winter, the latter more often in the spring. The name of a lane in this parish, Dun Kite Lane, preserves the memory of a bird which has not been seen in the neighbourhood within the memory of man. On the pools near the railway are a few

[1] "Som. Arch. Pro.," vol. xxxix."

Moorhens and Dabchicks; Coots are rarely seen. And among the moorland ditches Sedge Warblers, Reed Warblers, and Reed Buntings breed. Spotted Crakes and Water Rails are not unfrequently killed here in the winter, and it is possible that both species breed among the rhines. The rhines are often visited by Herons from Brockley, and during severe winters Bitterns are occasionally shot.

As in other parts of the moor, Water Rats are plentiful in the ditches, though their numbers vary much in different years. The pretty little Water Shrew, also, is not uncommon. The Amphibians, Fish, Mollusca, and Insects of the rhines have been sufficiently alluded to in the chapter on Weston. Large Pike have been taken in the pools near the railway. One caught in 1898 measured 42 inches in length, and weighed 21½ pounds.

The rarest plant found in the parish is the insignificant little *Trinia vulgaris*, only recorded from two other districts in England, but plentiful on Worle Hill. There, too, have been found the Dwarf Orchis and the White Mullein. Other interesting plants are the Alexanders, the Mountain St. John's Wort, the Ploughman's Spikenard, and the Horehound.

UPHILL

A CONSPICUOUS object from Weston Sands is the grey ruin of the old Church of St. Nicholas, once the parish church of Uphill, standing on the brink of the gap that parts Brean Down from the main range of Mendip. Some of its rude masonry is believed to be older than the brief paragraph in Domesday Book which describes the condition of the manor under the first of the Norman kings. And round the ancient building there can still be traced, in the short turf of the wind-swept hill, the faint lines of a record a thousand years earlier even than the Domesday Book. For close to the church are the earthworks, much defaced by time and still more by spade and plough, of the Roman guard-station which once defended the little port below;—the terminus of the Roman road down which the products of the Mendip mining country were carried to the sea. This road, which was traced by Sir Richard Hoare from the site of Old Sarum in Wiltshire and along the Mendip Hills to Uphill, a distance of rather more than fifty miles, appears to have come down to the shore of the river Axe on the south side of the hill, between two tumuli. It is supposed to have been

Uphill Old Church

in one of these tumuli that the Rev. David Williams, of Bleadon, about the year 1826, found a bronze signet-ring, engraved with the letter R, four bronze buttons, and fourteen small, ten-sided beads of deep-red glass, all of which are now in the museum at Glastonbury. An expert at the British Museum has, however, decided that these antiquities are not Roman. The ring and the buttons are of the sixteenth century, and the beads are no doubt contemporary. Sir Richard Hoare, who surveyed the line of the old Roman road, considered that its course to the eastward lay, not along the top of Bleadon Hill, but along the north side, above Hutton, three hundred yards below the existing cart-way; that it passed close to Upper Canada Farm, continuing along the south slope of Banwell Hill, until, just above Winthill House, it joined the lane skirting the field called Chapel Leaze, where there was probably a Roman settlement, coming down at length in front of Banwell Castle. The only part of this line which is still used is that between Winthill and the Castle. Colonel Bramble and the Rev. C. S. Taylor, however, are satisfied that the real line of the Roman road was identical with that of the cart-track along the top of Bleadon Hill; that it made a sharp turn to the north for a short distance along the edge of

Old Signet-Ring, Sixteenth Century

Loxton parish, followed the course of what is now called Bridewell Lane, again turned to the north up the road leading to Banwell Caves, and finally joined the line laid down by Sir Richard Hoare, from Winthill to the Castle. East of the Castle the ancient line follows the highway south of Banwell Park in which there is a Roman camp, and what is believed to have been an important boundary mark. At the distance of rather less than half a mile from the Castle the line leaves the highroad, and may be traced across the fields into a narrow lane that cuts the railway at a point half-way between Sandford and Winscombe stations. Farther on, under the name of Shipham Lane, it crosses the highroad close to the fourteenth milestone from Bristol. Thence it passes, first as Broadway and farther on as North Down Lane, to the north of Shipham, descending into the Black Down Valley, through an ancient cutting called the Hollow Way. Beyond this point it is for a long distance a mere cart-track along the side of Black Down, rising by a gentle gradient to a height of nearly eight hundred feet above the sea to Tyning Farm. Thence it may be traced along the open hill through the ancient mining settlement of Charterhouse, where there was a Roman camp, and where many very interesting Roman remains have been discovered. Beyond Charterhouse it passes near the Castle of Comfort, a name here applied only to a small wayside inn, but believed to be really ancient and to mean much the same thing as a camp of refuge. Not far from the inn are four large circular earthworks, the use of which is unknown, though it has been conjectured that they were sepulchral. From a point about two miles to the east of the Castle of Comfort the course of the Roman way is for nearly three miles the same as that of the modern road that crosses the highway from Chewton Mendip to Wells. Taking to the fields again a little to the north of the British camp at Maesbury, it crosses another much more important Roman road, the Fosse Way, about a mile and a half from Shepton Mallet, near a group of tumuli and another old encampment. It then joins the Frome Road for a short distance, goes across country again near East Cranmore and Leighton Camp, and finally leaves the county near Maiden Bradley, close to another old earthwork on Gaer Hill. In Wiltshire it was traced by Sir R. C. Hoare through Monkton Deverell and Warminster; and after passing the Roman stations of Stockton Wood and Grovely Wood, it at last reaches Old Sarum, whence it may have been continued to the shore of the English Channel.

Two names in Uphill, Wallborough and Cold Harbour, point clearly to the Roman occupation of the little port. Wallborough is the name of a mound to the south of the church, and Cold Harbour that of a field on the west side of the village, close to the sea. Wallborough, Borough Walls, Wallsend, and similar words are only found near the sites of Roman military stations. And along ancient lines of Roman road in this country are at least seventy places called "Cold Harbour"; and, as Mr. Isaac Taylor says, "about a dozen more bearing the analogous name of Caldicot or Cold Cot." Some regard the words as a corruption of *Colonia arborea*, "the settlement among the trees." But a more probable explanation is that the name was given to the ruin of a Roman villa, which might be used as a place of shelter by travellers. There is another Cold Harbour not far from Dundry, and a third near the village of Wookey.

There are few records of the discovery of Roman antiquities at Uphill. In the sand on the floor of the cavern at the foot of the hill, long used as a store by the volunteers in connection with the adjoining rifle range, the Rev. David Williams of Bleadon, its first modern explorer, found, in 1826, a fragment of Roman pottery and a coin of the Emperor Julian[1] (perhaps the first of the name, A.D. 133). Twenty years later, a pot containing 200 denarii is said to have been found in the same cave.[2] The port at Uphill was further strengthened by a camp at the eastern end of Brean Down, where other Roman relics have been found, including gold coins of some of the early emperors — Augustus, Nero, and the elder Drusus—and an engraved carnelian ring. The Roman name of the little harbour is unknown. The name "Ad Axium" is not classical, and was

[1] Rutter's "Somerset."
[2] Jackson, "Handbook of Weston-super-Mare."

invented by Sir Richard Hoare. It was suggested by Bishop Clifford[1] that the word Uphill dates from the days of King Alfred, and that in it we may trace the name of Hubba, a Danish Viking who is known to have harried the Somerset shore. In Domesday Book the name of the manor is Opopille. "Pill" is a common west-country word for a creek or inlet; and Bishop Clifford suggested that Opopille was a corruption of Hubba Pill—"Hubba's Harbour." The theory that the port was called after the Danish pirate is strengthened by the existence of another name, Hobbs's Boat, some distance farther up the river, half a mile south of the village of Bleadon, where there was formerly a ferry.

About ten miles to the southward is another name that may be connected with the old sea-rover. In the memorable Danish invasion which immediately preceded the battle of Ethandune and the Peace of Wedmore (A.D. 878), the enemy's forces, under Guthrum and Hubba, landed in Devonshire. It has been usual to add, "near Appledore." But neither the Anglo-Saxon Chronicle nor Alfred's friend and biographer Asser, who gives much fuller details, mentions Appledore, and the statement very likely arose, as Bishop Clifford pointed out, from a confusion, through a misreading of Leland, with another Appledore, in Kent, where another landing of Danish pirates took place, in 893. Roger de Hoveden says that the battle which followed the

[1] "Som. Arch. Pro.," vol. xxi.

landing was at Cymwich. Asser records that Hubba was slain before the Castle of Cynwit. There can be little doubt that the pirates came ashore at the spot where now stands the small seaport of Combwich, on the west side of the mouth of the Parret, which river was then and for some years after the boundary between Devon and Somerset; but that the fight was at Cannington, an isolated limestone hill about a mile distant from Combwich, on whose summit there may still be seen, as Bishop Clifford says, "an ancient encampment answering in every respect to Asser's description of the Castle of Cynwit." What happened, as we learn from John of Brompton, who wrote towards the end of the twelfth century, was that the invading army divided, and that the force under Hubba, being suddenly attacked by Odda and the men of Devon, was seized with panic. They were routed with great loss, and among the spoils of victory, as we read in both Asser and the Anglo-Saxon Chronicle, was "the war-flag which they called the RAVEN." It was only a temporary check to the invaders. They recovered the field. But their leader was among the slain. They buried his body, says John of Brompton, "with loud lamentations, and raised over it a mound which they named Ubbalowe; wherefore the place is so called to this day, and it is in the county of Devon." There is reasonable ground for thinking that this very grave may still be seen. About a mile from Combwich, not far from the bank of the river, Bishop Clifford found a large circular tumulus, surrounded by a trench, whose appearance and position, he says, "recalls the tombs of the Vikings." The tumulus is nameless, and no tradition points to the hero whose fall it may have been intended to commemorate. But about a mile from the spot is Uppercock Farm. *Kok* is Danish for "a heap": it survives in common speech in the word haycock. Uppercock may, as Bishop Clifford suggested, be a corruption of Hubba Cock; and that green knoll by the river may be the very mound of Ubbalowe, which his followers piled over the ashes of the dead sea-rover.[1]

In Domesday Book the manor, which then included both Uphill and Christon, and was among the possessions of Serlo de Burci, is thus described:—

"*Four knights hold from Serlo Opopille. Ewacre held it in the time of King Edward, and paid Danegeld for six hides and a half. There is land for ten plough-teams. In the demesne there are four plough-teams, with one serf, and seven villeins, and four boors with three plough-teams. There are seventy acres of meadow, and a hundred acres of pasture. It was and is worth six pounds.*"[2]

The Domesday paragraph is the earliest known

[1] "Som. Arch. Pro.," vol. xxi.

[2] A hide of land was a variable quantity, but probably averaged 240 acres. A plough-team corresponded to half that amount. Serfs were the absolute property of the Lord of the Manor, and could be sold like chattels. Villeins were the highest of the classes which had no sort of freedom, and belonged to the vill or manor. Boors were the highest class of labourers employed on the estate.—Eyton, "Domesday Studies."

written record of the history of the parish. But in an ancient document, compiled probably about 1413, and preserved among the archives of Axbridge, it is stated that the thirty-two burgesses of that town held under Athelstan, Edmund, Edred, Edgar, and St. Edward, "the right of hunting and fishing in all places, except preserves, from the place which is called Kotellisasch — now Cottle's Oak — (near Frome), to the rock which is called 'le Blacston' (the Black Rock at the mouth of the Axe), in the western sea." This right was probably for a time at least withdrawn, for in the records of the Perambulation of Mendip Forest in 1298—a royal commission appointed by Edward I. to carry out the promise of Henry III., "That all forests which our grandfather afforested should be viewed by good and lawful men"—it is mentioned that the estate described as Villa de Uphulle, then held by Philip de Lunget, was, with nineteen other Mendip manors, declared by the commissioners to be disafforested, having been included within the forest bounds by encroachment made since the accession of Henry II. in 1154.[1]

The present parish of Uphill extends from the Moorland Road on the north to the middle of the first bend in the course of the river Axe on the south side, having thus just a mile of open sea-board. Its boundaries include the Black Rock, which is not only one of the steering-marks for the little port, since its top is never covered by the waves, but, as has

[1] "Som. Arch. Pro.," vol. xxxvii.

been seen, it marked the western limit of the Forest of Mendip under the Saxon and Norman kings. The frontier of the parish for a short distance on the south is the Axe itself, which, insignificant as it is on the map of England, is the most important stream in the Mendip Country if only for the sake of its historical associations. For coal vessels and other small craft it was navigable as far up as Axbridge, until the erection of the flood-gates at Bleadon, under the Axe Drainage Act of 1802. There was also a river-port at Reckley, near Compton Bishop, on the branch called the Cheddar Water. To this there are interesting allusions in the Wells Cathedral Records, under the name of Radeclive or Redcliffe. Its particular object was the transport of ore from the Mendip mines to the sea at Uphill. There is a tidal-lock at Uphill, and on the stonework of it are these marks:—

M G   S B
C
15...   1606

The main line of the Great Western Railway and the Weston loop line both run through the parish of Uphill, but the station is on the Bleadon side of the boundary. There was, however, for many years a dummy or sham station on the Weston side of the bridge, where the loop now joins the main line, and of which substantial traces are still left. The story goes that an Uphill landowner, after driving a very hard bargain with the railway company for the land they needed for the line, made a final stipulation that there should be a station for his private and particular use. The company agreed. They put up a station. But there had been nothing in the agreement about trains. The grasping landowner got his platform, but until the day of his death no train ever drew up there. It is said further, that he carried the case to the courts, and finally ruined himself by litigation.

A pleasanter story connected with the making of the line is associated with the late Mr. Knyfton of Uphill Castle. The Bleadon cutting was in course of excavation when trouble arose with the navvies on the question of wages. The men would not listen to Brunel, who was there in person, and things began to look very serious. Brunel despatched a messenger for Mr. Knyfton, the nearest magistrate. "Without loss of time Mr. Knyfton started for the scene of action, and taking the Riot Act in his hand passed into the thick of the crowd, where he was greeted with menacing language and uplifted pickaxes. With calmness he talked to the men, telling them that law was stronger than force, and that all would be well if they acted in the spirit of their contract: if otherwise, a troop of cavalry from Horfield Barracks would probably be marching on Uphill. The navvies grew calmer, and by the tact, good temper, and resolution on the part of this ruler of the district, peace prevailed, and the frightened village shopkeepers were reassured." [1]

[1] Robert Arthur Kinglake, "Som. Arch. Pro.," vol. xxxiii.

In an old map of the time of Henry VIII., already alluded to, representing the "Coste of England uppon Seuerne," Uphill Church is marked, and standing near it on the seaward side is a blockhouse armed with two guns. In the drawing it looks much like the ruined tower of the old windmill on the other side of the church. It was also in the reign of Henry VIII. that Leland, the Royal Antiquary and Librarian, visited Somerset. He appears to have passed through this parish, and there is a brief note in his Itinerary to the effect, that "Uphil ys the Hed wher al the Water issueth to the Severne Se." In the next reign the little port was connected with what was an undoubted act of piracy, seeing that we were not only at peace with France at the time, but were actually allied with the French king, Henry of Navarre, the hero of Ivry. In the Calendar of State Papers of Elizabeth is the following passage:—

"[Endorsed] 6. Juny̆, 1592. De la Landes information for ye Merchantes of Bayonne spoiled by English shippes.

"To the Queenes ma^ties^ most honorable privie Councell.

"Right honorable Lordes, It hath byn an old sayenge, That he that beareth one wronge, seemeth to provoke an other, wch Bernard de la Lande deputie of the inhabitantes of the towne of Bayonne in France, and parties thereaboutes &c.

"Imprimis the said de la Lande doethe complaine for Peter de Hody burges and marchant of Bayonnė afore saide, sayenge that in the moneth of Aprill Anno Dñi

1591, he dide set forth a ship of his called the Gray honde of Bayonne, of the burthen of one houndred tonnes, for to make the voyage of newe founde launde, wch havinge there taken in her ladinge of one houndred and eight thousand of drye fishes, fowre thousand of greene fishes, and fowretenne hogsheades of trayne oyles, amountinge all the said marchandises, together with the said shippe, her ordenance, furniture and appurtenances to sixe thousand crownes of the summe, beinge on her retorne towardes Bayonne aforesaide, was mett by an Englishe shippe appointed warrlyke belonginge to Syr Walter Rawleigh knight, Whereof was m[r] John Flegon, who so furiouslye battered the same, that she was constrayned to yelde, and was brought to Uphill neare to Bristoll, w[ch] Peter de Hody havinge gyven order for the recoverie of the said shippe and goodes and allso havinge obteyned lettres from Madame the owne onely sister of the said frenshe kinge, to her M[tie], havinge for that effecte sent hether twoo menn, who have byn continuall sutters here eight monethes, but they could obteyne no Justice, So as havinge spent v.[c] crownes, they were fayne to leave of their sute, and to returne homwardes into Fraunce, for to save their lyfes, beinge every daie threatned by the owners and victellers of the said shippe of war, who beinge riche marchauntes in Bristoll have receyved the procedinges of the said marchandises, and with holde still the said shippe in their Custody."

[State Papers, Domestic, Elizabeth, vol. ccxlii., page 108 (or No. 44).]

At the present time colliers of from 90 to 120 tons come up to the wharf at Uphill, showing that the depth of water in the river is much what it was three hundred years ago.

During the siege of Bridgwater by the Parliamentary army under Fairfax, in the summer of 1645, an attempt was made to land Royalist reinforcements at Uphill, but the twenty ships that had been provided for the purpose were captured by Captain Swanley off the coast of Wales.[1]

In "Britannia Baconia," published in 1661, is an allusion to an extraordinary incident, the scene of which is quite unknown. It is probable that it is only a Chap-Book story of the time :—

> "It is reported that about Uphill (a parish by the seaside not far from Axbridge) within these half-hundred years, a parcel of ground swelled up like a hill, and on a sudden clave asunder, and fell down again into the earth, and in the place of it remains a great pool."

Uphill Castle is wholly modern. It was built by Mr. Payne about 1805, and was for some time used as a boys' school.[2] The late Thomas Tutton Knyfton, Esq., bought it, and, having built a tower and some castellated work, called the place Uphill Castle. Though Mr. Knyfton was a Somerset man, his ancestors belonged to Derbyshire, and the family took its name from the village of Kniveton, near Ashbourne, in that county. An old manuscript, alluding to a member of the house, observes: "Many and most of his family were knights."[3] In the Church of Mugginton, seven

[1] "Som. Arch. Pro.," vol. xxiii. [2] Mr. George Bennett's MS.
[3] "Som. Arch. Pro.," vol. xxxiii.

miles from Derby, is a brass in memory of a Kniveton who fought at Agincourt. The suit of armour worn in the battle by this very man is still in possession of the family, and was shown a few years since at an Art Loan Exhibition held at Weston-super-Mare.

It is said that the Rev. T. Gegg, of Axbridge, who owned the Uphill property before Mr. Knyfton, formed extensive plans for building on the land now occupied by the Golf Links, south of the Sanatorium. He began, the story goes, with a chapel. Difficulties arose, and the scheme was abandoned, and all that remains is a piece of the walling of the first and only building that was ever even begun. Mr. Gegg built the house called Uphill Grange, and it was he whose Boys' School was altered into Uphill Castle.

The steep brow from which the old Church of St. Nicholas looks out to sea down the fairway of the little river is no more than a hundred feet above high-water mark. But so low is the level of the far-reaching moorland at its base that no more commanding spot could have been chosen for a building to be dedicated to the patron saint of sailors, and which may well have been placed here, partly, at any rate, that it might be of use as a steering-mark for ships that were making for the port of Uphill. For more than half a century the old church has ceased to be the place of worship for the parish, but it still serves as a beacon for colliers crossing from the coast of Wales.

The church shows traces of various styles of architecture, from the rudest Norman to the latest Perpendicular; but it is usually said to belong mainly to three periods. Parts of the tower, especially the south side of it, at whose top there is a curious three-headed gargoyle, are probably much as they were left by the original builders, before the close of the eleventh century, before the completion of Domesday Book, and while William the Conqueror still occupied the throne. The chancel, too, has been very little altered, and if not as old as the tower, dates probably from about the year 1130. This is also believed to be the period of the stone fretwork in the belfry, which is probably part of the chancel arch. The plain and massive north porch, whose remarkable shape is no doubt due to a sinking of the foundations, is regarded as a rebuilding of the original Norman work; but the primitive south doorway just opposite to it, and long ago walled up, belongs to the very earliest period. On the large stone which forms the head of its arch there is cut a Maltese cross (perhaps the original Consecration Cross), and close by it there is a rude sun-dial. Not far from it is another dial, carved on a stone over the little south Norman window of the tower.

The heads of the tower windows show Early English alterations; and within quite recent times the remains of a thirteenth-century fresco, consisting of three figures, painted in warm monochrome, was still visible on the eastern wall. The fine Early English font long remained in a niche in the west wall of the nave, but being there much exposed to the weather it was removed in 1892 to the new church, where it has been in use ever since.

The western end of the church, with its window and canopy, is regarded as belonging to the Decorated period, perhaps to about the year 1350. Perpendicular masonry—that is to say, work of the period between 1377 and 1547—may be seen in the tower arches, in the stair turret, and in the north parapet of the tower.

Four of the five bells were cast by William Bilbie, one of the famous Chewstoke family of bell-founders, who flourished from before the reign of Queen Anne to the year of Waterloo. The bells are thus inscribed :—

1. THOMAS . KNYFTON . CHURCHWARDEN . WILLM . BILBIE . FECIT . 1775.
2. Ditto.
3. RECAST . 1840.
4. THOMAS . KNYFTON . CHURCHWARDEN . 1775 . WILLIAM BILBIE . CHEWSTOKE . FECIT . 1775.
5. THOMAS . KNYFTON . CHURCHWARDEN . WILLIAM BILBIE . FECIT . 1775.

I . TO . THE . CHURCH . THE . LIVING . CALL .
AND . TO . THE . GRAVE . DOTH . SUMMON . ALL .

The tenor bell is thirty-nine inches in diameter.

The old silver chalice and paten, after having been disused and in private hands for some years after the closing of the church on the hill, were restored to their rightful use by the present Rector on Christmas Day, 1890. On the same day there was presented to the new church a beautiful silver and ruby glass flagon. The old chalice, which bears the hall-mark of 1635, is a narrow goblet, six and a quarter inches high and three inches in diameter, and weighing rather more than seven ounces. The paten, which, in addition to the hall-mark, is inscribed "Uphill, 1742," measures six and a quarter inches across, and weighs a little over six ounces.

The church records, contained in thirteen volumes, five of which are still in use, go back to the year 1696. The first date actually given in the oldest volume is 1701; but on the second page is the entry of a birth dated five years earlier, having perhaps been forgotten: "Anstes, the daughter of Samuell Bayly and Mary, his wife, was born the 5th day of May 1696." Inside the cover of this book is written the name, "John Chappell, Rector"; he was appointed in 1660.

The Churchwardens' Accounts are still kept in the volume which was begun in 1779. In that year is the first of many entries relating to the repair of the old church:—

For 12 Thousand of Cornish Tyle, @ 11s. pr. Ths.	6	12	0
Forgot to put down 5s. for 5th of November 1778	0	5	0

For hauling two wagon load of Mortar and 1 load of Materials for the Church, and Liquar, 1s. 0 10 0
Paid for 3 yards of Velvet @ 13s. per yd. . 1 19 0

Many entries refer to "Forms of Prayer" in connection with occasions of public rejoicing :—

1795. Forms of Prayer for the Fast, the Prince's Marriage, and the King's Escape . 0 4 6
1796. Pd. a Form of Prayer for Sir Jno. Jervice's Victory over the Spanish fleet . 0 1 6
1797. Pd. for a Form of Prayer the 11th October for Admiral Duncan's Victory . . 0 1 6

Expenses connected with the re-casting of one of the bells are thus recorded :—

1840. Easter. Hauling the Bell to Bristol 0 6 0
Pd. for Beer for men taking down and hanging the Bell 0 6 3
Pd. for Re-casting the Bell . 15 3 4
Pd. for hauling it home . 0 6 0

The bodies of drowned sailors are sometimes washed ashore at Uphill. In 1847 is this entry :—

Paid to George Gould for picking up a dead body on the strand 0 5 0

In 1840 the question of building a new church was considered, on account of "the dilapidated condition and inconvenient situation" of the church on the hill. The foundation-stone of the new Church of St. Nicholas was laid in 1841 by the Bishop of the diocese, and in 1844 the building was consecrated. Services were, however, still held in the old church, on alternate Sundays, until April 5, 1846, when its use as a place of regular worship was discontinued. In 1864 the dilapidated roof of the church on the hill was taken down, and the chancel and belfry were converted into a Mortuary Chapel, which was partly roofed with stone slabs taken from the nave. The whole building was further repaired in 1890. In 1892 the old north porch, which had long been built up, was reopened, and the nave laid down with turf. A celebration of the Holy Communion, in Commemoration of the Dead, is held every year in the old church in the month of July.

In the Register of Bishop Ralph of Shrewsbury, preserved at Wells, are some allusions to this parish; the earliest is dated 1333:—

"Bishop Ralph to the Dean of Axbridge:

"We propose to 'visit' on Saturday next, after the Feast of S. Matthew the Apostle, the Churches of Blaedon, Uphulle, Weston, and the Chapel of Pokerston (Puxton), in the said Church of Uphulle. . . .

"We command you that you cite all and singular whom our Visitation concerns."

The next entry is in 1344:—

"The Rectors of Bleodon and Uphhulle, and their chaplains, are ordered to announce that false jurors have fallen under the sentence of greater excommunication."

Another entry runs thus:—

"Quit claim for ever by Walter Bursey, to Sir Thomas Lord of Berkelee, of all his right in the isle of Stepelholme, and all lands, &c., which the said Walter Bursey holds in Upphall and Crucheston (Christon). Witnesses: Lord John de Clyvedone, John Wroxhale, Sir Walter de Rodenye, Sir Edmund de Lyounds, Sir William Arthur, and others."

Uphill was one of the parishes which suffered from the terrible pestilence called the Black Death; and in 1348, when the disease was at its height, two new Rectors were instituted, Rog. Tylie and Joh. Muleward. The former was in succession to Will., called Laurenz of Eton, who no doubt died of the Black Death in 1348.[1]

Uphill Village School was formerly held in a room in the Castle grounds, but in 1872 the late Mr. T. T. Knyfton erected at his own expense a new building sufficient to accommodate 150 children. In 1889, a new classroom was added by his widow. The school premises are, therefore, the property of Mr. Greaves Knyfton, who lends them to the parish. The school is managed by a committee, and is supported by voluntary contributions. The average attendance in 1901 was: mixed school, 78; infants, 44.

The most famous name connected with modern Uphill is that of William Lisle Bowles, who has been called the father of the poets of Nature, and the forerunner of Wordsworth, Southey, and Coleridge. The latter wrote of him :—

"My heart has thanked thee, Bowles, for those soft strains,
Whose sadness soothes me like the murmuring
Of wild bees in the sunny showers of spring."

[1] Weaver, "Somerset Incumbents."

The poet's father, the Rev. William Thomas Bowles, was Rector of Uphill from 1769 until his death in 1786. He it was who planted the shrubberies in the Rectory gardens. The poet himself was born in 1762, and was thus a child of seven when his father came to the parish. In one of his poems, "Banwell Hill, or Days Departed," he says :—

> "I was a child when first I heard the sound
> Of the great sea! 'Twas night, and journeying far,
> We were belated on our road, 'mid scenes
> New and unknown—a mother and her child,
> Now first in this wide world a wanderer!
> My father came, the pastor of the church
> That crowns the high hill crest above the sea."

William Lisle Bowles wrote a good deal of poetry :—"Fourteen Sonnets" (1789), "Poems" (1798–1809), "The Spirit of Discovery" (1805), "The Missionary of the Andes" (1815), &c.; besides his "History of Bremhill," the parish of which he was made Rector in 1804. Made Canon of Salisbury in 1828, he died in that city in 1850, and was buried in the cathedral. His sonnets are regarded as containing his best work, but the verses which, in extreme old age, he wrote at Weston-super-Mare, the last of his many compositions, are among the most pathetic of them all :—

> "Was it but yesterday I heard the roar
> Of these white coursing waves, and trod the shore,
> A young and playful child—but yesterday?
> Now I return with locks of scattered grey

And wasted strength ; for many, many years
Have passed, some marked by joy, and some by tears,
Since last we parted. As I gaze around
I think of Time's fleet step that makes no sound.

. . . . . .

In yonder vale, beneath the hill-top tower,
My father decked the village pastor's bower ;
Now he, and all beneath whose knees I played,
Cold in the narrow cell of death are laid."

It is said that, in 1773, the Rev. John Langhorne happened to be at Weston while Hannah More was staying at Uphill. The two met upon the beach, and the former, whose poetry is less famous than his translation of Plutarch, traced with his stick these lines upon the sand :—

"Upon the shore,
Walked Hannah More.
Waves, let this record last !
Sooner shall ye,
Proud earth and sea,
Than what she writes, be past."

The lady, not to be outdone, returned the compliment by writing with her riding-whip :—

"Some firmer basis, polished Langhorne, choose,
To write the dictates of thy charming muse ;
Her strains in solid characters rehearse,
And be thy Tablet lasting as thy verse."

The western brow of the hill on which stands the old Church of St. Nicholas is Carboniferous Limestone, but the original arrangement of the rocks has been disturbed by a "fault," which extends for a considerable distance along the southern boundary of the parish, and the greater part of the hill is composed of Lower Lias, New Red Marl, and Dolomitic Conglomerate. The marl and the conglomerate are exposed in the railway cutting, where may also be seen, a short distance to the north of the station, a dyke of volcanic rock. One of the most interesting features in the history of Uphill is the series of caves and fissures, many of them containing the bones of extinct animals, which from time to time have been discovered in the process of quarrying limestone in the western face of the hill. The earliest account of these caves is that given by Rutter in his "Delineations," published in 1829. That writer describes how some workmen, who were quarrying stone at a point about thirty feet below the church, found a fissure containing a quantity of bones. These were shown to the Rev. David Williams, the Vicar of Bleadon, "who recognised them as belonging to animals of a country and climate differing from our own." Mr. Williams himself continued the exploration, and was rewarded by the discovery of bones of the Spotted Hyæna, Woolly Rhinoceros, Cave Bear, Ox, Horse, and other animals. The most abundant remains were those of the Hyæna; and since all the larger bones of other species were much gnawed and splintered, it seemed clear that this hollow had been a Hyæna den. The bones were all found near the mouth of the fissure, and were so firmly embedded in the detritus that they were with difficulty got out even with a pickaxe. Continuing the excavation, Mr. Williams discovered, some twenty feet farther down, a much larger cavern, about forty feet long and twelve feet high, and varying in width from eight to twenty feet. From the roof hung some fine stalactites, while many fossils projected from the surface of the limestone rock. "The floor was covered with the bones of sheep, and on digging into the mud and sand of which it consisted, several other bones of Sheep, Birds, Cuttle-fish, and Fox were found."[1] It was here, too, that the explorers came upon a fragment of Roman pottery, and a coin of the Emperor Julian. Rutter adds that when Professor Buckland visited the cave, he suggested that it had been inhabited by foxes, and showed that there were spots where these animals, "in their ingress and egress, had polished the irregular points of the rock projecting on their gangway as smooth as if they had been submitted to the lapidary's wheel." Some twenty years later, a new entrance to this cave was cut at the ground level, and in the course of the work a pot containing two hundred denarii was discovered. This cavern is still to be seen at the foot of the hill, almost directly under the old church, though it is not generally accessible, being closed with a door and used as a storehouse for explosives. The majority of the bones were given by Mr. Williams to the Bristol Museum, a few went to Professor Buckland, and others were given to

[1] Rutter's "Delineations."

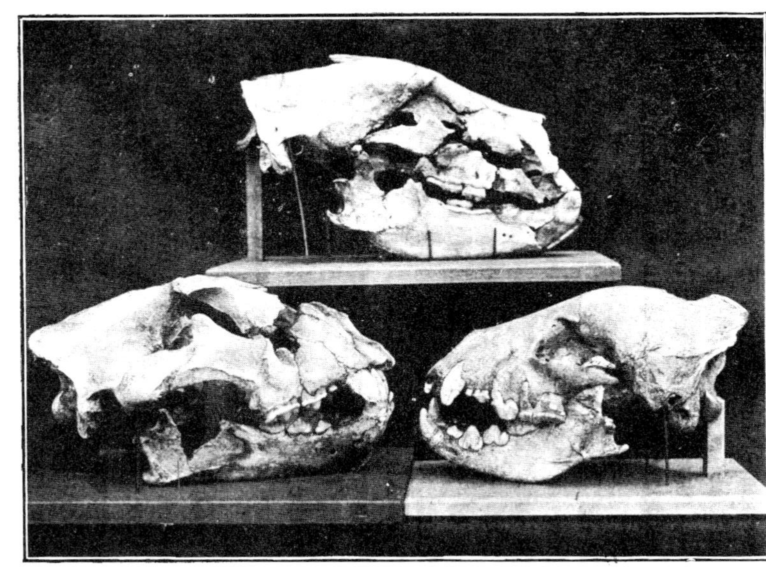

Cave Lion — Cave Bear — Cave Hyæna

SKULLS OF EXTINCT ANIMALS FROM A MENDIP BONE-CAVE

the Geological Society in London. Nothing is known of the whereabouts of the two hundred denarii.

In 1863, as we learn from a letter written to the *Geologist* in that year by Dr. Charles Pooley, of Weston-super-Mare, another cave was discovered at Uphill, about sixty feet from the ground. Besides the usual stalagmitic breccia, it contained an unctuous loam very rich in animal remains. In this cave-earth Dr. Pooley found bones of the Wolf, Fox, Wild Boar, and Otter, the antlers of a Stag, and some human remains, including a thigh-bone and part of a skull.

In 1896, at points from forty to fifty feet below the top of the quarry cliff, several more fissures were found, and these having been thoroughly explored by Mr. Edward Wilson, on behalf of the Bristol Museum, yielded great quantities of animal remains. The most abundant bones were again those of the Spotted Hyæna, of which enough were found "to indicate the presence of scores of individuals."[1] Next in quantity were the bones of the Horse. Other remains were those of the Woolly Rhinoceros, Elephant, Mammoth, Cave Bear, Red Deer, Fox, Badger, and Squirrel. Bones of the Rabbit, Sheep, Mole, and Fowl were also found, but they, of course, must have been introduced into the cave at a later period than those of the extinct animals. The same remark applies probably to the rude flint implements and weapons. And although

[1] "Proceedings of the Bristol Naturalists' Society," vol. ix. pt. iii.

coprolites were met with among the bones, the explorers of the cave consider that all the ancient remains were washed into the fissure where they were discovered, and that the actual Hyæna den has not, in this instance, been found.

In other caves and fissures near the same spot there have been found from time to time parts of human skeletons, which, it has been conjectured, had fallen from tumuli on the hill above, when the mounds were destroyed by the spade or plough. The writer was present when, in 1881, in a small cavern high up in the face of the quarry, there was found under the broken stalagmite floor a human skull, together with some pieces of charcoal, as if the place had been used as a habitation. The skull was that of a very old man, whose teeth, though undecayed, were much worn, as if by the use of flour imperfectly ground in a quern.

The neighbourhood of Uphill has more attractions for sea-birds and wild-fowl than any other part of the short Mendip coast-line. At high water the estuary of the Axe is an arm of the sea eight hundred yards across. When the tide goes down there is nothing left of the river but an insignificant little stream of tawny water, a few feet wide, almost lost between its vast and dreary banks of brown mud. These muddy shores, and the broader flats of the bay itself, provide feeding-ground for a host of Curlews and Redshanks, Dunlins, and Ringed Plovers, among whose ranks are occasionally seen Knots and

Sanderlings and Purple Sandpipers. The sewage-outfall near the ferry and the fishing-nets farther down attract many Gulls. Cormorants, Razorbills, and Guillemots, from their wilder and more rocky haunts upon the opposite coast of Wales, sometimes stay about the nets for a day or two. Gannets are more rarely seen; one was shot near the Black Rock in January 1894. From the southern side of the parish there stretches away a wide tract of low-lying moorland, cut up by innumerable ditches, the haunt of Snipe and Heron and Water-rail. Legion is the name of the birds that have been shot in the river. The commonest of the many ducks are of course Teal and Widgeon and Wild-duck. The last sometimes breeds within the boundaries of the parish. Hard winters bring Geese and even Swans, together with Scaup Ducks, Pochards, Golden-eyes, Scoters, Mergansers, and other more or less familiar species. The Sheldrakes that nest on Brean Down sometimes lead their broods nearly as far as Uphill wharf, in order that the young argonauts may gain their first experiences on the smooth waters of the river. Rough weather has been known to drive in for shelter such wanderers as the Great Northern Diver, the Little Auk, both the Storm Petrel and Leach's Petrel, the Manx Shearwater, and the Pomatorhine Skua. Both the Common Tern and the Grey Phalarope sometimes put in to the river on their way south in the autumn. And few winters pass in which a flock of Snow-buntings is not seen among the sand-hills.

The fish caught near Uphill are much the same as those of other parts of the bay. In the tidal water of the river there are also Eels, Mullet, and Sea-bass. The small and prettily tinted bivalves, whose empty shells are so abundant on Uphill sands, belong to the genus *Tellina*, of which there are here probably two species only, in spite of many differences of colour, due largely to age. Quite as numerous, but less noticeable on account of their extreme smallness and their inconspicuous colouring, are the minute spiral shells of the two similar genera, *Hydrobius* and *Rissoa*. With these is often to be seen another small and similarly shaped shell, formerly called *Conovulus*, but now known as *Melampus denticulatus*, from the "teeth" that are so easily seen in its mouth. It inhabits the brackish ditches, and was once classed with fresh-water shells. In addition to these the Axe brings down many kinds, both of land and fresh-water Mollusca, and their empty shells are often to be found near the bank of the river. *Paludina vivipara*, a large fresh-water shell, not unlike the great garden snail, but having its mouth closed when alive with an operculum, is among the species thus found; but no living specimens have been seen in the district, at least for some years. A handful of "river drift"—grass, straws, twigs, and dead leaves, accumulated in a creek or back-water in flood time—often yields a rich harvest, especially of such small and not easily recognised species as *Vertigo pygmæa*, *Helix pulchella*, or *Achatina acicula*, which are so minute that their beauty of form and sculpture cannot be fully appreciated without the aid of a magnifying glass.

The notes on "Marine Life" in the chapter on Weston-super-Mare will apply in great measure to this parish.

If the list of the Uphill flora is not a long one, it includes a few plants of great rarity. The most remarkable is the wild Asparagus, only known in three other botanical districts in the British Islands. Another very rare species is *Ruppia spiralis*, a small floating plant, without an English name, which grows in brackish water. Three other notable flowers are the Twiggy Mullein, the Broad-leaved Cress, and the Rock Hutchinsia. Among the sand-hills grow both the common varieties of the Evening Primrose, two well-established aliens from America.

The Snowdrops alluded to in Rutter's "Somerset" still grow at Uphill. We call them wild, but they are nowhere native to this country, having been, it is believed, introduced from Italy about the time of Queen Elizabeth. They are mentioned under the name of Bulbous Violets by Gerard, the contemporary of Shakespeare, but not by Shakespeare himself, who, had they been familiar in his day, would surely have made use of flowers so beautiful. Those at Uphill may well have escaped from cultivation, growing as they do so near the Rectory garden. But the clumps that flourish beneath the noble beeches and horse-chestnuts, in that beautiful field at the parting of the ways, may be the descendants of flowers that grew there before the trees were planted. Nature has done much both for them and their surroundings, and may have provided the mist of bluebells that glorifies the meadow later in the year. But it was the hand of man that scattered in the grass the

> "Daffodils
> That come before the swallow dares, and take
> The winds of March with beauty."

BREAN

THE parish of Brean—or Breane, as it is perhaps more usually spelt by its inhabitants, many of whom, moreover, pronounce the name in two syllables—is bounded on all sides except the south by water. On the east is the river Axe, on the north and west is the Bristol Channel, and on the south is the parish of Berrow. The promontory of Brean Down, the most western extremity of the Mendip Hills, is the only ground in the parish which is appreciably raised above the level of the sea. The remainder is an almost absolute plain, lying so low that it would be constantly flooded at high tides were it not for the embankments along the river Axe, and for the sea-wall and the sand-hills on the edge of Bridgwater Bay. The sea-wall, believed to be very ancient, is for the most part buried by the drifting sand, but it is occasionally laid bare by high tides and rough weather. In 1607 the coast defences gave way not far from Burnham, and a tract of country, twenty miles long and five miles wide, was flooded ten or twelve feet deep. In a Chap-Book printed in London that year and entitled, "A true Report of certaine wonderfull overflowings of

Brean Church and Rectory

Waters now lately in Summersetshire," is this passage:—

"So (besides other small villages standing in vallies) is Brian Downe, a village quite consumed."

Another Chap-Book, called "More strange news of wonderfull accidents hapning by the late overflowings of waters in Summersetshire," gives further details; and after naming "thirtie Townes and Villages in the West Country . . . utterly overflowed and their cattell destroyed (or the greatest part of them), besides men, women and children," the writer goes on to say: "The parrish of Breane is swallowed (for the most part) up by the waters. In it stood but nine houses, and of those seaven were consumed, and with them xxvi persons lost their lives." By far the larger part of the parish is occupied with this broad alluvial plain, whose rich meadows are divided by innumerable ditches, or rhines as they are called in the West Country, which serve instead of walls or hedges. Much of this is grazing land, and a notable industry of Brean is the preparation of Caerphilly cheese, a variety made specially for Welsh miners, and sent across for that purpose to Cardiff.

At the time of the Norman survey the manor belonged to Walter of Douai, and the following details of it are given in Domesday Book:—

"*Walter himself holds Brien. In the time of King Edward Merlesuain held it, and paid Danegeld for two hides. There is land for eight plough-teams. In the demesne there are three plough-teams, with one serf, and nine villeins, and seven boors and eight cotters, with three plough-teams and a half. There are thirty acres of pasture. It is worth a hundred shillings.*"[1]

Collinson, who traces the history of the manor from the reign of Edward III. to 1786, the time when he himself was writing, quotes a deed of the year 1637, by which Thomas Bond of Ogborn St. George, in Wiltshire, conveyed most of the property to William Cann of Bristol, "together with all messuages, lands, commons, waifs, estrays, wrecks of sea, courts and perquisites of courts, fishings, royalties, rents, reversions and services belonging to he said manor." In the same deed it is stated that Thomas Bond had already conveyed to Henry, Lord Danvers, and to Anthony Garrard and their heirs, "a newly built house, part of the manor, and four hundred acres of land, parcel of the demesne; also the down or warren called Brean Down, and the passage or ferry belonging to the said manor, together with the right of presentation to the living, and rights and royalties upon the demesne lands before recited." From the allusion to thc Down and

[1] A hide of land probably averaged 240 acres. A plough-team meant about 120 acres. Serfs were mere slaves, the personal property of the Lord of the Manor, but not belonging to the estate. Villeins were the highest of the classes which had no sort of freedom, but they had land and chattels of their own, though these belonged to the estate. Cotters were of similar but rather inferior condition. Boors were probably the highest class of farm-labourers employed on the estate.—Eyton, "Domesday Studies."

the ferry, we may perhaps conclude that the "newly built house" is the farm at the eastern end of the hill, which probably dates, therefore, from early Stuart times. The present Lord of the Manor is Wm. Wyndham, Esq. of Salisbury. The inhabitants of the parish have increased somewhat since Collinson wrote, when forty persons, occupying between them eight houses, made up its scanty population. The inhabitants now number 112, and the inhabited houses have increased to twenty-three.

The Church of St. Bridget is a plain and primitive little building, whose tower is so low and inconspicuous—hardly showing, indeed, above the roof of the nave—that from the summit of the Down, two miles away, it is almost impossible to distinguish it from the houses that stand near. The tower was, however, once of ordinary height, but was struck by lightning in 1729, and afterwards cut down to its present shape. On the west side is a stone with this inscription:—

John Ginckens
Churchwarden
Anō Dom̄ 1729

Some remains of the old tower windows can still be traced inside the belfry. In the chamber under the tower is a holy-water stoup, which seems large for the size of the building. When the church was restored a few years ago, the chancel was entirely rebuilt; and its only ancient features are the piscina or holy-water drain on the south wall near the altar, and the arch of the door. About seventy years ago, a small vestry was built on the south side of the chancel; and it was in breaking away the plaster of the wall, to make an entry from this vestry into the chancel, that the old doorway was discovered. The centre window on the north side of the nave is old, the other two were put up when the church was restored in 1883. When the nave was paved, the brick flooring described by Collinson was taken up, and underneath it was found a still older floor of pebbles. Below this, at the west end of the nave, were discovered several skeletons, lying close to the surface. With one exception the bench-ends are modern, but they have been copied from the old specimen still preserved under the tower. The most striking feature of the church is the boldly carved octagonal font, from the south side of which the ornamentation appears to have been partly cut away. The simply ornamented wooden pulpit is Jacobæan, as may be seen from the quaintly arranged inscription near the top of its south-western side :—

GEORGE ❀
GVDRID
GAVE ❀ THI
S ❀ 1620 ❀

Behind the pulpit is a recess, which may mark the

position of the rood-loft and stair. On either side of the chancel-arch are two carved stone heads.

FONT IN BREAN CHURCH

That on the left side is the head of a woman, with curls, and a general style of wearing the hair said to be characteristic of the time of Richard II. (1377-1399), which may be an indication of the reconstruction or alteration of the church. The arch of the doorway from the interior into the tower is, however, apparently much earlier.

The communion plate of Brean Church consists of a plain silver chalice, dated 1773, a modern glass flagon, and a plain silver paten, also modern. An antique paten, said to have been in use some sixty or seventy years ago, seems to have disappeared.

In the tower hang three bells, all of them very ancient, and in all probability cast some years before the Reformation. The curious crown stamp on the first of them, and the divisional stops used in the inscriptions on the other two, are marks employed by a bell-founder whose name is unknown, but whose initials were T. G., and who flourished about the year 1500.[1]

The bells are thus inscribed :—

Sancte Micail.
Quos Convoco Virgo Maria.
Sancte Dionisi Ora Pro Nobis.

In the churchyard is a tombstone on which were formerly some lines beginning :—

"If health were a thing that money could buy,
The rich they would live, and the poor they would die;"

but the inscription is no longer legible. The north side of the churchyard was chiefly reserved for the interment of the bodies of drowned sailors, many of

[1] Ellacombe, "Church Bells of Somerset."

which were washed ashore on Brean sands before the building of the Burnham lighthouse. It was after some of these sorrowful waifs had been committed to the dust, about thirty years ago, that an iron heart was set up in their memory. It bore the lines, now almost worn away:—

" The cruel winds and yawning waves
Hurried me to my doom;
While wife and children dear
Waited for me at home."

It has now also a bullet-hole through it, a record of the time, more than twenty years ago, when it was taken from its place and set up on the sands as a target. The present Rector had it restored and let into a stone socket to prevent a second removal.

The existing church records of Brean are comparatively modern. The oldest Registers go no further back than 1730, and even these have been re-copied from the commencement down to the year 1807. The entries are few, and present no points of special interest. It is, however, remarkable that in the seventy years from 1730 to 1800 only sixteen burials are recorded, which, with the present population, would give a death-rate of rather less than four per thousand.

The first page of the book of Churchwardens' Accounts is headed: " Robert Chaplain's disbursements for the Church and Ospitall for the parrish of Breand for the year 1727 " ; and the first entry is of the contribution to the hospital, which, as already noted, was established at Woodspring :—

It. pd. the 4 quartr's Ospitall . . . 00 13 00

It is only within comparatively recent times that bodies washed up by the waves received Christian burial. In old days the remains were merely buried in the sand, just above high-water mark. As already pointed out, a corner of Brean churchyard was reserved for such poor waifs of the sea; and in the Churchwardens' Accounts are entries of payments made to men who had found dead bodies on the shore.

Brean parish is so remote from the world that it is not surprising to find superstitions and quaint old beliefs still lingering in it. Among these are strange things in the way of medicine. There are people in Brean who still, it is said, consider spiders as efficacious remedies for ague, a common disease in that low-lying district. Sometimes the spider is killed and made into a pill with bread. Sometimes a live spider is put in water, and when "he do curly up," both water and spider are swallowed together. In an old book of local accounts, dated 1771, are some curious prescriptions for sick cows. One "infaliable Receipt" runs thus:—

"Take an ounce of Dragons blood, an ounce of Bol Armeniack, half an ounce of Irish Slait, one handful of nettels boild in milk. Two candels Give with this Drinch."

"For the same:—

"Take three liv eals and pour them down the throat of the beast."

The most remarkable feature of the parish is the headland of Brean Down, the longest of the three promontories that break the coast-line of the Mendip Country, and by far the most picturesque and interesting of the three. Though but an insignificant point upon the map of England, it is to the naturalist and the antiquary one of the most attractive spots in the district. It is but a mile from the outskirts of a much-frequented town; but the tidal waters of the Axe, the little mud-stained river that separates it from Weston sands, forms for its wild life so effectual a safeguard that even the Raven still finds sanctuary among the rugged cliffs along its southern verge, while its grassy slopes and rocky ledges, the shingle and the sand-hills, and the fringe of the far-reaching moorland at its feet, have all their characteristic birds or flowers or insects.

The isolated situation of the Down, together with the steepness of its sides, made it, in early times, particularly easy to defend, and it shows at many points distinct signs of human occupation. It has all, however, been under the plough within the memory of persons still living. Forty years ago the whole available southern slope was cut up into allotments. Other parts of the hill have still more recently been under cultivation, and in this way many barrows and earthworks have no doubt been defaced, or have even entirely disappeared.

At the eastern end of Brean Down there was a Roman camp, which doubtless served as an additional defence for the little port of Uphill, half a mile away. Of this camp one angle only now remains. The rest of the works have been destroyed by the quarries which have been cut in the north side of the hill. On this spot, when, about thirty years ago, the quarrymen were taking off the turf before beginning to dig for stone in a fresh place, they found some Roman coins, including gold pieces of Augustus, Nero, and the elder Drusus, the last being much the rarest of the three. All were in a fine state of preservation. The lettering on the coins of Nero and Augustus was as clear as when they were struck. There are special points of interest in connection with these pieces of money. Among all the thousands of Roman coins which have been found in Somerset, very few gold coins are known ; and the Aureus of Augustus, in particular, is an example of almost the earliest regular gold coinage ever issued by the Roman government. The coins of early Rome were all of copper. Silver money was not coined until 269 B.C. Some gold coins were in use during the Republic, but, with the exception of a few, now of great rarity, which may have been struck in Campania, they all came from foreign mints. The commonest was probably the Macedonian stater. The first regular gold coin, called the Aureus denarius, or, more briefly, Aureus, a piece equal to twenty-five silver denarii, rather less in diameter than an English sovereign, but thicker and a few grains heavier, was struck about the time of Julius Cæsar. His nephew and successor, Augustus, reduced the weight of the Aureus to 120 grains, or three grains less than a sovereign, and this is exactly the weight of the one discovered on Brean Down. Among other coins found at the same time were two silver denarii of Vespasian, one of which, struck to commemorate the Conquest of Palestine, bears on the reverse a seated figure, with a trophy of armour hung above it, while below is the single word IVDAEA. Other Roman relics have at various times been discovered on the Down. Among them was a beautiful carnelian ring, once exhibited at a meeting of the Somersetshire Archæological Society.[1]

On the highest point of the hill, 321 feet above the sea, are some loose stones, usually regarded as the remains of a beacon or fire-signalling station, and round them may be traced the earthworks of another ancient encampment, probably British, where many fragments of simple and undecorated pottery have from time to time been brought to the surface by the rabbits. There are other signs of fortification along the north slope of the hill, and on that

[1] "Som. Arch. Pro.," vol. ii.

side, too, are some pits, perhaps the centres of huts, like those on Worlebury, in one or two cases showing remains of walling.

There are only two buildings on Brean Down—the now dismantled fort at the western extremity, and the farm below the south slope of the hill, near the landing-place of the ferry. Close to the farm, approached by a slight path to the right of the road, is the only well on the Down—except the much better one within the farm precincts—with a stone archway, and a time-worn flight of steps, not unpicturesquely set in a little hollow in the side of the hill. Below it is some rough masonry, apparently ancient. A layer of cinders in the gravel above this, containing scraps of old iron, suggests that it is the remains of a forge.

Beyond the walled garden belonging to the farm is the military road, which, after climbing the slope, is continued along the northern face of the Down to the fort at the western end. These works, constructed in 1867 as one of the four links in the chain of defences across the Bristol Channel, were armed with seven seven-inch muzzle-loading guns, and were planned for a garrison of about fifty men. Early one morning in July 1900, the fort was the scene of a tremendous explosion, when one of the magazines was blown up, wrecking the earthworks, overturning the guns, and scattering fragments of the buildings in all directions. The only man killed was the gunner, who, it is believed, had fired his carbine into the magazine. In the following year, the old guns were sold by auction.

On the north shore of the Down, a little way to the east of the fort, there lay for many years the ruins of the stone pier, which, while in course of construction as the first step in the Brean Down Harbour Scheme, was long ago swept away by a storm. The idea was that a point near the seaward end of the Down would be an excellent position for a port, because of the great depth of water there at all states of the tide, and because of the nearness of the main Great Western Line and the consequent shortness of the journey to London.

A survey of the Down was taken in 1867 in connection with the proposed branch railway, but the unfinished pier was destroyed a few years later, and, finally, the scheme was abandoned. The foundation-stone of the pier was laid by Lady Wilmot in 1864, just a month after a similar ceremony at Birnbeck. The stone was several fathoms under water, and a buoy was attached to it to mark the spot. The rising tide lifted both buoy and foundation-stone, and later on they were discovered adrift not far from the Steep Holm. The pier was ultimately destroyed by the great storm of December 1872, and a few stones that still lie on the shore at Brean are all that remains of the Company's £365,000.

It is a wide expanse both of land and sea upon which the eye looks down from the summit of the hill. To the north, at the end of a broad sweep of yellow sand, is Weston-super-Mare, clustering along the slopes of Worlebury and stretching far out over the moor. Along the western horizon, across the brown waters of the Channel, lies the coast of Wales —Cardiff, with its forest of masts and its long plumes of smoke, and, far inland, the dim shape of Brecknock Beacon. Far to southward stretches away a broad alluvial plain, dotted with white hamlets and cut up by innumerable ditches. In the middle distance, rising like an island out of the wide green level, is the isolated hill of Brent Knoll, with the earthworks of an ancient British cattle-station on its summit, and the slender spire of East Brent Church just showing at its foot. Before the erection of the lighthouse at Burnham, the spire of East Brent was regularly whitewashed, so as to serve, like the old tower of Uphill, as a steering-mark for ships in the Channel. Hard by the Knoll is the square tower of Lympsham, half-hidden among clustering elms; and far off across the moor, in whose green level gleams the winding silver of the Axe, is the Tor of Glastonbury, from whose crest looks down like a watch-tower the ruin of the ancient Church of St. Michael.

On the southern side, two miles away, is the little village of Brean; and beyond it there shows above the sand-hills the square tower of Berrow. Beyond Berrow stands the white shaft of Burnham Lighthouse, and still farther off are the smoke and the towers of Bridgwater. On the far side of Bridgwater Bay show the faint outlines of the Quantock Hills, with Exmoor, still more faint, beyond.

In sunny weather a mirage may often be seen from the Down, and to a less extent on the beach itself. While the tide is still far out there sometimes appears, close up to high-water mark, a sort of phantom sea, which not only looks exactly like a smooth sheet of water, but reflects in its magic mirror the tower of Berrow Church and the ragged line of sand-hills. When, as more rarely happens, it is visible on the other side of the hill, it reflects the esplanade at Weston and all the buildings of the town.

Against the southern side of the Down, where the beach meets the foot of the cliff, is a great heap of drifted sand, in which human bones are sometimes brought to light by the rabbits, and in which several complete skeletons have been found. These may be remains of the ancient inhabitants of the camps above, or of drowned sailors, whose bodies it was the custom, until late in last century, to bury on the beach, just above high-water mark.

Rabbits are not indigenous to Britain, though the date of their introduction is unknown. But there were rabbits on Brean Down so long ago as 1361, when Robert Brene, who then owned the property, made a grant to one Thomas Hege "of all his rabbits in his parcel of Brenne Downe." [1]

Kingfishers have more than once dug their burrow

[1] Collinson.

at the foot of this great heap of sand, strewing their floor with empty cases of shrimps instead of with fish-bones. There is no fresh-water near the spot, and the Kingfishers seem to find better hunting-ground along the edge of the tide than in the muddy waters of the Axe. It is no uncommon thing, however, to see one of these beautiful birds hovering like a hawk over one of the moorland ditches and then plunging down beneath the surface. Among the most noteworthy of the many birds that haunt the Down are Sheldrakes, which have much increased in number of late years. As they usually lay their eggs in rabbit-holes—more rarely choosing an open space among the bushes—they are known in the district as Burrow Ducks. They are shy birds, and not very easy to see if they are suspicious of danger. But at low tide they are often visible on the mud, their boldly marked plumage showing plainly out against the sombre background. In summer, especially in the early morning or the late evening, they may be seen flying up to their nests, which are generally not far from the edge of the cliffs. When the breeding season is over, both old birds and young go out to sea, apparently not returning to the Down until late in the following spring.

From time immemorial a pair of Ravens have built their eyrie in the cliffs of Brean, usually rearing their broods in safety, though they seem to allow no others of their clan to gain a footing near the ancestral nesting-place. Ravens are not really rare in the Mendip Country, and when, as has sometimes happened, one of the Brean birds has been shot, the survivor has had no difficulty in finding another mate. Many Jackdaws build in crannies of the cliffs, and in rabbit-burrows. But the Rock Doves that sometimes bear them company are regarded by ornithologists rather as escaped Blue Rocks, survivors perhaps of rural pigeon-matches, than as really wild. Both the Sparrow-Hawk and the Kestrel rear their broods among the rocks, but the Peregrine Falcon, though formerly a resident and still not unfrequently seen, has no eyrie now nearer than the Steep Holm. There is not a great variety of sea-fowl on the Somerset side of the Channel, and none breed among the rocks of the Down. Eggs of the Oyster-catcher, or Sea Pie, as the fishermen call it, have several times been found in the shingle towards Brean village, and a clutch of three Redshank's eggs was once taken on the Black Rock. More common than either are Ringed Plovers, of which a few pairs stay every year to breed near the shore.

From autumn to spring many kinds of wild-fowl haunt the mouth of the Axe. Few winters pass in which some storm-driven stranger does not put in for shelter to the mouth of the river, too often, alas! in vain. All through the winter months the mud-flats on both sides of the Down are thronged by Curlews and Dunlins, Plovers and Oyster-catchers, and all the ordinary tenants of the season. There are always Scaup Ducks on the bay in winter, and in hard weather they sometimes appear in flocks of thousands. Though keeping for the most part well out to sea, these beautiful birds occasionally come close inshore, and have even been seen foraging on the sands opposite the Weston Sanatorium. The parish boundary is in the middle of the river, but the birds that, at various seasons of the year, frequent the mouth of the Axe, have been already alluded to in the chapter on Uphill.

Most characteristic of Brean Down is the Rock Pipit, a weak-voiced, lark-like, little bird, which, though not often seen on the hill itself, is common among the rocks about its base. On the other hand, the rarest bird recorded for Brean is probably Montagu's Harrier, of which a specimen was shot there in 1864.[1] Cormorants are occasionally seen; and in October 1892 a Shag was shot somewhere between Brean Down and the river Parret.[2]

Most of the birds of Brean are land birds. But even in their voices there are suggestions of the sea. The Starling on the chimney of the farm copies to the life the call of the Curlew and the hoarse clamour of the Gulls, and has been heard to imitate even the creak of tackle on board a little coaster anchored in the river; while the Skylarks that nest in the rich meadows weave into their own sweet songs

[1] "Som. Arch. Pro.," vol. xxxvii.
[2] "Som. Arch. Pro.," vol. xl.

the wail of the Lapwing and the whistle of the Plover.

One of the chief attractions of Brean Down is the abundance and variety of its plants. After a wet June, which best suits the shallow, sandy soil, more than a hundred different kinds of wild-flowers have been found in blossom there, mainly on its southern slope, but including also the beach and the sand-hills, and the ditches on the edge of the moor, in the course of a single summer afternoon. By far the rarest flower is the beautiful little White Rock Rose, which, except for a few points on the hill above the village of Bleadon, where of late years it has established itself, is elsewhere found only at Torquay. At Brean Down it is so abundant that in favourable years its delicate petals whiten parts of the south slope of the hill like a slight sprinkling of snow. Other rare plants are the *Trinia*, the Wild Cabbage, the Broad-leaved Cress (*Lepidium latifolium*), one of the Mouse-ear Chickweeds (*Cerastium pumilum*), the Milk Thistle, the Ivy Broom-rape, and the lesser Broom-rape, and both the Evening Primroses, *biennis* and *odorata*, two established aliens, the former from North America, the latter from Patagonia.

Other characteristic plants are Henbane, Hound's-tongue, Bugloss, Fœtid Iris, *Chlora perfoliata*, the Grass Pea, the Bee Orchis, and the Dwarf Orchis, also known as the Burnt Tip Orchis, from the dark colour of its unopened flowers. Samphire grows freely among the rocks on the south side, though no one appears to gather it for pickling, as Rutter says was done in his time. There are two ferns which are more plentiful on Brean Down than in any other spot in the Mendip Country. Sea Spleenwort is nowhere common on this coast, but it grows at several points among the Brean cliffs; and near the western end of the promontory there is a little cave whose rocky walls are thickly hung with its shining fronds. On the hill itself, Moonwort is very abundant for a limited period at the end of April and the beginning of May, growing freely even in the paths and sheep tracks, although from its diminutive size it is no doubt often overlooked.

The Down is a good place for the insect-hunter. Its flowery slopes are the haunt of many Moths and Butterflies, especially of Chalk-Hill Blues, Graylings, and Burnet Moths. Marbled Whites and Cream-spot Tiger Moths have also been taken, the latter sometimes in great numbers.

The promontory is wholly composed of Carboniferous Limestone, whose strata, dipping to the north, are broken on the southern side into picturesque and rugged cliffs. Perhaps the most characteristic fossil is the familiar horn-shaped coral *Cyathophyllum*, of which many examples may be seen in the living rock at the foot of the hill. In fissures on the south side there have been found many bones and antlers of Reindeer. Reindeer have long been extinct in these islands, but unlike most of the other large mammals whose remains have been discovered in the various caves of the Mendip Country, there is ground for thinking that they were still to be found in Britain within historic times. In the Saga of Orkney, written about the close of the twelfth century, is a passage which may be thus translated: "The earls were accustomed almost every summer to cross over into Caithness, and there, in the forest, to hunt the red deer and reindeer." Some authorities think that the closing words, "edr Hreina," should be translated, "or reindeer;" but Professor Brandt of St. Petersburg, Professor Boyd Dawkins, and others, accept the version before given.[1]

The sand-hills that line the shore of Bridgwater Bay may seem to the casual observer little better than a wilderness. But in the summer, at any rate, they possess many attractions for the naturalist. There, on the warm sand, the Sea Convolvulus opens its great flowers. There on the edge of the shingle flourish the Hound's-tongue, the Sea Holly, the Yellow-horned Poppy, and many another salt-loving species. A few pairs of Sheldrakes breed in the rabbit burrows, and Oyster-catchers and Ringed Plovers sometimes lay their eggs among the pebbles above high-water mark. There, too, may be seen, about noon on a sunny day in the late spring, the rare Sea Tiger-Beetle. A still rarer species is a yellow geodephagous beetle, *Nebria complanata*, entirely confined to the shore of the Bristol Channel.

[1] Harting, "Extinct British Wild Animals."

Occasionally the sand-hills are visited in summer by swarms of Cream-spot Tiger Moths. Among the stems of the Marram, the tall sedge whose roots hold the loose sand from drifting farther in over the fields, are to be found quantities of a prettily marked spiral land-shell, *Bulimus acutus*, only to be met with near the sea. There is also some excellent hunting-ground for a naturalist among the many ditches of the moor. Of a crowd of interesting water-plants, perhaps the most striking, though far from the rarest, is the tall and beautiful Flowering Rush. Of Dr. Pooley's list of 111 species of Weston *Diatomaceæ*, a good many were found in the Brean marshes or on the shore of the Down. In the dwarf willow-bushes overhanging the ditches, moorland birds such as Reed-Sparrows and Sedge-Warblers, sometimes make their nests, while the water itself contains a great variety of fresh-water shells, insects, and lower forms of life.

The fisheries in the neighbourhood of Brean have declined in value of late years. But a good many different kinds of fish are still caught, or at some time or other have been seen by the fishermen. The fish and the few other marine creatures to be found here are much the same as in Weston Bay. At Brean, as is the case all along this part of the coast, the most conspicuous shells on the sands are the brightly coloured little bivalves of the genus *Tellina*, of which there are locally probably not more than two species. Very abundant, too, though less easily seen, are the tiny spiral shells of the two very similar genera, *Hydrobius* and *Rissoa*. The ordinary shells to be found among the rocks belong, as in the other bays, to six species: the common Whelk, three kinds of Periwinkle, the Limpet, and a shell called *Purpura lapillus*, much smaller and of a more slender shape than the Whelk. At times, after very rough weather, great quantities of very large "Cuttle Bones" are washed up on the beach on the south side of the Down; and the live Squid themselves are occasionally seen by the fishermen.

It is not often that ships are wrecked on Brean sands. In a great gale in the autumn of 1896, a Norwegian barque of about 1000 tons was driven ashore between the Down and the village, and her crew of twelve men, together with their dog, were rescued by the Burnham lifeboat. The vessel was lightened with the hope of getting her off at high tide, but tugs failed to move her. A return of the gale drove her still higher up the beach, and she was ultimately sold and broken up. She was originally a British ship, and was called *Maipu* after a Chilian river. It is a remarkable fact, that the four English vessels which have borne this name have all been lost. There is a tradition in the district that a large Portuguese ship was wrecked off the Down some centuries ago; and the spot is still pointed out on the north side, where after rough weather, fragments of the glass and pottery, which are supposed to have formed her cargo, have often been washed up by the sea. Cups which, some sixty years since, were found there unbroken, were of brown glazed ware, with two handles, and bore the letters A.R., surmounted by a crown. This device may perhaps refer to Alphonso VI., who was crowned King of Portugal in 1656, and who, eleven years later, was on account of his vices and misgovernment compelled by his wife and brother to abdicate the throne. Although few vessels are wrecked on this coast, many curious things, including even West Indian Buck-eye Beans that have probably drifted all the way across the Atlantic, are from time to time left by the tide upon the beach near the two cottages that seem to cower for shelter behind the old sea-wall. In every piece of woodwork about these two houses one seems to read a message from the sea. The garden-gate of one is made of planks which the tide has laid upon the sand; the posts from which it hangs are pieces of a mast. Mahogany panels from the saloon of some lost steamship have been worked into the walling of the garden-shed. Every fire that burns upon the hearth is a fire of driftwood, the jetsam

"of wrecks upon the main,
Of ships dismasted, that were hailed,
And sent no answer back again."

THE ISLANDS

THE two Holms, the rocky islets so conspicuous from the Weston beach, may be called the outposts of the Mendip Hills, with which at one time they were undoubtedly connected. The Steep Holm is included in the parish of Brean, but the Flat Holm, or Flatholm, as it is usually spelt, is part of the parish of St. Mary's, Cardiff. They are much alike in area, each measuring about sixty acres in extent. But while the Steep Holm is long and narrow—about half a mile in length, and three hundred yards or less in breadth—the Flat Holm is a broad oval, some six hundred and sixty yards long, and five hundred and forty yards across, so that their real outlines are just the reverse of what they seem to be from the Somerset shore. Holm is a Scandinavian word for "island," and is almost always applied to an island in a lake or river, such as Stockholm in Lake Maelar, and Lingholm in Windermere.[1] The names were doubtless in this case given by the Norsemen, who found these rocks convenient stations from which to plunder both sides of the Channel. In the Anglo-Saxon Chronicle the

[1] Isaac Taylor, "Words and Places."

Holms are called Bradanreolice and Steopanreolice; that is to say, Broad Reel Island and Steep Reel Island, perhaps in allusion to their shape as seen from the fairway.

The Steep Holm

The Steep Holm, three miles west-north-west of Brean Down, to which, no doubt, it once was joined, rises abruptly from the sea. Its rocky sides are bold and precipitous, in some places very picturesque, and landing is possible at only two points. Boats usually put in at the shingle beach at the eastern end, opposite Weston, whence a track, passing to the left of the now ruinous and deserted inn, leads to the summit, two hundred and fifty feet above the sea. But inside the Calf Rock, on the south side, there is another, and perhaps more ancient, landing-place, from which a path leads up to the site of the ruined Priory. Small as the island is, it has an interesting history. Its isolated position, its distance from the mainland, the difficulty of getting to it, and the ease with which it could be defended, have combined to make it, at various periods, a sanctuary and a stronghold.

It is usually said that the historian Gildas, who lived between 516 and 572 A.D., retired to the Steep Holm for the sake of its solitude and remoteness, and that there he wrote his melancholy book, *De Excidio Britanniæ*, describing the downfall of

Peregrine Falcon

Britain. But the statement appears to rest on a passage in Leland, who wrote nearly a thousand years after the time of Gildas, and who, although he frequently refers to the works of that author, says nothing about any of them having been written on the Steep Holm. The following is a translation of the passage alluded to:—

"There are those who think, and I myself am disposed to agree with them, that he made his way to the Severn Sea, and that he inhabited one of the islands there, against which beats the fury of the stormy water. There are two islets in that part of the Severn Sea, one of which is called Stepeholme, the other Flatholme." After observing that he is going to give new names to these two islands, "Præruptaria" and "Planaria," in order, perhaps, to harmonise better with the Latin of his Chronicle, Leland continues: "There are many reasons why it seems to me probable that Gildas first fixed upon one of these islands as the scene of his retirement, and that he took up his abode there. But as the devices of man are never certain and enduring, so, in the spot where he had promised himself the deepest solitude and the most complete repose, he had often to submit to uproar and disturbance. His troubles were caused by pirates who, conscious of their evil deeds, steered their galleys to the small islands of the Severn Sea, since these had few inhabitants, and were therefore well adapted for hiding-places and for storing plunder. He endured for some time the crimes, the thefts, and the outrages of these ruffians. But when he found that there seemed likely to be no bound or limit to their wickedness, he saw that he should have to change his place of residence. As he was thinking it over, his eyes rested on Somerset. In that district was a colony of hermits, called Avallon, a name which I translate 'Fruit Garden.' Of this he had often heard many things about both its origin and its sanctity. Having fortunately got hold of a small vessel, he set sail, and soon reached the longed-for shore. Setting out without delay on his journey, he got safely to Avallon. This spot modern writers have called Glessoneybury; but I, in my Latin treatise, shall call it Glessoburgum." After observing that he has been able to find out very little about the writings of Gildas, Leland says further: "William of Meildune writes, in his book on the History of Glessoburgum, that Gildas died among the Avallonian hermits."[1]

Nothing more is known about the pirates who disturbed the solitude of Gildas. The Anglo-Saxon Chronicle records that in the year 918 a great fleet from Brittany, under the command of the Earls Ohtor and Rhoald, put in to the mouth of the Severn, and "spoiled the North-Welsh everywhere by the sea coast where they then pleased." The freebooters were worsted at length by the men of

[1] Leland, *Commentarii de Scriptoribus Britannicis*, cap. xxxi,. *De Gilda Sapiente*.

Hereford and Gloucester. Earl Rhoald was killed, and the invaders promised to leave the country. They attempted two more descents, however, one to the east of Watchet, and another at Porlock. But the royal troops had occupied the whole of the Somerset coast, and the pirates were beaten off. So roughly were they handled that, in the words of the Chronicle, "few of them got away, except those alone who there swam out to the ships. And then they sat down, out on the island of Bradanreolice (The Flat Holm), until such time as they were quite destitute of food; and many men died of hunger, because they could not obtain any food. Then they went thence to South Wales, and then out to Ireland: and this was during harvest." This is the account given in Manuscript A. But Manuscripts B, C, and D, and the Chronicle of Henry of Huntingdon, say that the pirates took refuge on the Steep Holm. The latter is certainly the more likely. Its loftier and more precipitous sides, and its two not very practicable landing-places, would make it a much easier place to defend.

In 1067, the year after the Battle of Hastings, we learn from the Anglo-Saxon Chronicle that "Harold's mother Githa, and the wives of many good men with her, went to the Steep Holms, and there abode some time, and afterwards went from thence over sea to St. Omer's."

At a later period the island came into the possession of the family of Bec of Eresby in Lincolnshire,[1] and in the reign of Edward I. it was granted by John Bec to Henry de Laci, Earl of Lincoln.[2] The next owners appear to have been the Berkeleys, who held it, as we learn from the family records, at least as late as the reign of Henry V. At some remote period a small Priory was founded on the island at a point where the Garden Battery now stands. This was restored by Maurice the Third of Berkeley about the close of the thirteenth or the beginning of the fourteenth century, as appears from the following passage in the family archives :—

> "This lord Maurice (1281–1326), new built the friery for the fryers and brethren in the Holmes, an Iland in Seavern and not far from his manor of Portbury."

The last allusion to the island in the Berkeley Manuscripts is in the life of Thomas the Fourth (1352-1417):—

> "In the 13th of Richard the second, the lady Elizabeth his mother dying, this lord entred upon the lands which shee held in Joynture and dower. . . . And upon the Isle of Stepholmes, in the County of Somerset." [3]

Of the further history of the Steep Holm Priory nothing is known, but traces of the building can still be seen. Before the construction of the

[1] Collinson. [2] Dugdale.

[3] "MS. Memoirs of the Lives of the Berkeleys," 1066 to 1618, written by John Smyth of Nibley, 1618, and preserved in the Muniment Room of Berkeley Castle.

batteries in 1867, there was standing a piece of walling about seven feet high, of good workmanship, and faced with dressed stone of the island. At the base of it was a plinth, three feet broad, of brown sandstone. Most of this wall is now buried, but part of it, from which the facing has been taken away, is visible near the roofless ruins at the top of the path, one of which is perhaps the remains of the building which, according to Rutter, was erected here in 1776, to provide shelter for storm-bound fishermen.

During the construction of the Garden Battery, so called because it stands on what was supposed to have been the garden of the friars, the foundations of the Priory were in great part laid bare. One chamber was so well preserved that it was repaired, and used as a living-room by the foreman in charge of the works. In clearing out the earth, in order to lay down a wooden floor, it was found that the whole space inside the walls of this building was packed with skeletons, lying close together side by side only a few inches below the surface. Near the same spot were found many bones of deer, a number of brass rings of primitive workmanship, a coin bearing the figure of an archer, together with some old pieces of money, said to show no legible device or inscription. There is a tradition that a former tenant of the island once dug up a pot of coins, but all trace of them appears to be lost. Built into the wall of the Side-arm Store belonging to the Tombstone Battery, is part of the lid of an ancient stone coffin, a piece of hard blue lias, with a moulding, and with a cross cut in it, and upon this has also been inscribed the date of its discovery, 1867.

In 1832 the Corporation of Bristol sold the Steep Holm to Colonel Tynte of Haswell, Bridgwater, and the present owner is Mr. Kemis Tynte of Cefn Mabley, near Cardiff, from whom the War Department holds part of the island on lease. Colonel Tynte built himself a house near the landing-place, and for a time he lived there. He then leased the island, and the house was turned into an inn. The innkeeper claimed the right of selling drink without a licence, on the ground that the island was in no parish, and was beyond the jurisdiction of the Excise. About twenty years ago this so-called right was challenged by the authorities, and the Court of Queen's Bench having decided that there was no ground for the claim of exemption, the inn was abandoned, and it has since become a ruin. The only persons now living on the Steep Holm are the few gunners in charge of the fort, where, however, there are quarters for about fifty men. A little to the right of the inn is the only well on the island. It contains a spring of good drinking-water, but in times of drought it becomes almost or quite dry.

It has always been believed by the islanders that the Steep Holm was a sort of sanctuary, where no one could be arrested for debt or for any other offence against the law. And about sixty years since a Weston innkeeper is said to have taken refuge on the rock to avoid imprisonment for debt, and to have lived there for seven years, occasionally going home on Sundays, and always returning to sanctuary the same night. Collinson gives the Steep Holm under the parish of Uphill. Ten years ago, however, it was united for rating purposes with the parish of Brean.

The two Holms are links in the chain of defences which stretches across the Bristol Channel; and on the top of this island are six batteries—the Garden, the Rudder Rock, the Split Rock, the Summit, the Laboratory, and the Tombstone Batteries, armed altogether with ten seven-inch muzzle-loading guns. In 1899 the War Office, having decided to replace these obsolete weapons with heavy modern breech-loaders, and being, it is said, in doubt whether the new guns should be in barbettes or behind shields. a dummy 9.2-inch gun, protected by a Harveyed shield of nickel steel, about thirty feet long and three inches thick, was mounted in the Rudder Rock Battery. And at this the second-class cruiser *Arrogant* (ten guns, 5750 tons, and 10,000 horse-power)—the men in charge of the fort having been withdrawn to the shelter of the cliffs on the eastern side—fired, as she steamed past the island, some hundreds of rounds from her 6-inch, 4.7-inch, and smaller guns, at ranges varying from 1800 to 2000 yards. The shield, struck by many shells, was greatly damaged, while the concrete wall of the battery was completely demolished by the bombardment.

During a great storm about the year 1810, a large West Indiaman, called the *Rebecca*, was wrecked near the Steep Holm. Casks of rum from her cargo were washed ashore on Weston beach, and, in defiance of the scanty force of Preventive men then available, were seized upon and tapped by the villagers. Farmers from the country round came to the spot with carts, and carried away milk-pails full of spirit. In the autumn of 1901 a large Spanish barque, the *Anita*, struck on or near the island. All hands were lost, and the adjacent coast was strewn for miles with pieces of her wreckage.

Island life must always possess special attractions for the naturalist. And even within the scanty limits of this little rock there is to be found at least one peculiar form. This is the Great Round-headed Garlic, a fine plant with flower-stems five feet high, and believed to be the ancestor of the common leek of cultivation. Originally a native of Switzerland, Southern Europe, and Western Asia, it occurs in these islands only in three isolated and widely separated localities—in the Channel Islands, on an island in Galway Bay, and here on the Steep Holm. The Steep Holm plant, however, is a variety, and is entirely confined to this particular spot. The Single Pæony, for which the island is famous, may be called a flower of even greater rarity still, since it is to be found wild nowhere else in this country. This beautiful plant, which came from Southern Europe, may, like the giant Garlic, the Alexanders, and perhaps also the Caper Spurge, have been introduced by the inmates of the Priory; but its right to be included in the British Flora is quite as great as that of other species whose claims are not contested. In spite of the raids of selfish and unscrupulous dealers and collectors, it still grows on a steep grassy slope above the landing-place, and in recent times it seems to have established itself at other points on the island.

There are no trees on the Steep Holm, but Privet and Elder grow freely among the cliffs, which in some places are thickly draped with ivy. There is, however, a great variety of plants, which, in addition to the rarer species already mentioned, include the Wild Cabbage, the Ivy Broom-rape, the Golden Samphire, and the Rock Sea-Lavender. Of commoner flowers the most striking are the Hemlock, the Fœtid Iris, the Wild Mignonette, Beet, the Chlora, the Bee Orchis, the Hound's-tongue, and the Red Valerian or Good Neighbours.

The native Mammalia are few. Bats are said to inhabit the cave, and some have been disturbed from the ruined inn and from the old building behind it. But there are no rats, mice, shrews, or moles. There are still a good many rabbits ; but if these are the descendants of those alluded to by Rutter, they show no trace of that red fur that he says characterised the Steep Holm rabbits of his time. The cliffs are said to have been formerly frequented during the breeding-season by great numbers of sea-birds, whose eggs were collected and sent to sugar-refineries in Bristol. This year, however, only about fifty Herring Gulls, a few pairs of Lesser Black-backed Gulls, and a small number of Kittiwakes nested among the rocks on the north-west, while several pairs of Sheldrakes were observed to have nests in crevices or in rabbit-burrows towards the south-east. Shearwaters and Oyster-catchers were also seen on or near the rock during the breeding-season, and in winter time the sprat-nets attract a good many Guillemots. Both Ravens and Peregrine Falcons still have eyries in the cliffs, and eggs of the Hobby were taken here in 1849.[1] Other birds lately seen on the Holm in the early summer, and believed to breed upon the island, are Kestrels, Sparrow-hawks, Rock Doves, Meadow and Rock Pipits, Skylarks, Swifts, and Swallows.

There are no snakes on the island, and no frogs or toads or newts. But there are a few Slow-worms, which are strange creatures to find on an isolated rock like this. The last recorded specimen was seen in 1901. The only Butterflies seen, in three expeditions to the Steep Holm, were Painted Lady, Dark Green Fritillary, Small Heath, Large and Small Whites, and the Common Blue. The commonest Moth in summer is the Burnet. Among other species taken were the Cinnabar, the Lackey, the Herald, and the Yellow Shell. The only land-

[1] "Som. Arch. Pro.," vol. i.

shells that have been noticed are seven species of *Helix—aspersa*, *nemoralis*, *rufescens*, *virgata*, *caperata*, *pygmæa*, and *pulchella*; *Pupa secale*, *umbilicata*, and *muscorum*; *Clausilia laminata*, *Cyclostoma elegans*, and several kinds of *Zonites*.

Since the Steep Holm is composed entirely of Carboniferous Limestone, the fossils found there are naturally similar to those of the same formation on the mainland. Recent visitors noticed in particular *Productus giganteus* and *Euomphalus æqualis*, together with *Encrinites* and various other corals. The rock contains lead-ore, but it does not appear to have been worked, as there is some evidence was the case on the sister island. On the northern side is a cave, running deep into the island. It is difficult of access, and its entrance, although above high-water mark, can only be reached at low tide. It was visited about twenty years ago by two men, who brought away a number of stalactites of great size and beauty. They also saw bats in great numbers clinging to the roof. The explorers crawled through a narrow passage into a much more spacious chamber beyond. From the roof of this there hung many very fine stalactites, and the floor was covered with a sheet of water.

The Flat Holm

The Flat Holm, two miles and a half due north of its neighbour, is five miles and a half from

Anchor Head. It is, however, much nearer to the Welsh coast, being only two miles and a half from Lavernock Point. Politically also it belongs to Wales, for although in Collinson's time it formed part of Uphill, it is now included in the parish of St. Mary's, Cardiff. It belongs to the Marquis of Bute, and is rented partly by the War Office and partly by the Cardiff Corporation. It is not half the height of the Steep Holm, but is slightly more in area, measuring roughly about seventy acres, though the grazing land of the farm is reckoned at forty acres only.

The conspicuous feature of the island is the Lighthouse, whose tower, ninety feet high, stands at the south-east corner, twenty yards from the edge of the cliff, on ground that is a hundred and ten feet above high-water mark. The first lighthouse, built in 1737, measured only sixty-nine feet to the top of the gallery-course, and its light consisted of a beacon-fire. In 1817 the packet-ship *William and Mary* was wrecked on the Wolves, a group of rocks about half-way between the Holm and Lavernock Point. Sixty lives were lost. And a rough, unhewn stone near the landing-place long marked the spot where, it is said, the bodies of fifty sailors were buried in a common grave. This memorial has now disappeared, and it is believed that it was built into the walls of the hospital. It was perhaps in consequence of this disaster that the lighthouse tower was raised in height, and it may have been then that a lantern was set up instead of a coal fire. For in the outer masonry of the tower, at a point which probably marks the original height, these words are cut: TOP OF TOWER BUILT 1820. The magnificent dioptric oil-lantern now employed, one of the finest in use, has eight concentric wicks, and gives a light of 50,000 candle-power, clearly visible at a distance of eighteen miles. The master of a tug once reported to the chief light-keeper that he had seen the light when twenty-five miles from the island. The lamp is one of the kind known as group-flashing; and by means of clock-work, is made to show for twenty-one seconds, is then obscured for three seconds, shines again for three seconds, and is once more eclipsed for three seconds, making in all a period of half a minute. Two men only are in charge. Stores and letters are brought to them weekly from Cardiff, and there is both telephonic and wireless telegraphic communication with the Welsh shore. It is interesting to remember that some of the earliest experiments in wireless telegraphy were made between the Flat Holm and the mainland, by Mr., now Sir William Preece. The lighthouse has no fog-signalling appliances, but is provided with rocket-apparatus for calling the lifeboat, or for summoning the doctor at night.

The *William and Mary* is not the only vessel that has come to grief on the Wolves. In 1899 a steam-trawler struck there and became a total wreck, and in 1894 the steamship *Escombe*, from Newport, ran on the same rocks and foundered.

Early in February 1902 the Flat Holm was the scene of a remarkable phenomenon. In the night a shower of mud fell on the island, covering the glass of the lighthouse with a dirty white coating that stuck like glue, and which was only removed with great difficulty. The immediate application of a hose and of long brushes made little impression on it, and it was not until next day that the light-keepers, with a ladder, and with buckets of hot water and a leather, were able to get the lantern clean again. It appears that during the early part of 1902 a quantity of fine dust, believed by meteorologists to have been carried in the atmosphere from the Desert of the Sahara, fell on an area of some 2000 square miles, including Cornwall and other parts of the south-west of England. The material that enveloped the Flat Holm lantern may have been some of this dust changed to mud by clouds or rain.

The Flat Holm, like the sister island, is a link in the chain of Severn defences. The fortifications consist of four isolated works—the Lighthouse Battery, the Well Battery, the Farm Battery, and the Castle Rock Battery, armed in all with nine seven-inch muzzle-loading guns, mounted on Moncrieff disappearing carriages. There are quarters for about fifty men, but the garrison at present consists of a master-gunner and six artillerymen. No remains of old buildings were found while the batteries were in course of construction, as was the case on the Steep Holm; indeed, there is no record that any coins, or pottery, or similar antiquities were ever discovered on the island. But on digging out the ground in preparation for a water-tank the workmen came upon a raised sea-beach, in which were found not only shells, but horns of red deer, and a piece of a human skull.

The Flat Holm has several times been used for the isolation of cholera patients, who were at first provided only with tents. Some years ago, however, the Cardiff Corporation built a hospital here, for the reception of suspicious cases on ships arriving at either Barry or Cardiff. This is still standing; but it has been superseded by a new and substantial structure, erected at a cost of some thousands of pounds. Connected with it is a crematorium, in which in October 1900 were cremated the remains of a sailor supposed to have died from bubonic plague.

In the centre of the Holm are an inn and farm-buildings, occupied by the tenant of the island, who also has charge of the hospital and crematorium. The only crops grown are garden produce. The rest of the farm is for grazing. The inn-keeper and his family, with his workmen, the garrison, the light-keepers, and Lloyds' signalman, make up altogether a population of about twenty. The Vicar and Curate of St. Mary's, Cardiff, visit the island once a year, and hold a service in the barracks of the fort. A little to the east of the inn are two graves, in which, according to the tradition of the island—a tradition, however, which has no evidence to support it—were buried two of the murderers of Thomas à Becket. There are two springs on the Flat Holm. One of them, the Dripping Well, which can only be reached at low tide, is in a broad fissure running several yards into the cliff; where, from the rocky roof, water drips into a natural basin. The shaft of the other well, whose depth is estimated at thirty feet, is lined with masonry, and when the water in it is low, passages can be seen leading off from it, arched with stone; and it is the belief of the islanders that the well was originally a lead-mine. The supply is intermittent, ebbing and flowing with the tide; at low tide there is about four feet of water in it, at high-water none. It is brackish and only used for cattle. In the face of the east cliff is a cave called the Smugglers' Hole. A plainly marked path leads to it, and men are still living who claim to have seen it well filled with kegs of brandy that had never paid the Queen's dues.

The wild animals living on the island are few; and the natural history of the Flat Holm is altogether less interesting than that of its neighbour. Rabbits are now almost extinct. It is said that those that remain could be counted on the fingers of one hand. There are no rats or house-mice, and, so far as is known, no moles or field-voles. In fact, the only wild mammal besides the rabbits and a few bats that shelter in the caves is the Wood-mouse or Long-tailed Field-mouse, a specimen of which was lately examined by the writer. The only birds that are known to breed on the islands are Starlings, Skylarks, Tree Pipits, and Blackbirds. But there is some reason for thinking that Sparrow-hawks nest in the cliffs. Gulls rarely even alight on the Holm, but in the sprat-season great numbers of Guillemots frequent the fishing-nets.

The lighthouse does not appear to lie in a route much frequented by migratory birds. Not many are seen passing, and very few strike the glass of the lantern. Only two birds, a Woodcock and a Guillemot, were killed in this way during the spring of 1901. Starlings strike the glass very hard at times, making noise enough, the light-keeper says, for a Wild Duck, but they are hardly ever found dead. As on the Steep Holm, there is one reptile, the Slow-worm, a specimen of which was seen in the summer of 1900. The insects, the land-shells, and the plants are much the same on the two islands, except that on the Flat Holm there is no Single Pæony and no Great Round-headed Garlic. Many sprats are caught in the winter near the island, and cod and other fish are taken with the line.

BLEADON

THE large parish of Bleadon, whose southern boundary follows the windings of the Axe, includes wide areas both of hill-country and of moorland. The railway station is on the edge of a broad expanse called Bleadon Level, partly encircled by the river, from which it is protected by high earthen dykes. The Level was twice flooded during the last quarter of the nineteenth century, but on each occasion the cattle grazing on it were rescued without loss. This low-lying district, a belt of pasture between the Axe and the villages of Shiplate and Wonderstone, and a curious strip of moor on the other side of the hill, which, although barely three hundred yards wide, stretches past Uphill and extends nearly to the road between Weston and Locking, are all hardly twenty feet above high-water mark. On the north, the parish boundary runs along the highest part of Bleadon Hill, a little to the north of the Roman road from Old Sarum to the sea; and here, about a quarter of a mile from Upper Canada Farm, is a point 549 feet above sea-level, the highest ground in the Mendips west of Crook's Peak. Near this spot is the conspicuous clump of trees called

Sculpture in the Porch of Bleadon Church

in the district "The Caterpillar," from the resemblance which a distant view of it, from nearly every side, presents to some crawling animal with multitudinous legs.

Bleadon village, a scattered hamlet pleasantly situated along the southern slope of the hill, and partly also on the fringe of the moors which here stretch far away to the southward, begins about half a mile from the station, though the church is half a mile farther on. The points of interest connected with the place are the ancient British encampment on Pirn Hill; the cavern, since destroyed by quarrying, in which the Rev. David Williams, who was Rector of Bleadon for thirty years, found, early in the nineteenth century, the remains of many extinct animals; and the fine old Church of St. Peter, whose noble tower is so conspicuous across the level moors.

Of the early history of the manor nothing is definitely known. It was the opinion of Sir Richard Hoare that the Roman road, which passed through Charterhouse, and along which was probably brought the produce of the Mendip lead-mines, and which came down to the sea at Uphill, traversed the northern border of the parish for about seven hundred yards, a line which is not now used for traffic. Modern authorities, however, are satisfied that the old road ran along the top of Bleadon Hill, and that the present cart-track follows the original route. Half a mile east of the railway station is the site of the British encampment, on the slope of

Pirn Hill, and just below the Roman road. There is no record that it was ever explored, though there is a tradition that a pot of gold coins was found there many years ago. In the year 1053, according to a passage in Dugdale's *Monasticon*,[1] Githa, wife of Earl Godwin and mother of King Harold II., gave the Manor of Bleadon to the Monastery of Winchester; and in Domesday Book, in the list of possessions of Walchelin, Bishop of that see, the following details are given:—

"*The same Bishop holds Bledone. It was and is still for the maintenance of the monks. In the time of King Edward it paid Danegeld for 15 hides. There is land for 17 plough-teams. Of this there are in the demesne 10 hides, and there are 3 plough-teams, and 8 serfs, and 16 villeins, and 10 boors, and 11 plough-teams. There are 50 acres of meadow, and pasture one mile long and half a mile broad. It was and still is worth 15 pounds. Of these 10 hides Saiulf holds from the Bishop 1 hide, and there he has 1 plough-team, and 1 serf, and 1 boor, and 16 acres of meadow, and one acre of coppice. It is worth 20 shillings.*"[2]

An old tradition connected with Bleadon is quoted by the author of "Worlebury," from an anonymous

[1] Vol. i. p. 190, ed. 1817.

[2] A hide probably averaged 240 acres; a plough-team 120. Serfs were chattels, the absolute property of the landlord. Villeins belonged to the estate, and were sold with it. Boors were the highest class of farm-labourers. — Eyton, "Domesday Studies."

writer, "variously said to have been a Mr. Jay, of Nettlecombe, in West Somerset, who died about 1684, and a Mr. John Gibbons, who was living about 1670," and whose tract, "A Discourse about some Roman Antiquities discovered near Conquest," is bound up with Hearne's edition of Langtoft's "Chronicle." Speaking of the Danes, the author says :—

"Their 5th invasion was at Uphill, Bledon, &c., where I have enquired of the inhabitans, whether they had, at any time, heard of any Deanes, that came, in the dayes of yore, to Steep homes near them. They told me, that the generall tradition of their Country hath beene, that a fleete of Deanes fled, to shelter themselves in the said Isle, and sometime they brake out into England, and sometimes into Wales, for sustenance; at length coming to Uphill, and Bledon, &c., they fastned their ships to the shoare, left them, and marched up into the Country for booties, and that all the inhabitants fled away before them, one poor lame woman excepted, which hidd in a Rock near the ships, and when she was near spent with hunger, she was necessitated to adventure down the ships for releif, saying to herself, with the Lepers, *if they kill me, I shall but die:* but coming thither, and scearching from ship to ship, and finding no living Creature, at last espying an hatchett, took it, and with it chopped of all the Cables which ancored the ships to the shoare, and sent them to Sea, where they quickly perished. The Danes having gotten intelligence of the loss of some of their ships, speedily retreated, to save themselves and the rest, but the people of the Country, having intelligence, that all their ships were cast away, took courage, pursued them to Bledon, there fought, and destroyed them with such a bloody slaughter, as that frome thence the place took, and ever since hath kept, the name Bledon, alias Bleed-down or bloud-down, to this day. And some of them have informed me, that, when their Husbandmen plough their grounds, they find multitudes of Men's Teeth there, which being naturally the hardest bones in the body, and obdurated with chewing (in some grounds), are almost as permanent as little stones. And a Gentleman there, within 7 yeares past, having bought a peice of Moorish ground, lying at the foot of the said Bledon, when his labourers renewed the dyke filled up about it, they found great heaps of Men's skulls, and other humane bones, as entire as ever they had been."[1]

This explanation of the name of the village does not satisfy modern philologists, who can throw no light upon the origin of the word except that its second syllable is the Celtic *dun*, "a hill."

In the census of Church property in England and Wales, made under the authority of Pope Nicholas IV. about the year 1291,[2] the annual value of Bleadon Church is entered at £16, 13s. 4d. And a little later the sum paid yearly by Bleadon to the Prior of Winchester is given at £4, 6s. 8d. In a document drawn up in 1542, by order of King Henry VIII., the Winchester property at Bleadon is stated to be worth £36, 18s. per annum.[3]

The date of the original building of the Church of St. Peter is unknown, but it is recorded in the

[1] C. W. Dymond, F.S.A., "Worlebury."
[2] "Tax. Eccles. Angl. et Wall.," p. 197.
[3] Dugdale's *Monasticon*, vol. i. p. 217.

Wells Registers that a chancel and a high altar were dedicated here in 1317. The tower, though of stern and simple design, and having, as has been observed, a rather blank look, from the shortness of its windows, most of which, moreover, were blocked up by the builders, is no mean example of Perpendicular architecture. It has an open parapet and pinnacles, with a spirelet at the north-east corner; and round the top of it are some striking gargoyles, one of which represents a musician playing on a kind of bagpipe. Over the picturesque western doorway is a fine four-light Perpendicular window. Within the church porch, on the right, is a remarkable piece of sculpture built into the wall, where it was discovered some thirty years ago, buried beneath the plaster. This curious work of art, which dates probably from the fourteenth century, represents the Virgin carrying the Infant Christ on her left arm, with a cross behind her, and with two kneeling figures on her left and right, one of whom, to judge from the hammer in his belt, may be intended for Joseph the Carpenter. Over the group is a carved canopy, resting on two grotesque heads. Traces of colour in red, green, and yellow, and a number of silver stars, were visible on the cross and on the framework behind the kneeling figures when the sculpture was first found, but they have now disappeared. It is possible that the whole work was once the head of the cross which still stands near the churchyard. There are several such groups on existing Somerset crosses. Over the door into the church is a curious carved figure of an angel.

The nave, which is of the Perpendicular period, with plain windows and a timbered roof, seems narrow, as we see it now. But a blank space in the wall is believed to mark the spot where formerly stood a Chantry Chapel, dedicated to St. Paul. Of this, however, no other trace remains, unless the two ancient stone effigies that lay so long upon the churchyard grass represent the founder of the chapel and his wife. These figures, which in 1899 were removed to the interior of the church—the man to an arched recess on the right of the altar, and the woman to the space between the wall and the pulpit—have suffered much from the frost and the rain of two centuries, and few details of the woman's dress can now be made out. She is apparently veiled, and her hands are in the attitude of prayer. The effigy of the man has a coat reaching to the knees, with a low-crowned, narrow-brimmed hat, and he has a staff by his side. Over his head is a carved canopy, and, like the other figure, he has a satchel at his side.

One bay of the chancel is Perpendicular, with modern coloured windows, but the two eastern bays are Decorated. About the year 1800 the chancel was shortened by twelve feet, and the east wall of it remained blank for nearly sixty years. The large three-light eastern window was put up in 1859 by Mrs. Merle, partly in memory of her father and partly in memory of her uncle and grandfather, both of whom were Rectors of Bleadon. Until 1859 the only windows in the chancel were the three on the south side, one of which was a "leper's" window, and was formerly unglazed. To the right of the altar is an arched recess which may have originally contained the recumbent effigy now reposing in it, and which has been lately removed from the churchyard, or it may have been used for representations of the Easter Sepulchre. The canopied piscina—that is to say, the stone basin and drain used in Pre-Reformation times for pouring away the water in which the sacred vessels had been washed—now built into the north wall of the sanctuary, was found in 1899 in the churchyard, close to the church wall, during the digging of a grave. To the south of the altar is a finely canopied priest's door. In 1901 a tiny window, a foot high and less than four inches wide, was brought to light among the ivy on the outer wall, and through it may be seen, with the aid of a ladder, the long-blocked-up stairs to the rood-loft. The plain round font may perhaps belong to the twelfth century. Both it and the finely carved octagonal stone Perpendicular pulpit have evidently been moved from their original positions.

On the floor of the church are several old inscribed sepulchral slabs, but none, apparently, of any great antiquity. Two vault-stones, lately found in the church, bear inscriptions dated 1658 and 1678. On the first of these is the name of John

Whippey, July 20, 1658. Three other names were, however, cut in the same stone during the following century. To one of them, George Yeo, who died in 1763, is this epitaph :—

> "Torn from the embraces of his second wife,
> And their fond children, happy in his life,
> Lost to the poor too, who exclaim in woe,
> Striking their bosoms, here lies Mr. Yeo."

Near the recumbent statue in the recess in the chancel wall is an epitaph which deserves to be remembered :—

SACRED TO THE MEMORY OF
JOHN PRANKERD, ESQ.
OF THIS PARISH
On the 22nd of June 1839
AGED 85 YEARS
HE DIED AS HE LIVED
AN HONEST MAN.

The oldest inscription in the churchyard is that found in 1900 on the under side of a large stone, and apparently in memory of the same John Whippey whose name is on the vault-stone, already mentioned as having been found in the chancel. In addition to the date, July 20, 1658, this stone bears the words :—

CRISTUS SOLUS MEA SALUS

and

> "Under this stone here lyeth
> A youth whom vertue magnifieth."

In the tower hang five bells, all comparatively

modern. Only the first and fifth bear any lettering. The treble is merely marked :—

BILBIE : 1710. J.C. V.C. C.W.

The tenor is thus inscribed :—

BILBIE CAST WE. IOHN : CHAMPION : VMFRY CHAMPION : CH : WARDENS. WHEN : ALL : WE : WAS : CAST. 1711.

The beams of the belfry are, however, older than that, for in one of them is cut "1627. T.G. WA." In 1832 the tower was struck by lightning. Some of the stones which had filled up the holes left by the builders' scaffolding were thrown out, and their places still remain vacant.

The Bleadon Church plate is very ancient, and consists of a plain silver paten and an engraved silver chalice, both of which are probably Elizabethan, though the marks are almost obliterated.

The Bleadon parish records have suffered both from the lapse of time and from the carelessness of custodians. The oaken chest which was provided for their safe keeping, in compliance with the Ecclesiastical Mandate of 1603, still stands in the vestry. Its three old locks, too, still remain. But the keys, one for the minister, and two for the churchwardens, "so that neither the minister without the two churchwardens, nor the churchwardens without the minister, should at any time take that book out of the said coffer," have long been lost. And all that remains of the old Registers are thirty-five leaves of parchment, fastened with red tape, and without a cover. At the top of the first sheet are the words, "Bleadon register . . . in the year of our Lord God, 1713." The actual records, however, begin some years earlier. The first baptism, though not entered until the eleventh page, is dated 1706, and the first burial 1712. Here and there occurs a note, showing that some entry had been made in the wrong place. In 1754, for example, we read: "The last two names, Sarah and Mary Ann, I entered amongst ye Burials by mistake." After the entry recording the death of the Rev. Henry Norman, who had been Rector of the parish for thirty-five years, the writer of the notice added, "during which time he always behaved like a good and faithful shepperd. God grant that this parish may have a successor equally serviceable." But some later hand, surely not of the successor himself, has drawn a pen through these significant words.

The Black Death, which in 1348 and 1349 devastated a great part of the British Islands, and whose history is briefly outlined in the chapter on the Mendip Country, visited Bleadon. In the Bishop's Registers at Wells are these entries, relating to the institution of Rectors in this parish:—

1337. Joh. de Middleton.
1348. Tho. de Bokenhulle.
Tho. Raly.

From which it would appear that two Rectors died, probably of the plague, in 1348.[1]

Two Rectors of Bleadon have left their mark, one in science and one in literature. The Rev. David Williams, who, for thirty years, from 1820 to 1850, was not only incumbent but principal landowner of the parish, is best remembered in the district for his researches among the Mendip Bone Caves. It was he who explored the caverns of Bleadon, Hutton, and Burrington. But his geological studies were by no means confined to the district where he lived so long. He left behind him at his death a manuscript describing in detail the geology of Somerset, Devon, and Cornwall; and he contributed papers to the British Association, to the Geological Society, and to various scientific journals. Parts, though by no means the whole of his valuable collections, are now the property of the Somersetshire Archæological and Natural History Society.

Another famous name connected with this parish is that of the Rev. Meric Casaubon, D.D. Born in Geneva in 1599, he took his degree at Christ Church, Oxford, in 1621, and three years later was made Rector of Bleadon. He was here only four years, and when in 1644 the struggle between the King and the Commons deprived him of office, he was holding a Living in the Isle of Thanet. His writings are less known than those of his father, the

[1] Weaver, "Somerset Incumbents."

more distinguished Isaac Casaubon. But that he was a man of mark in his time is clear from the facts that he was asked by Cromwell to write a History of the Civil War, which, however, he declined to do, and that he was invited by Christina, Queen of Sweden, to visit and report upon the universities in that country. Another Living was bestowed upon him at the Restoration, and this he retained until his death in 1671.

The books of Parish Accounts, the oldest of which, that of the Overseers of the Poor, begins in 1718, are similar in character to those of neighbouring parishes, and contain no items of special interest.

Near the churchyard, though it is said that the place where it stands was formerly within the sacred precincts, is a fine old village cross. The steps and socket are much older than the shaft, and date, so Dr. Pooley thought, from about 1380. The shaft, which was much injured by lightning in 1832, is probably not earlier than the close of the seventeenth century. Part of the original column, with a ring attached to it for fastening up horses, stands against the wall of a neighbouring cottage. Another fragment of the old shaft was placed at the top of the modern one under the finial. The sculpture now built into the wall inside the church porch may have formed the head of the original cross.

Bleadon village stands chiefly on a patch of Dolomitic Conglomerate; and a narrow strip of the same formation borders, on the west and north, the belt of Red Marl which skirts the Axe and sweeps upwards towards the hills, and on which are the two little hamlets of Shiplate and Wonderstone. Wonderstone may, as has been suggested, take its name from "the beautiful Breccia so called, which consists of yellow translucent crystals of carbonate of lime, disseminated through a dark-red earthy dolomite."[1] Shiplate, or Shiplake, as it is called on some maps, may, as Isaac Taylor says of Shiplake in Oxfordshire, be from the Anglo-Saxon *Sceap-loca*, "a sheepfold."[2] The wide area of Bleadon Level, and the low-lying land nearer to the village, are alluvial, and the hill itself, except for the beds already noticed, is a mass of Carboniferous Limestone. Bleadon was anciently a mining village, and shafts in search of lead were chiefly sunk in this rock. In this rock, too, was discovered the fissure, now quite destroyed by quarrying, where the Rev. David Williams found the remarkable deposits of bones of extinct animals. These remains were mostly those of the Wolf, Tiger, Cave-bear, Elephant, Ox, and Horse. Some of these creatures must have been of gigantic size. The Cave-bear, for instance, can have stood little less than nine feet high. The Ox, too, which Mr. Williams suggested should be called *Bos Bleadon* from the place of its discovery, must have been a

[1] Jackson, "Visitors' Handbook to Weston-super-Mare."
[2] "Names and their Histories."

beast of prodigious dimensions. The size of the Elephant whose remains were found in the fissure may be imagined from the fact, that the explorers found a fragment of tusk six feet long and two feet in circumference, measurements which would probably represent an original length of about sixteen feet. We may compare with this the tusk of an African Elephant, believed to have come from the Kilimandjaro district, which was sold not long ago at Zanzibar. This tusk, the largest known, measures ten feet four inches along the curve, and its length in a straight line is eight feet four inches. Its girth where it becomes solid is two feet two and a half inches, and it weighs 236 pounds.[1]

An important feature of the parish, especially in a district whose streams are so few, is the river Axe, which here makes a great loop to the southward, partially enclosing the rich pastures of the Bleadon Level. The source of the Axe is in Wookey Hole, near Wells, where the river issues from the cavern, after a subterranean course, as is believed, of some miles. The length of it is no more than twenty miles, but it is a stream of no small historic interest, for it long formed the border-line between the conquering Saxons and the still untamed Britons who inhabited what was then a part of Wales. In old days it was navigable for coal vessels and other small craft as far up as Axbridge. But the construction of flood-gates at Bleadon, under the Axe

[1] *Field*, March 16, 1901.

Drainage Act of 1802, put an end to its use for traffic beyond this village. The landing-place was again changed when the railway-bridge was built across the river, and the coal-smacks, which are of from thirty to forty tons burden, now discharge their cargoes at a wharf about a mile west of Hobbs's Boat. This building, now a tavern, was once the ferry-house. But when, many years ago, in order to improve the navigation, a new bed was cut for the river at a point about a mile south of Bleadon Church and the old course abandoned, the ferry was no longer used. This is the place which, as remarked in a previous chapter, Bishop Clifford believed to have been, like Uphill and Uppercock Farm, named after Hubba, the Danish sea-rover, who plundered these shores in King Alfred's time, who fell in battle on the banks of the Parret, and whose grave-mound is still to be seen not far from the little river-port of Combwich.

The Axe has two tributaries, the Lox Yeo and the Cheddar Water, both on the right bank, and both joining the main stream near the foot of Crook's Peak, though flowing from opposite sides of the hill. The Lox Yeo rises in powerful springs at Max, near Winscombe, close to the site of the old mill. The Cheddar Water issues from a cave at the entrance of Cheddar Gorge, flowing through a subterranean passage from Charterhouse.

The fisheries of the Axe, which once were of sufficient importance to be the subject of special licences from the Dean and Chapter of Wells, were for a long period ruined by poisoned water from the lead-works at Charterhouse, and by chemical refuse from paper-mills lower down the stream. These sources of pollution have now ceased, and a local Anglers' Association has done a great deal by watching the stream, and by turning down fish, to improve the character of the fishing. There are fine trout on the upper part of the Cheddar Water, and in the Axe there are Pike, Perch, Rudd, Roach, Dace, Eels, and a few Trout. In the Lox Yeo there are Trout, Pike, Eels, Lamperns, Flounders, and smaller fish, such as Loach, Miller's-thumbs, and two kinds of Sticklebacks. No doubt some of the fish that have been turned down in the Axe have also made their way up the tributary streams. Otters were once numerous on the Axe, but it is long since any were seen in the Bleadon district. One very interesting plant, the rare and beautiful White Rock Rose, sometimes called the White Cistus, so plentiful on Brean Down, though found nowhere else in the kingdom except at one spot near Torquay, has of late years completely established itself on Bleadon Hill.

HUTTON

DUE north of Bleadon, and occupying like that parish part of the high ground of the western extremity of Mendip, and also, like Bleadon, stretching far across the moor to within a quarter of a mile of the road from Weston to Locking, lies the parish of Hutton, which includes, besides the chief village, the little hamlets of Oldmixon and Elborough, and the farm and cluster of buildings called Ludwell. A large part of this area is on the dead level of the great alluvial plain which is shared by all the parishes in the district, and is thus little more than twenty feet above high-water mark, though the ground on the top of the hill is rather more than three hundred feet above the sea. The moorland levels are monotonous and comparatively uninteresting, except to the naturalist. But that part of the parish which extends along the hillside, with its steep grassy slopes, with here and there the grey limestone breaking through, its woods and its scattered timber, its meadows and orchards, its picturesque cottages, its old manor-house and its still older church, is a typical piece of quiet-coloured

West Country rural landscape. Characteristic, too, of the West Country is the glen called Hutton Combe, which, approached by a lane turning off the main road to the east of the village, below the ruined windmill, winds away into the hills.

Hutton is a quiet spot, a place that suggests the American poet's—

> "eastern village
> Of uneventful toil;
> Where golden harvests followed quiet tillage,
> Above a peaceful soil."

Nor is there any record that its life was ever more stirring than at present, except perhaps in the old mining days, of which some faint memory still survives in the half-obliterated mouths of the old lead-shafts and ochre-pits and calamine-workings that can be traced on the hill, and in the fields and woods. Yet the names of all the four places in it can be found in records hundreds of years old. Ludwell and Oldmixon, or, as they were then spelt, Ludewell and Holdmixon, are mentioned in a document dated 1272.[1] Detailed accounts of Hutton and Elborough are given in Domesday Book; and the history of the latter can perhaps be traced three centuries earlier still. The Manor of Hutton is thus described by those who surveyed it for William the Conqueror in 1085, among the lands, originally belonging to Glastonbury Abbey, but which, as we may gather from an earlier entry in Domes-

[1] Hundred Rolls.

Hutton Church

day Book, had apparently been seized by the King, and were at the time of the Survey held by Geoffrey of Coutance, that fighting bishop who was by his master's side at Hastings:—

"*Azelin holds from the Bishop Hotune. In the time of King Edward two thanes held it as two manors, and paid Danegeld for five hides. There is land for five plough-teams. In the demesne there is one plough-team and seven villeins; and six boors have two plough-teams. There are thirty acres of meadow, and two hundred acres of pasture, and fifteen acres of coppice. It was worth four pounds; now sixty shillings.*" The Exeter Domesday adds, as possessions of the manor, sixty goats.

Of the smaller Manor of Elborough, at the eastern end of the parish, Domesday Book gives the following details:—

"*Azelin holds from the Bishop Lilbere. Alward held it in the time of King Edward, and paid Danegeld for three hides. There is land for four plough-teams. In the demesne there are two plough-teams, with one serf and one villein, and five boors with one plough-team. There are twenty acres of meadow, and forty acres of pasture. It was worth sixty shillings; now forty shillings.*" [1]

It has been suggested that the fall in the value

[1] A hide of land was a somewhat variable quantity, but it probably averaged 240 acres. A plough-team corresponded to half that amount, or 120 acres. Serfs were the absolute property of the Lord of the Manor, and could be bought and sold like cattle.

of these two manors, as in several others in the same district, and even much farther inland, was the result of the destruction caused by the piratical descent on this coast in 1067, the year after the Battle of Hastings, by one of the sons of Harold. Having been beaten off from Bristol, the raiders, as we read in the Anglo-Saxon Chronicle, "went to Somersetshire, where they went up the country"; [1] which they no doubt plundered to the best of their ability.

Collinson, in writing of Elborough, alludes to a passage in the Chronicle of John of Glastonbury, which appears to mean that Cynewulf, or Kenwulf, a king of the West Saxons, who was assassinated in A.D. 755, gave the manor to Æthelward, who bestowed it on the Abbey of Glastonbury. The original passage runs: "Cyneuulfus de Elenbearo dat. Æthelardo, qui G." [2] But it is quite possible that it is only one of the many inventions by which the monkish chroniclers sought to account for the possessions of the Abbey.

The history of Hutton Manor has been traced in various old records by Mr. Emmanuel Green, F.S.A., and is given at length in the thirty-first volume of the "Proceedings of the Somersetshire Archæolo-

Villeins belonged to the vill or manor, and were the highest of the classes which had no sort of freedom. Boors probably lived near the manor-house and were the highest class of farm-labourers employed on the estate.—Eyton, "Domesday Studies."

[1] The Rev. J. A. Bennett, "Vestiges of the Norman Conquest of Somerset." "Som. Arch. Pro.," vol. xxv.

[2] *Johannis Glastoniensis Chronica*, vol. ii. p. 371.

gical Society." The first known mention of the place after the time of Domesday Book is in the reign of Henry III., when, by a judgment of the Mendip Forest Court, the village of Hutton was condemned, in company with Christon, Loxton, and Banwell, as the parishes nearest to the scene of the crime, to pay a fine, because two men of Bleadon, who had chased and killed one of the king's deer, had absconded, and failed to appear before the Court. Hutton and Christon had to pay half a mark. Loxton was fined a mark, and Banwell twenty shillings.[1] In the same reign, in the year 1259, Paganus Fitz-John brought a successful action against Adam le Waleys, owner of Hutton Manor, and recovered his father's lands in Ladewell, which his powerful neighbour had seized.[2] In the Hundred Rolls of 1272, the first year of King Edward I., is an allusion to three local landowners of the time: Adam le Waleys Lord of Hucton, Paganus de Ludewell, and Ralph de Holdmixon. In 1279 Paganus de Ladewell (as the name is then spelt) again had trouble with a grasping neighbouring proprietor. This time it was the Prior of Winchester, Lord of the Manor of Bleadon, who had taken wrongful possession of certain "common of Pasture" in Bleadon, which belonged to the free tenants of the Manor of Hutton.[3]

[1] *Placita Forestæ*, Somerset, No. 1, 39 Henry III.
[2] Patent Rolls, 43 Henry III., 13d.
[3] *Placita Quo Warranto*, 8 Edward I.

In 1298, in the Perambulation of the Forest of Mendip, made under Edward I., the owner of the Manor of Hutton, "with woods and marshes and properties pertaining to it," is given as John de Waleys.[1] At a later period, after several changes of ownership,[2] the Manor passed to the Paynes, descendants, no doubt, of Paganus of Ludwell, with a modernised family name. John Payne, Esquire, the first known holder of Hutton, in this line, died in 1496, as is recorded on his monument in the village church. It is probable that he built, or rebuilt, the old part of the court, whose style is that of the middle of the fifteenth century, though the earliest documentary mention of the house is in 1529.[3] In 1604, Nicholas Payne sold the property to Dr. John Still, Bishop of Bath and Wells, who died two years later, and whose amazing monument is one of the sights, though not one of the glories of Wells Cathedral. It was Bishop Still, so it is believed, who built the Jacobæan portion of the court. He is said to have been the author of the play called "Gammer Gurton's Needle," one of the very earliest of English comedies. The evidence is, however, of the slightest. It was not until 1782 that Isaac Reed identified "Mr. S., Master of Art," the reputed author of the play, with Still, mainly on the ground that, when "Gam-

[1] Collinson. [2] "Som. Arch. Pro." [3] Ibid.

mer Gurton's Needle" was written, there was no other Master of Arts in Christ's College whose name began with S. It has been shown, however, that there were thirteen Masters of Arts of the College then living whose names began with S; and during Still's lifetime the work was never attributed to him. The play itself is comparatively little known except to students of literature; but a song in it, in praise of "Jolly Good Ale and Old," is worth reading for the sake of its sound, if not of its sense, especially when we remember that it was written by a dignitary of the Church:—

"I CANNOT EAT BUT LITTLE MEAT.

"I cannot eat but little meat,
My stomach is not good;
But sure I think that I can drink
With him that wears a hood.
Though I go bare, take ye no care,
I nothing am a-cold;
I stuff my skin so full within
Of jolly good ale and old.

I love no roast but a nut-brown toast,
And a crab laid in the fire;
And little bread shall do me stead;
Much bread I nought desire.
No frost nor snow, nor wind, I trow,
Can hurt me if I wold;
I am so wrapped and thoroughly lapped
Of jolly good ale and old.

And Tip, my wife, that as her life
  Loveth well good ale to seek,
Full oft drinks she till ye may see
  The tears run down her cheek:
Then doth she trowl to me the bowl,
  Even as a malt-worm should,
And saith, 'Sweetheart, I took my part
  Of this jolly good ale and old.'

Now let them drink till they nod and wink,
  Even as good fellows should do;
They shall not miss to have the bliss
  Good ale doth bring men to;
And all poor souls that have scoured bowls,
  Or have them lustily trowled,
God save the lives of them and their wives,
  Whether they be young or old."

The next owner of Hutton was the Bishop's son Nathaniel, who died in 1626, and whose monument, bearing a striking and memorable epitaph, is in the church. The manor then passed into other hands, among them those of the Brent family, to some of whom there is a monument in the churchyard, and from whom Alfred Bisdee, Esquire, the present Lord of the Manor, obtained the property by purchase.

In the little village of Oldmixon, at the extreme west of Hutton parish, was born, in 1637, a more voluminous writer, at any rate, than Bishop Still, and a man of mark in his time. This was John Oldmixon, historian, pamphleteer, and poet. His best-known work is his "History of England," in three volumes folio. But he was a bitter partisan, and the most conspicuous feature of the book is its hostility to the House of Stuart. He wrote several plays, of which the most successful was the last, "The Governor of Cyprus," a tragedy, acted at Lincoln's Inn Fields, in 1703. For his opera called "The Grove, or Love's Paradise," performed at Drury Lane, in 1700, the music was written by Purcell. He is said to have written, in 1716, a ballad called "The Catholic Priest," which was an attack on Pope's "Homer."[1] Pope retaliated by putting Oldmixon in the "Dunciad":—

> "In naked majesty Oldmixon stands,
> And, Milo-like, surveys his arms and hands;
> Then sighing, thus, 'And am I now threescore?
> Ah why, ye Gods, should two and two make four?'
> He said, and climbed a stranded lighter's height,
> Shot to the black abyss, and plung'd downright.
> The Senior's judgment all the crowd admire,
> Who but to sink the deeper, rose the higher."[2]

Oldmixon was not the equal of Pope, and never wrote anything to compare with even those famous verses that begin—

> "Happy the man whose wish and care
> A few paternal acres bound,
> Content to breathe his native air
> In his own ground."

But that the old Hanoverian partisan had a pretty

[1] "Dictionary of National Biography."
[2] "Dunciad," book ii. lines 283–290.

touch of his own, is clear from these often-quoted lines :—

> "I lately vowed, but 'twas in haste,
> That I no more would court
> The joys that seem when they are past
> As dull as they are short.
>
> I oft to hate my mistress swear,
> But soon my weakness find ;
> I make my oaths when she's severe,
> But break them when she's kind."

The poet's father, John Oldmixon of Oldmixon, died in 1675, and his widow in 1689, when their son was only sixteen, and there is no evidence that the latter spent more than a very few years in his native village. Oldmixon is a name not altogether unknown in the history of Somerset. Nic. de Oldmixene was Rector of Portishead from 1325 to 1348, and Will. de Oldmyxton was Rector of Croscombe from 1401 to 1424. Another Will. de Oldmyxton was patron of the Living of Hutton in 1529. And during the eighteenth century the name Oldmixon occurs in the Rate Books of the Parish of Hutton.

The Hutton Communion Plate consists of four pieces. The oldest is a silver chalice of very simple design, bearing the initials of the maker, R.G., but no hall-mark. From its shape, and the absence of any hall-mark, it is believed to be early eighteenth-century work. The next in age is a silver paten, on a foot, with the inscription :—

THE GIFT OF IOHN PAINE RECT^{R} 1755

The hall-mark shows the actual date of the paten to be 1721 or 1722. John Paine was instituted Rector in 1744, on the nomination of John Windam. The silver flagon given to the church by Humphrey Brent is thus inscribed :—

> "This Flagon is my Gift to ye parish Church of Hutton in ye County of Somset ; to be there used at the Sacrament of our Lord's Supper : upon Condition that ye same be, at all other times, in ye Custody of me, my Heirs or Assigns, Inhabiting there, for the use aforesaid."

On a shield below are the Arms, on a Field gules, a Wyvern passant, with the name and date, H. Brent, anno 1737. A second paten, though of mediæval shape, is of modern workmanship.

Sir Richard Hoare, who, in 1826, surveyed the Roman road from Old Sarum to Uphill, considered that its course could be traced across the entire breadth of the parish, traversing the northern slope of the hill, at a distance of from three to five hundred yards from the modern road, and passing close to Upper Canada Farm ; a track not now used as a road in the parishes of Uphill, Bleadon, or Hutton.

But Colonel Bramble and the Rev. C. S. Taylor are satisfied that it ran along the top of Bleadon Hill, and did not cross Hutton at all.

There appears to be no record of the discovery of any ancient coins or pottery in any part of the parish of Hutton. Some forty years ago, when men were lowering the road at Rowans, as the hill on the way to Banwell is called, a row of four or five skeletons was laid bare. The place where one was lying is still visible in the rock by the roadside, filled up with stones. Traces of earthworks, much defaced by the plough, may be seen in the adjoining field. Near the same spot another skeleton was found a few years ago by workmen engaged in enlarging the quarry at the foot of the lane leading to the old windmill. The skeleton was some two feet below the surface, and resting on the rock. There seems to have been no trace, in either instance, of coins or pottery or weapons.

The Church of St. Mary, which stands on a slope about fifty feet above the village, possesses no very striking architectural features. But its fine old Perpendicular tower and the magnificent ivy that covers so much of the venerable building make it one of the most picturesque churches in the district. In Collinson's time, that is to say, at the close of the eighteenth century, the body of the church consisted of only a nave and a chancel. About fifty years later, in 1849, a south aisle was added, and the chancel was rebuilt and raised, and at the same time what is said to have been a fine southern porch was destroyed.[1] Both nave and chancel have an open timber or waggon roof, with a beautiful cornice of finely carved flowers; and the stone vaulting of the ringing-chamber under the tower is a particularly fine piece of work. One of the striking features of the church is the beautiful carved stone pulpit, which, like the fine octagonal font, dates probably from the early Perpendicular period (1377–1545). In the old coloured glass in the south window may be seen four shields, representing, with various impalements, the arms of Thomas Payne, who died in 1528, and whose brass now stands in a recess to the left of the altar.

Perhaps the most interesting objects in the interior are the brasses, two of them in memory of members of the Payne family, and one bearing the epitaph of Nathaniel Still. The oldest of the Payne monuments, that of John Payne, Esquire, who died in 1496, is in the floor within the altar rails, in front of the High Altar, a position which suggests that the deceased had been a benefactor of the church. It may have been this man who, as Collinson says—without alluding to this monument—founded a chantry here "for a priest to perform mass for the souls of his two wives, Elizabeth and Marianne, and for the souls of all his ancestors deceased." On this brass are represented standing figures of the knight and his lady—or one of his ladies—

[1] "Som. Arch. Pro.," vol. xxxi.

with their eleven children, and with this inscription :—

Hic iacet sub lapide marmoreo Jo̅hes Payne de Hutton Armiger Et Elizabeth vxor ei^s qui quidem Jo̅hes obyt v^o die Augusti Ao: Dm̅. M.CCCCLXXXXVI. quor: aı̅abs: ppiciet: De^s: Amen.

The knight is in full plate-armour, with a skirt of chain-mail, and is armed with a dagger and long two-handed sword. It is the military costume of the time of King Henry VII., and is such as might have been worn at the Battle of Bosworth, eleven years before the date here given.

In an arched recess to the left of the altar is another Payne brass, with effigies and shields, all set in cement. This is in memory of Thomas, son of the John Payne of the older monument, and of his wife Elizabeth. It is thus inscribed :—

Pray for ye soules of Thomas Payne, Squier & Elyzabeth hyis wiffe which departid ye XVth day of Augvst ye yere of o^r Lord God MCCCCCXXVIII.

In this case, the two principal figures are kneeling, each at a sort of reading-desk. The man wears plate-armour, much like that of his father, who died thirty-two years before, but with no chain-mail, and with a much shorter sword. Such, no doubt, was the equipment of squires who followed King Henry VIII. or his nobles at the Field of the Cloth of Gold, seven years earlier than the date on this tomb. Behind the father kneel eight sons, and behind the

Brass of John and Elizabeth Payne, in Hutton Church

2 A

mother three daughters, all eleven bareheaded, and with flowing locks. Under the tower are three slabs which were removed from the chancel, two of them very old. On one of them is a modern brass plate with this inscription :—

Thomas Payne, armiger qui obiit XXIII° die Martii a° DM MDLXXXII.

Part of the original epitaph can still be traced round the margin of the stone. A similar slab now placed in the belfry bears a very worn and no longer legible incription, possibly in memory of Nicholas Payne, who in 1604 sold the manor to Bishop Still.

At the west end of the south aisle, having been removed from its original place when the organ chamber was built,[1] is a brass in memory of Nathaniel Still, with effigies of himself, his wife, and his five children, and with this epitaph :—

In memory of Nathanill Still of this parish Esq.,
who dyed the second day of Febrvary anno dno 1626.

"Not that hee needeth monvments of stone
For his well gotten fame to rest vppon
But this was reard to testifie that hee
Lives in theire loves y[t] yet svrviving bee
For vnto vertv who first raised his name
Hee left the preservation of the same
And to posterity remaine it shall
When brass and marble monvments shall fall."

By marriage with Nathaniel Still's daughter, the Manor of Hutton passed to the Codringtons, to one

[1] Jackson, "Visitors' Handbook to Weston-super-Mare."

of whom, William Codrington, who died in 1728, there is a brief inscription on a slab formerly in the floor of the church, but now placed upright in the belfry. On the chancel wall is a curious old mural tablet to Robert Willis, who died in 1719, which is decorated with two cherubs' heads most suggestive of West Country farmers. In the floor are several ancient slabs, chiefly of the seventeenth century.

In the tower hang five bells, two of which were cast in 1708 by Edward Bilbie, one of the famous Chewstoke family, and the other three by unknown bell-founders of the previous century. The bells are thus inscribed :—

1. E : BILBIE . 1708 SH . GL . W .
2. AN : NO : DO : MI : NI : 1675 G : S : L : B . CW . TP.
3. ANNO DOMINI 1627.
4. ANNO DOMINI 1637.
5. ED . BILBIE CAST WE 1708.
   SAM HAIS . GO . IONES WARDENS
   WHEN I DO CALL COM SERVE GOD ALL.[1]

In a bell-cot on the south-eastern gable of the nave there no doubt once hung a "sanctus-bell," but this has long since disappeared.

In the vestry is preserved a statuette of alabaster, now much mutilated, which is believed to have originally stood in the niche now placed in the east wall of the south aisle. The drapery is very gracefully treated, and the pose of the figure suggests the hand of a true artist. The subject can only

[1] Ellacombe, "Church Bells of Somerset."

be a matter of conjecture, but it may have been intended for an angel.

The earliest Register of Marriages commences in 1747, that of Burials in 1743, and of Christenings in 1744. The entries in these present few points of interest. A curious Christian name for a woman is Chrysogon. In 1750 are allusions to two people who bore it — Chrysogon Dark and Chrysogon Lewis. There are many references to the family of Brent, one of whom, in 1741, bought the manor from the Codringtons.

"1759 Feb 27 Humphrey Brent Esq deceased Decr 18 1758."

If the details are correct, burial did not take place for two months after death.

"1769 Augt 27 John Brent Doctor of Physic died."

From 1781 to 1788 the entries are on loose scraps of paper, which have since been sewn together. It will be seen on reference to the book in which these are now preserved that it was quite a common thing for the Hutton children not to be baptized until a good while after their birth. Such entries as "being near three years old," or "being more than one year old," are frequent. The parson who, in 1793, married William Pimm and Diana Brooks, made this memorandum :—

"When I came to that part of the ceremony on the woman's part "Obey him," &c., Pimm bawled out,

"Stop, sir, please to read that over again. The women don't rightly understand it."

The Churchwardens' Accounts begin in 1725, and from that year until 1734, when such entries cease, payments were made on behalf of a hospital, probably at Woodspring:—

1725. Paid the Hospitall money . . . 1 4 ½
1730. Paid the County Bridge money and Hospital at bleadon 00 06 00

As Mr. Ernest E. Baker says, this may mean that there was a hospital at Bleadon, or, which is more probable, it may merely mean that the rate was paid in that village.

The winter of 1794-1795 was one of great severity throughout England. The frost lasted from 24th December 1794 to 14th February 1795, with the intermission of one day only. Hutton was evidently among the places that suffered from the effects of this inclement season. The Churchwardens held a special meeting, took into consideration "the poor and their nessessetous wants, and agreed to give them a farther supply of coals, and apply it with equal justice as the Overseers have not attended to the Pet'tions of the Poor as he ought to have done during this severe season." The parish stocks of Hutton are no longer visible, but as lately as 1823 the sum of 15s. 9d. was paid for their repair. Still farther back, in 1799, is this entry:—

Paid the Blacksmith's Bill for irons for the stocks and whiping post 13 9

The Accounts are not concerned solely with village affairs. It is recorded in these pages that prayers were offered in Hutton Church in 1802, after King George III. had been shot at in his box at Drury Lane; in 1805 "on account of a complet victory over the French fleet off Trafalgar by Adm'l Nelson who lost his life in the battle;" and again in 1815, "for the splendid victory gained by the Duke of Wellington over Buonaparte at Waterloo, which decided the war."

There were also county affairs to be attended to, and Hutton, like other parishes, helped to keep up the bridges and gaols:—

1725. The gole and Mashell se[1] money .	00 13 06
1731. Pd Thomas Stock the gole and bridge money	0 8 6
1733. Pd ye constable at Cros the county stock money and goal . . .	00 07 10

In 1758 some of the travelling expenses of Overseers were disallowed, on the ground of extravagance, with this note:—

"I sign this Overseers account in hopes that his successor in office will not presume to act for the future than what is above expressed."

Adjoining the church on the south-east is the old manor-house called Hutton Court, a remarkable example of domestic architecture. The eastern part of it, including the large square tower, is believed

[1] "Marshalsea," here an old word for county rate. —Halliwell.

to date from the middle of the fifteenth century, and may have been built on the site of a still older dwelling, by the John Payne whose tomb is before the High Altar in the church. The most striking feature of this part of the building is the noble dining hall, a spacious and well-proportioned room, with a fine timbered roof. The western part of the Court is Jacobæan, and is attributed to Bishop Still, who owned the manor in the early days of James I. In one of the bedrooms is a mantelpiece of that period.

The present Rectory House stands on the site of the old one, and was built in 1870 by the Rev. G. H. Gibbs, who was Rector from 1869 to 1896. The school was built in 1874 on a portion of the glebe which was given for the purpose by the Rector and the Patron of the Living. The average attendance of scholars is fifty-six. The old schoolhouse stood near the church, and its site now forms part of the churchyard.

The level ground in Hutton parish is alluvial, being part of the great Severn plain which is shared by every parish in the district. In all this low-lying region, which is about a thousand acres in extent, and in the middle of which once stood the old Weston Junction railway station, there is not now a single dwelling-house. The land is all down in grass, and the fields are to a great extent divided by rhines instead of by hedges. Some of these ditches are connected with the slow-moving stream called the Weston Rhine, which finds its way into the sea at Uphill. Hutton village, like Oldmixon, Ludwell, and Elborough, stands on the Red Marl, and above each of the minor hamlets there is a narrow strip of Dolomitic Conglomerate, an important formation, useful as a handsome and durable building-stone, and formerly famous for its calamine-workings. The hill above the village, Hutton or Bleadon Hill, is wholly composed of Carboniferous Limestone. It was in this rock that both the lead-mines and the ochre-pits were sunk. And it was while sinking a shaft in search of ochre that some miners, about the year 1650, discovered the cave or fissure from which Dr Catcott, in 1759, and at a later period, the Rev. David Williams of Bleadon and "Professor" Beard of Banwell, obtained the bones of many extinct animals. Rutter's account of the original discovery is as follows:—

"The miners having opened an ochre-pit, came to a fissure in the limestone rock filled with good ochre, which, being continued to the depth of eight yards, opened into a cavern, the floor of which consisted also of ochre; and strewed on its surface were large quantities of white bones, which were found dispersed through the ochreous mass. In the centre of the chamber, a large stalactite depended from the roof, beneath which a corresponding pillar of stalagmite arose from the floor." [1]

It was a hundred years later when Dr. Catcott, in company with some friends, visited the

[1] Rutter, "Delineations of Somerset," p. 101.

spot, and, as he says, "descended into a cavern about ninety feet deep, around whose sides, and from the roof, the bones projected, so as to represent the inside of a charnel-house." The explorers took away some of the bones, but seeing signs of collapse in the walls of the cavern, they withdrew, intending to visit the place again. Soon afterwards, however, the pit fell in, and was not examined again for seventy years. About the year 1826, the Rev. David Williams, having read Dr. Catcott's narrative in that author's "Treatise on the Deluge," and having found after patient search some fragments of bone among the rubbish near the mouth of an old pit, and being also assured by a miner that this was the traditional spot, sank three shafts, the third of which struck directly into Catcott's cavern. With the assistance of Beard, fresh from his discoveries in the Bone-cave at Banwell, Dr. Williams made a thorough exploration of the place, which seems to have been a fissure filled with ochreous rubble, in which were great quantities of bones, principally those of the Elephant, Tiger, Hyæna, Wolf, Boar, and Horse. No bones of the Ox, so abundant in the Banwell cave, were discovered at Hutton, and, on the other hand, no remains of the Horse were found at Banwell. After the exploration the pit was filled in. But the mouth of it can still be seen in the centre of a group of Scotch firs, in a field adjoining the road, not far above Upper Canada Farm.

Hutton, a commoner village-name in the north

than in the south of England, is derived, says Mr. Isaac Taylor, from the Anglo-Saxon *hoh*, "a point of land shaped like a heel or hough, stretching out into a plain or sea."[1] In Oldmixon, or Holdmixon, as it is spelt in the Hundred Rolls of 1272, "Hold" is perhaps another form of "Wold," "a wood." Of the other two ancient place-names in the parish, Ludwell is less likely to mean "Our Lady's Well" than the "Public Well"; and Elborough almost certainly means "The Burial Mound of Ælla."

With its varied features of wood and hill and moorland, Hutton has naturally no little variety both of animals and plants. In the woods above the village, whose carefully guarded seclusion and rough and broken ground make them an almost ideal haunt for such animals, both Badgers and Foxes are occasionally seen. In the ditches of the moor are many Water-rats; in some years they are very numerous indeed. Less often seen are the Water-shrews—beautiful little creatures, that at times may be watched playing on the surface of the water like so many kittens.

The birds of Hutton Hill are, so far as is known, chiefly such ordinary woodlanders as do not interfere with the interests of game-preserving. The Lesser Spotted Woodpecker is occasionally observed; and the Green Woodpecker, the Wryneck, and the Nuthatch all breed among the orchards. Nightingales

[1] "Names and their Histories."

return year after year to the same stations in Hutton Combe, and along the edge of Hutton woods, but they are not common in the neighbourhood. This year a pair of Hawfinches were seen from the Rectory windows, and have very probably nested somewhere near.

Conspicuous among the birds that regularly frequent the moor are Hawks, particularly Kestrels, which, although their homes may be in distant cliffs or woods, are fond of hunting over these level meadows. On the ponds that were made during the construction of the railway are a few Dabchicks, Moorhens, and Coots. The shy Water-rail and the rare little Spotted Crake are to be found more in the ditches than on the more open water. The tall hedges that fringe the ponds, and the thick-growing foliage along the rhines, are favourite haunts all through the summer of the Reed and the Sedge Warbler. Brockley Herons often come down to fish among the ditches; and a hard winter generally brings a Bittern or two to receive the welcome which the average Englishman is tempted to extend to every unusual bird. The Kingfisher, too, is a bird of the moor, and may sometimes be seen hovering like a Hawk, before plunging down into the water. There are often large flocks of Peewits on the moor in the winter, and a few breed there, as do others on the hill. Some years ago a man disturbed a Peewit from a field above the village. As she rose, three young birds were seen standing on the grass.

The man walked up to the spot, which was only a few yards away, but to his astonishment the three youngsters had disappeared. After looking closely at the ground for several minutes, he discovered one crouched on the grass between his feet; the other two he failed to find at all.

It is quite possible to cross the moor without seeing any specially remarkable birds or beasts. But the ditches, at almost any season of the year, are crowded with interest. Their quiet waters hide a marvellous wealth of life—fish, newts, insects of many kinds, fresh-water shells of great variety and beauty, together with countless creatures still lower in the scale, very many of which can only be seen to advantage, if seen at all, with the aid of a microscope. Besides the two Sticklebacks, so remarkable as nest-builders, the fish of the Weston Rhine, and of all the other rhines that are connected with it, are chiefly Eels and Flounders, both very interesting species, whose life-history has been briefly described in the chapter on Weston-super-Mare.

The moorland ditches are too often cleaned out to make them very attractive to the botanist. One of the prettiest flowers found there is the Frog-bit, with its round leaves and dainty little white three-petalled blossoms. Among the plants of Hutton woods are the Purple Gromwell, Bird's-nest Orchis, *Narcissus biflorus* or Primrose Peerless, Wild Snow-drop, Spurge Laurel, Butterfly Orchis, and Great Woodrush. A much rarer flower, however, than any of these is the insignificant little *Trinia*, a small, umbelliferous plant, rather suggestive of the carrot, found on the rocky slopes of Hutton Combe in 1874, and since then at many points in the Mendip Country, but occurring in only three of Watson's 112 British Botanical Districts. There is some fine timber in Hutton, especially near the Court. But the most remarkable tree in the parish is probably the magnificent ivy that adds so much to the beauty of the church tower, and whose stem is now 39 inches in girth at a height of nearly a yard from the ground. It is about ninety years old, as has been ascertained from the testimony of a parishioner, whose father well remembered the circumstance of its being planted, having had his ears boxed on the occasion for throwing his ball against the church tower.

TRINIA VULGARIS

LOCKING

LOCKING parish lies almost entirely on the flat. The greater part of it is no more than twenty feet above the level of the sea. The two small risings near Locking and Lockinghead respectively are barely thirty feet higher than the adjoining moor, and the site of the church, the most elevated ground in the parish, is only fifty-five feet above mean high-water mark. Low as it lies, however, Locking is a beautiful little village. The road that slopes gently up past the old manor-house is overshadowed by the tall elms of a populous rookery. The church is very picturesque, with its fine and ivy-mantled tower, and with the yews and limes of its quiet graveyard. And the road along the top of the ridge to the east of the village looks across a beautiful hollow, with rich meadow-lands and noble timber.

The most ancient work of man in Locking parish is probably a mound, the use and origin of which, however, are not yet clear, on the top of Carberry, a slight rising in the moor close to Lockinghead Farm, a building which stands back half a mile or more from the road that joins Locking and Weston. On the summit of this knoll, which is rather more than fifty feet above the level of the sea, is what appears to be a circular tumulus, about a hundred feet in diameter, and about eight feet high. Near it, and partly enclosing it, are two low banks of earth. On the top of this tumulus the tenants of the farm were preparing to put up a flagstaff at the time of the Coronation of King Edward VII., when, at a depth of about twenty inches below the surface, they came upon some buried masonry. Further digging revealed a small subterranean chamber, nearly square, nine feet four inches by nine feet two inches, built of dressed Lias, and with a flight of stone steps leading down into the interior. The masonry has a singularly modern appearance, but this may be partly owing to the character of the stone, which lends itself to regularity of treatment. Among the few objects of interest found so far in the course of digging out the earth with which the chamber was filled, are a much-worn silver penny of Edward IV. or V., many nails, apparently of iron, fragments of pottery, some of it quite modern, but some, particularly two pieces of an urn, evidently ancient, and some bones, one of which was pierced with holes.

Further excavation may throw some light upon this curious structure, which is probably much more modern than the tumulus itself. It does not appear to have been sepulchral. It is too small to have been a place of defence. It may perhaps be no-

Font in Locking Church

thing more than a cellar connected with a windmill or other building of which no trace now remains aboveground (see note on page 400).

The natural history of the parish presents no striking points of interest, and is much the same as that of adjoining districts. One rare plant grows in the village itself, the Pale Linaria (*Linaria repens*). This little Snapdragon, whose creamy, blue-veined flowers have a slight but pleasant scent, and which is found at only two other spots in the county, still flourishes in crannies of the Lias walls near Locking Church.

Locking is not alluded to in Domesday Book, as it then formed part of the great manor of Banwell.[1] We hear of it first in connection with the Priory of Woodspring, or, as it was originally called, Worspring. In a charter of the reign of Edward II., dated 1325, it is stated that, at the time of its foundation at Dodelyng, Galfridus Gilbewyn had endowed the Priory with "his whole manor of Lokyng, with all belonging to it, except four freemen, with their tenements, which the aforesaid William de Courtenaye kept for himself." Farther on in the same document are given the names of three other Locking landowners, Henry Engayne, Henry de Pendeney, and Richard de Hordwell, who made over more or less of their property to Prior John and his Canons.[2] After the suppression of

[1] Eyton "Domesday Studies."

[2] Patent Rolls, 18 Edw. II., p. 2, m. 33.

the monastery, the Locking property which had been held by the Prior, was estimated by the Royal Commissioners at £24, 18s. 11d. At the time of the Dissolution this property was granted to Sir William St. Loe, who, in 1542, sold it, with the advowson of the church, to Thomas Clarke. Thence it passed in succession to the families of Norris, Carlile, and Plomley.[1] In 1685, John Plumley, then the Lord of Locking Manor, joined the Rebellion of the Duke of Monmouth. After the Battle of Sedgemoor he escaped, and remained for a time in hiding among the hills. But he was taken and executed. His estates were forfeited to the Crown, and were bought by Edward Colston, or, as his name appears in the list of ratepayers in the Locking Churchwardens' Accounts for 1714, Edward Couldstone. In 1708, according to Collinson, this gentleman settled the property on "his great school in Bristol." And the Merchant Venturers, as trustees of the Colston Charities, are still the Lords of Locking Manor.

Attempts have been made to connect the name of this village with that of a Scandinavian deity, Loki, the god of Strife, the spirit of Evil. But, as Professor Skeat says, "Locking cannot be from Loki, for the simple reason that these names generally go back to a man's name, at any rate when they end in 'ing,' which means 'son of,' or 'sons of.'" The founder of the settlement may possibly

[1] Collinson.

have been a Norseman. There are several spots in the district whose names are believed to be of Danish origin; the Holms and Wick St. Lawrence, for example, possibly Birnbeck, and perhaps also, as Bishop Clifford thought, Uphill and Hobbs's Boat. In addition to these, Mr. Isaac Taylor has pointed out the How Rock, at the end of Brean Down, and the Langford Grounds, the sandbanks near the mouth of the Yeo, both of which names he regards as Danish. The latter is especially interesting, since it may mean that the Norsemen knew the Bristol Channel by the appropriate title of Long Fiord.[1]

The ground on which the village stands is one of the lower spurs of Mendip, and consists of a ridge formed partly of Red Marl, partly of Lower Lias, and partly of Rhætic or Penarth Beds. Many walls in Locking are built of Lias, and the church itself is of the same material. The Church of St. Augustine, standing a little way back from the road, is finely situated; and its beautiful graveyard commands a view over a wide stretch of country—the hamlet of Elborough, the long line of hill that extends from Banwell to the sea, Brean Down—the Bristol Channel, and the Steep Holm. About the year 1820, the body of the church was rebuilt and enlarged. But the tower is old, and in spite of its stucco covering is very picturesque, with its boldly carved windows, the Priest's Door at the south-east corner, and its magnificent growth of ivy. The

[1] Isaac Taylor, "Words and Places."

church has two very striking and valuable possessions: its curious old font, and its noble carved stone Perpendicular pulpit. This pulpit is one of the very finest in the whole county; but its beautiful carvings are sadly marred by the gaudy paint with which some unknown hand has attempted to adorn it. The font which stands under the tower, consists of a nearly square stone basin, supported on a very massive central shaft, with four slender pillars round it. At each corner of the bowl is the grotesque figure of a man, with remarkably short legs, and with arms outstretched in such a manner that, in the middle of the nearest sides of the font, the hands of one man meet those of his two neighbours. The figures are in armour, not very noticeable at the first glance, in coats of leather with iron bosses on their breasts, and with helmets such as were worn in the time of Richard I. The sides of the font are covered with curious carvings; those on the south face, which was formerly turned to the wall, being much less elaborate than the others. To judge from the style of the armour worn by the effigies at its corners, the font dates probably from the last ten years of the twelfth century, 1190 to 1200, which may also be the time of the founding of the church. The first known Vicar, however, was Richard de Lincumb, who held the living from 1307 to 1310. Drawings of the font made sixty years ago show it without the pillars at the four corners. It is believed that these were added when extensive repairs were carried out in the church, about half a century ago. The oaken cover is modern, and it is said that, in order to make it fit, the stonework was cut away, and the tops of the knights' helmets lowered.

In the tower hang four bells, the second of which is very old, having its legend in antique lettering, and bearing a stamp which is found on several mediæval bells.[1]

The bells are thus inscribed :—

1. No inscription.
2. Iste: est: Johannes.
3. CAST BY I PYKE BRIDGEWATER IOHN KINGSTON FOUNDER.
4. I TO THE CHURCH THE LIVING CALL AND TO THE GRAVE I SUMMON ALL. CAST BY C DAVIS BRIDGEWATER. WM COOMBES RD LANCY CHURCH WARDENS.

On an oak beam in the belfry is cut an inscription, which either was never finished or has been partly erased :—

IOHN PLVMLEY
LORD OF TIE MAN
1631

This stands, no doubt, for the father or the grandfather of the unfortunate John Plumley, who, fifty-four years later, joined the Monmouth Insurrection.

[1] Ellacombe, "Church Bells of Somerset."

In the Locking Churchwardens' Accounts for 1659 is this side-note :—

"Delivered unto Nicolas Wooseel, the 17th of Aprill 1659 one silver chalice and one pewter fflagon." The silver chalice has disappeared, but the pewter tankard, together with a paten of the same metal—though bearing a silver hall-mark—was found some years ago in an old chest, in a much battered condition, and both are still preserved. The plate now in use, however, is modern, presenting no features of particular interest, and consists of the following pieces :—

A small silver paten, dated 1777, and marked with the letters I.S., which are believed to be the initials of John Scofield, the maker.

A plated flagon, and two plated chalices, marked underneath, "Parish of Locking, 1843."

A large plated paten, marked "Parish of Locking, 1846."

The earliest existing Church Registers of Locking begin in 1750. The old books dating from 1600 have been lost sight of for some years. A recently discovered volume of Churchwardens' Accounts, covering the period from 1633 to 1683, contains many curious and interesting entries. It is worthy of note that these accounts were regularly kept during the Civil War, a time when many such records were temporarily discontinued. In this old volume each year's account is accompanied by a list of ratepayers, from whose contributions the greater part of the church's income was derived. There were also two small pieces of land which yielded some revenue :—

1634. Receaved of Barnard Cayser for one-half acer of haye . . . . iis. viiid.
Receaved of John Phippen for the yard of mead . . . . xviiid.

The expenses of the wardens were of the usual character. Bells and windows were constant sources of outlay. The bells appear to have been too heavy for the tower, and both it and they needed frequent repair. Such items as "twoe bells ropes," "oyle for the bells," "amending the clippers," "a new Baudrepp for the seconde bell," occur on every page. The services of the glazier were in frequent request, partly owing, no doubt, to the fact that the parishioners were in the habit of playing fives against the church tower, a practice which the wardens do not seem to have been able to check, as is shown by the following extract :—

1635. It. spent when I was called to Wels to prevent those that played fives in the churchyard being the 28th of Januarie . . xviid.

In the previous year there had been a somewhat similar complaint :—

1634. It. spent when we were called to Wells for not preventing bowlers playinge in the churchyard . . . . vis.

In this book also we find allusion to the Woodspring Hospital :—

1654. Impt. for hospitall and maymed souldiers for one wholle yeare . . . . 10s. 8d.

Several interesting entries refer to books of various kinds which were purchased for the church :—

1633. It payd for a booke wh is called the kinges libertie for recreation . . . . vid.
1648. Itm. primus (?) for binding of the Bybell . . . . xs.
1662. Item for a chaine for the Booke of Martyrs . . . . iiiid.
1663. It for the Common prayer booke and the gettinge of him . . . . . . viiis. viiid.

As in other parishes in the district, outdoor relief appears to have been given to all who asked for it, and the pleas are of every imaginable character. The following are a few examples :—

It given unto an Irishman that came with his mother in a cart . . . . . . vid.
It given unto fower English peoples wch were robbed by Pyrattes . . . . . vid.
It given unto two poore women wch had their husbanses slayne in the kinges Service the vith of November . . . . . . vid.
Itm. given to a doctors wife . . . . iiid.
Given unto a man wch had scalled himself in the fire in going to save his children . . iiiid.

Contributions were also made towards the assistance of places and people at a distance. Thus the parishioners of Locking sent money to help in the repair of Keynsham Church, in rebuilding the church at Berwick-on-Tweed, and in relieving distress caused by a fire at Stratford-on-Avon.

The Civil War left a temporary mark in the church. In 1635, the King's arms were put up in the building. They must have been taken down in Commonwealth times, for in 1661 they were restored to their original place, and the restoration cost the parish much expense:—

1661. Item pd. the painter for the Kings Armes	£2
Item for bringing the King's Armes from Bristoll to Banwell and thence to the church	iis.

Other items were for "bords," "nailes," and "spickes," for fixing "the sd Armes to the wall."

The Dutch War, and the depredations of Algerine corsairs during the ignominous reign of Charles II., swelled the list of applicants for outdoor relief. The following are for the year 1665 alone:—

Item given to nine poore people which had lost by the Hollander	viiid.
Item given to a poor Irishman who had lost by the Hollander	ivd.
Item given to twelve pore people which had lost by the Turcks	6d.
Item given unto three poore Seamen which had lost by the turcke Aug 26	4d.

The Locking Churchwardens paid, as the law

required, for the destruction of "vermin," and there are many entries in the accounts of sums paid for heads of polecats, hedgehogs, and sparrows. For example:—

Pd to Hen Plomley for a dosen and half of sparrowes heades . . . . . . iiid.

It Pd to Hen Plomley for three polecatts heads . . . . iiiid.

Thomas Torr Churchwarden for 3 Hedgehogs as I catcht myself 0 0 6

Polecats are rare animals in the Mendip Country in our time, and certainly the Locking wardens did their part in exterminating them. With the disregard of spelling which characterises so many of these old account-books, the authorities wrote not only polecat, but poul kat, powlecatt, polecatte, pollcatt, polcat, poalcat, pollcat, and paullcat.

After 1683 there is a gap in the Accounts, and the next volume begins in 1714. In that interval many things had happened. James II. had come and gone. William of Orange had landed at Torbay, and had struggled and suffered and fought, and had gone to his account. And now Queen Anne was dead. But more than all that, the Lord of the Manor, John Plumley, had gone to join the Duke of Monmouth, had shared in the rout of Sedgemoor, had lain in hiding among the hills, had returned to Locking a condemned man, and had, so the village tradition runs, been hanged as a rebel almost within sight of his own door. In the book of 1714 John Plumley no longer heads the list of ratepayers. His place is taken by "Edward Couldstone." The old name is not, however, quite forgotten, and the names of Joseph Plumley, Francis Plumley, and Widow Plumley, still appear in the lists of the time among the ratepayers of the parish.

To the left of the road from Weston to Locking, a short distance to the east of the foot of the slope that leads up towards the church, is Locking manor-house: at the back a picturesque and rambling old building, and with its front partly covered by a beautiful magnolia. This house, and its estate of about 150 acres, are the only parts of the manor which do not belong to the Merchant Venturers of Bristol. About the year 1750 this property, so it is said, was, in order to pay off a debt, sold to a Mr. Jenkins, in whose family it remained until some twenty years ago. On the death of his last descendant the estate was again sold, and is now the property of Mr. R. A. Hill. Among the former owners was the Rev. Stiverd Jenkins, officiating minister of Weston-super-Mare, who resided here. It was he, so it is said, who brought in bullock-wagons from the top of Mendip or, as others say, from the moor near Glastonbury, the score or so of great stones, believed to be the remains of a stone circle, which still stand round the lawn of the manor-house. The tallest of these monoliths measures 9½ feet in height, and 10 feet in girth; and there are others which are 8 feet, 8½ feet, and 9 feet high.

The house is believed to have been built in the time of Queen Elizabeth by one of the Merchant Venturers, but it has been ruthlessly modernised and altered. A few years ago all the oak beams which crossed the ceilings were removed, and the whole front was rebuilt. The house still contains, however, some interesting traces of its former importance. In the dining-room is a finely modelled plaster mantelpiece, probably imitated from some Jacobæan masterpiece in Bristol. About twelve years ago a way was cut through the dining-room wall, which was four feet in thickness. In the wall were found parts of a fireplace and an old stairway, which, it has been suggested, were the remains of a secret chamber. The house was once surrounded by a moat, which has been excavated to a depth of fifteen feet; and round the building have been found many old stone drains, showing that it was once much more extensive than at present.

Two traditions are connected with the manor-house. One is that there is a great treasure buried somewhere within its precincts; the other is that the place is haunted by the ghost of the widow of the ill-fated John Plumley, who was Lord of Locking Manor in 1685, and who joined the Monmouth rebellion. No one now living appears to have seen this phantom; but the late parish clerk, who died at a great age a few years ago, had many tales to tell of its appearance. The story goes that John Plumley, whose two sons were killed on the field, escaped from Sedgemoor and remained for a time in safe hiding at various places among the Mendips. It is quite possible that Plumley's Den, one of the caves at Burrington, received its name because he found shelter there. He returned after a while to his native village, and was hiding in the little wood still known as Plumley's Copse—though but scant traces of it are now left—south-east of Lockinghead Farm, when the attention of a party of soldiers, who were quartered at the farm, and who were engaged in searching for rebels, and no doubt for John Plumley in particular, was attracted to the spot where he was concealed by the barking of his favourite dog. It is said that he was dragged from his hiding-place behind a large stone, which still marks the spot, and hanged on a great elm hard by, about a hundred yards from the knoll called Carberry, close to Lockinghead. The traditional tree is still pointed out, but it was struck by lightning a few years ago and burned for two days. Overwhelmed with horror and despair, the unfortunate man's widow threw herself and the dog, who, through his devotion to his master, had been the innocent cause of the catastrophe, down one of the wells in the garden. And the story was long current in the village that the figure of a lady in white, carrying a dog in her arms, was sometimes seen in the twilight gliding down the Ghost's Walk, at the back of the manor-house, and vanishing between two yew-trees by the mouth of a long disused well.

NOTE.—With regard to the works now under examination at Lockinghead, it might seem that some light is thrown upon them by the fact that at first sight the word Carberry certainly suggests a camp, but *Car* does not always stand for *fort*;[1] and *bury* sometimes means a *tumulus*. The adjoining field, in which some nearly obliterated mounds can just be made out, is called The Barrows.

[1] Isaac Taylor, "Names and their Histories."

BANWELL

THE parish of Banwell, which is one of the largest in the Mendip Country, lies partly in the great alluvial plain and partly in the hills. The village itself stands, as Leland well said of it, at the roots of Mendip. But the parish extends up the steep slope above the little town, and reaches even to the banks of the stream that loiters through the meadows of the great Mendip valley. The highest ground in the parish is on Banwell Hill and Banwell Park, of which the former is just 300 feet, and the latter 318 feet above the sea. On the other hand there are parts even of the town itself which are not 40 feet above high-water mark. Many places in the moor that stretches away to the northward are less than half of even that slight altitude; and there is a spot near the hamlet of East Rolstone which is only 16 feet above the level of the sea. At some remote period the estuary of the Severn covered all the low-lying country between the present coast-line and the Banwell hills. And were it not for the old walls and the heaps of drifted sand along the coast five miles away, the parish might still at times be flooded by the sea.

The last time this happened was in January 1607, when, through the giving way of the sea-wall near Burnham, a tract of country twenty miles long and five miles wide, and including thirty villages, among which were Banwell, Congresbury, Puxton, and Yatton, was flooded ten or twelve feet deep by the sea-water. "In this civill Warres betweene the Land and the Sea," to quote from a Black-Letter Chap-Book of the time, "many Men, Women, and Children lost their lives: to save which, some climbed uppe to the tops of the houses, but the rage of the merciles tide grew so strong, yt. in many, yea most of the Villages aforenamed, the Foundations of the buildings being washed away, the whole frame fell down, and they dyed in the waters: Others got up into trees, but the trees had their rootes unfastened by the selfe-same destroyer, that disjoynted barnes and houses, and their last refuge was patiently to die."[1]

Banwell is a place of great interest, both as regards its present features and its ancient history. Its Bone Cave is known by name wherever geology is studied. Its church is one of the finest in a district whose churches are pre-eminently distin-

[1] A true report of certaine wonderfull ouerflowings of Waters, now lately in Summerset-shire, Norfolke, and other places of England: destroying many thousands of men, women, and children, ouerthrowing and bearing downe whole townes and villages, and drowning infinite numbers of sheepe and other Cattle. Printed at London by W. I. for Edward White and are to be solde at the signe of the Gunne, 1607. Reprinted by Ernest E. Baker, F.S.A., 1884.

Banwell Church

guished for their beauty. The crest of Banwell Park is crowned by the time-worn ramparts of an old Hill Fortress, built in the first place by the Britons, and occupied later by the Romans. On the same hill, lower down the slope among the trees, is a remarkable Roman landmark, of which no other example is known in Somerset and very few in all England. Every wayfarer from Banwell to Woodborough follows for a short distance at least the Roman road down which the heavy ingots from the Mendip lead-mines were carried to the sea. And there is some ground for thinking that the Romans established a settlement below this road, between Banwell Castle and the hamlet of Winthill. Near the centre of the little township, perhaps on the very ground now occupied by the parish church, once stood the Abbey which, on a Christmas eve more than a thousand years since, King Alfred bestowed upon his friend and biographer, the Welshman Asser. Hard by it rose in after years a palace that was occupied in turn by many bishops of the see. And at Towerhead, a mile to the eastward, under the wooded slope of Banwell Park, may still be seen some traces of the summer residence built by Bishop Godwyn in the days of Queen Elizabeth.

It is possible that Banwell was built on the northern side of the hill instead of on the warm slope that looks across the great Winscombe valley, for the sake of the fine spring of water that rises in the centre of the village; a spring that has never yet been known to fail during the driest summer, and that only once, in modern times at any rate, in the winter of 1802, has been even partly covered with ice. It was no doubt this spring which gave the place its name. "Banwell," says Mr. Isaac Taylor, "is Bananwyl."[1] "If," writes Professor Skeat, "Isaac Taylor is right, Banwell means 'Bana's Well,' where Bana is the epithet of a man." Banan is the genitive case of Bana, which in Anglo-Saxon usually means "a slayer," that is to say, a man who has killed another in battle, or in a duel. There is more water in this parish than in most other parts of the district. From the pool in the village runs the straight-cut water-course called the Wick or the Banwell River, which joins the estuary of the Yeo, and finds its way into the sea not far from Wood-spring Priory. Two of the parish boundaries are streams. The Lox forms its frontier for a long distance on the south, and its eastern limit is fixed by the course of the Towerhead Brook. Collinson, writing in 1791, says that the spring in the village was medicinal, and that it was once famous for curing scrofulous disorders. In his time, too, it turned a grist-mill near the church. Rutter speaks of a second mill, "an extensive writing-paper manufactory." In this, at a later period, was made paper for Bank of England notes. In Rutter's time the pond was "ornamented by a graceful weeping-

[1] Isaac Taylor, "Names and their Histories."

willow on a small island in the centre, and a pair of handsome swans." The island was made, and the willow planted on it, in 1810. The grist-mill still finds work to do. But in 1850 the paper-factory was turned into a brewery, and the chief industry of the village at the present day is the making of beer. The willow, too, has disappeared. Swans, however, are still a striking feature in the beautiful view of the church tower, seen across the pool in the centre of the village.

Banwell Camp, hidden among the trees of the Park, occupies a large area on the summit of the hill. Its dimensions are difficult to determine. As is usual with British hill forts, it is irregular in form, measuring about five hundred yards in extreme length by about three hundred and fifty yards in breadth, and it covers about twenty acres. Its defences, which are of loose stones, are very slight—two or three feet high inside, and from seven to ten feet high on the outside, from the top of the rampart to the bottom of the outer ditch. Within this space are some traces of Roman occupation, and it is believed that a Roman camp was constructed inside the older British fort. Within the smaller camp is a mound, in which, according to Rutter, foundations of buildings have been discovered. That writer adds that, within the memory of persons living in his time, many cartloads of freestone had been taken from the spot. There appears to be no record of any systematic exploration, but flint implements and rude pottery have at various times been found there. A fine bronze-winged Celt or axe-head was dug up on the north side of the hill, about the year 1882, and is now in the Bristol Museum. It is shaped like a small hatchet, and is not quite six inches long. The end

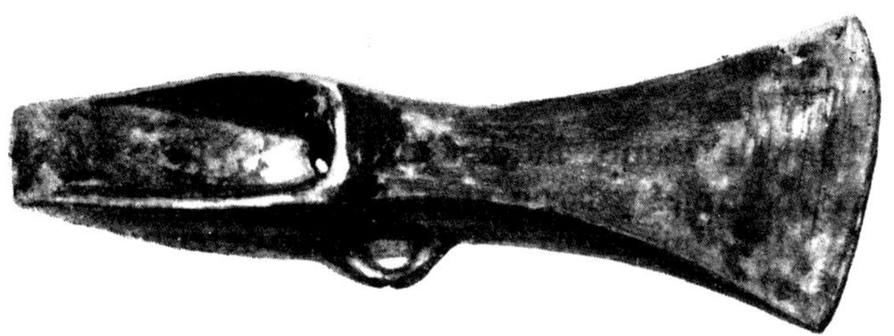

Ancient Bronze Axe-head

opposite to the cutting-edge is socketed on both sides so as to allow of its being let into a wooden handle, and on the lower side is a loop by which the implement could be further secured. In the summer of 1901 several flint flakes and a well-worked leaf-shaped flint arrow-head were found in the camp itself. In the collection of coins left by Mr. George Bennett, of Rolstone, is a small British silver coin found in the neighbourhood, but there is no record of the actual spot where it was discovered. It bears on one side the archaic figure of a horse, imitated probably from the gold stater of Philip II. of Macedon, which served as a model for some at least of the coins that were current in this island before the landing of Cæsar.

Not far from the entrance-gate of the Park is a small enclosure, believed to be of Roman origin, though it was probably not a military work. It is nearly rectangular in shape, about 75 yards long and 64 yards wide, surrounded by a rampart of earth and stones, 12 feet broad, and varying, according to the slope of the hill, from 5 to 10 feet in height. Within its area is a very solid earthen structure, in the shape of a cross, whose arms, 12 feet broad, extend nearly to the walls of the enclosure. Excavations made here showed that the foundations of the cross were of masonry; but little else was found, besides bones and fragments of pottery. The whole structure has been called a camp; but antiquaries now think that it was not a fortification but a boundary-mark, such as the Romans were in the habit of making in a newly conquered country. Similar landmarks have been found in various parts of England, one of them near Swansea, but this is the only one known to exist in Somerset.[1]

The Roman road already alluded to, which ran from Old Sarum in Wiltshire to the little port of Uphill, passed close to the foot of the southern slope of the Park, and it is still used for a short distance east and west of Banwell Castle. To the east, in the direction of the Mendip mining country,

[1] The Rev. Prebendary Scarth, "Som. Arch. Pro.," vol. xxxi.

the road from Banwell to Woodborough follows the old line for about half a mile. Where the modern road turns sharply to the right, the ancient way keeps straight on, a hardly distinguishable track, across the fields. Joining a very narrow lane that leads from Towerhead on the other side of the hill, it crosses the railway between Sandford and Winscombe stations, cuts the highroad close to the fourteenth milestone on the way from Bristol, passes to the north of Shipham, and descends into the Black Down valley through a cutting called the Hollow Way. For some miles beyond this point, past Charterhouse, the site of the mining settlement where the lead was raised which was carried down it to the sea at Uphill, past the Castle of Comfort, and keeping to some of the highest ground on Mendip, it can only be traced with difficulty.

In the opposite direction, towards Uphill, due west from Banwell Castle, the Roman road can be followed for about five hundred yards along the lane to Winthill. When this lane turns down to the left, the ancient way takes to the fields and becomes a rough cart-track, often hardly to be made out, until it once more joins the road leading down from the caves. It is the opinion of Colonel Bramble and the Rev. C. S. Taylor that the Roman road here turned sharply to the left, following the line of Bridewell Lane, skirting the north side of Christon Plantation, and then ran along the top of Bleadon Hill to its terminus at the mouth of the river Axe, near Uphill. Here it came down to the sea between two tumuli, to the south of the ruined Church of St. Nicholas.

The earliest allusion to Banwell is to be found in the writings of John Asser, a Welsh monk who, on account of his abilities and learning, was, about the year 880, invited to Court, where he became the friend and adviser of King Alfred. Alfred made him abbot of more than one monastery, and finally appointed him to the Bishopric of Sherborne, where, in the year 910, he died. In 893 Asser wrote an account of the life and exploits of his royal master, under the title of *De Vita et Rebus Gestis Alfredi*. And in recording the events of the year 886, after describing how an illness had attacked him, and how he had determined to persist in asking the king's leave to return home, he says :—

"He called me to him at twilight on Christmas Eve, and gave me two letters, in which was a long inventory of all the goods in the two monasteries of Amgresbyri[1] and Banuwille. On the same day he delivered to me the two monasteries with all their contents, and a very valuable pall of silk, and as much incense as a strong man could carry, adding these words: He did not give these trifles through any unwillingness to bestow more valuable things in future; for in the course of time, he unexpectedly gave me Exancestre. . . . He then gave me permission to ride at once to these two monasteries filled with so many good things, and then to return to my home."

Of the Banwell Monastery nothing further is

[1] One MS. says Cungresbury.

known, not even the name of the Order of the monks who paced its cloisters. Leland, writing in 1540, just after the dissolution of the great religious houses, says: "There was at Banwelle in the tyme of Alfride King of the Westsaxons a notable Monasterie of ——," and the blank is still unfilled. Of the building itself not a stone remains. Its very site is a mere matter of conjecture.

There are but brief references to Banwell for more than a century after Asser's time. In 904 Bishop Denewulf and the Convent at the Old Minster at Winchester gave the Manor of Banwell, together with estates at Crowcombe Heathfield, Compton Bishop, and Stoke by Shelbourne, to Edward the Elder, in consideration of the remission of certain rights which the king possessed over the Winchester Manor of Taunton.[1] And in 998 A.D., King Edgar, in a Charter of Liberties to Winchester Cathedral relating to Taunton, mentions the above grant, and also states that King Edward gave all the four manors, including Banwell, to the Brethren and Sisters at Cheddar Minster, in exchange for some land at Carhampton.[2] From the Autobiography of Giso, who was Bishop of Wells from 1059 to 1087, it appears that the manors of Banwell and Congresbury, with other property, were given by King Canute to Dudoc, who afterwards, in 1033,

[1] Kemble, Codex Dipl., mlxxxiv. Birch, Cart. Sax., 612. Thorpe, Dipl., p. 155.

[2] Kemble, Codex Dipl., dxcviii. Birch, Cart. Sax., 1219. Thorpe, Dipl., p. 234.

became Bishop of Wells. Dudoc left the property to the see; and Giso adds that the bequest was confirmed by Royal Charters "of the time of the most pious King Edward," of which charters, however, no trace can now be found. Giso goes on to complain that when Dudoc died, Earl Harold, in defiance of the will, seized the two manors of Banwell and Congresbury, and continued to hold them until the death of Edward the Confessor. Giso, so he declares, protested. And after an interval of some years, Harold promised ample restitution. That Harold held the manor is clear from Domesday Book. Whether he got possession of it by fair means or foul is another question. Later authorities—a writer of the fourteenth century, known as the Canon of Wells, Godwyn, who was consecrated Bishop of Bath and Wells in 1584, and Collinson the county historian—represent that Harold's seizure, as they termed it, reduced the Canons of Wells to beggary, and that Giso was compelled to fly the country. Of this, however, Giso himself says nothing. And it is doubtful, as was pointed out by the late John Richard Green, if the earl ever took anything from the see that really belonged to it. Banwell was Dudoc's private feof. At his death it is quite probable that it would revert to the Crown, and equally probable that it would at once be bestowed upon some royal favourite. In this way Harold may have become the owner of the manor.

There are, however, contemporary charters which seem to give colour to Giso's version of the story, for while they confirm the grant of the Bishopric of Wells, and of the lands that Dudoc had held, to Giso, they contain hints that there had been a seizure of some kind. One of these charters thus begins :—

"King Eadward greets Earl Harold and Abbot Aylnoth and Shirereeve Godwin and all my thegns in Somerset friendly; and I have you to know that I have given Giso my priest this bishopric here with you and all its belongings . . . as full and as freely as Duduco or any bishop before him had in all things. And if there be any land taken out of that bishopric I will that it come in again."

Harold's own charter, so far from containing, as Mr. Green says, "any acknowledgment of wrong, is the strongest proof of Harold's unconsciousness of having done any wrong at all. It runs indeed in a strangely friendly fashion :—

'Harold King greets Ailnoth Abbot and Tovid and all my thanes in Somerset friendly; and I have you to know that I will that Bishop Giso have sac and soc over his land and over his men, and toll and teme and infangtheof in borough and out as fully and freely as he had aforetime in King Eadward's days in all things . . . and I will that no man do him wrong in anything.'

"If Harold were the wrong-doer the clause is the language of sarcasm rather than of restitution.

But there is no question either of the one or of the other. The words are those of one who was on good terms with Giso, and who has not the slightest suspicion of a wish on the Bishop's part for more than he possessed in King Edward's days."

Among the documents in possession of the Dean and Chapter of Wells is a copy of a charter by which William the Conqueror, two years after his accession, confirmed Banwell and other Somerset lands to Giso. This document, after alluding to an estate "in a place which is called by the inhabitants Banawelle," adds that "King Harold, fired by avarice, had taken them away." The wording of the last phrase may have been due to Giso's own prompting. William would be ready to listen to any tale against the "Usurper" whom he had overthrown at Hastings. The signatures to this charter are of great interest. First come the royal names:—

✠ Ego Willhelmus rex Anglorum crucis titulo meam confirmo donacionem. [I, William, King of the English, confirm my gift with the sign of the Cross.]

✠ Ego Mathyld regina eodem signo adhibeo confirmacionem. [I, Matilda the Queen, add my confirmation with the same sign.]

The next to sign were the Archbishops of Canterbury and York, Stigand and Aldred. After them come eleven Bishops, and it is curious to note that nearly every prelate found a different word to express his assent to the objects of the document.

✠ Ego Stigandus archiepiscopus consensi et subscripsi.
✠ Ego Aldraedus archiepiscopus confirmavi.
✠ Ego Odo episcopus frater Regis conroboravi.[1]
✠ Ego Hugo episcopus consolidavi.
✠ Ego Goffrid episcopus consignavi.
✠ Ego Heremannus episcopus consensi.
✠ Ego Leofricus episcopus non renui.
✠ Ego Gilmaer episcopus annui.
✠ Ego Willhelmus episcopus laudavi.
✠ Ego Egelricus episcopus confirmo.
✠ Ego Walterus episcopus favi.
✠ Ego Wulfsig episcopus confirmavi.
✠ Ego Remigius episcopus consignavi.

Then follow the names of four abbots, several earls, Robert the king's brother,[2] Richard the king's son, and various other men of mark. An examination of the signatures reveals the very remarkable fact that at Whitsuntide in 1068 the Royal Court was more English than Norman. Another very interesting feature of the document is its minute description of the boundaries of the ancient Manor of Banwell, which then included not only the modern parish of Banwell but Puxton, Churchill, and Compton Bishop. In the last named were reckoned five hides at Huish near Highbridge,

[1] The Fighting Bishop of Bayeux, who did good service at Hastings, but afterwards rebelled against his brother.

[2] Robert of Normandy, defeated at Tenchebrai in 1106 by Henry I., and imprisoned in Cardiff Castle until his death, twenty-nine years later.

which now form part of Burnham.[1] Banwell parish is a large one, measuring as it does 4829 acres; but the Banwell of Bishop Giso's time, and of the time of the Great Norman Survey, was no less than 10,474 acres in extent.

The next allusion to Banwell is in Domesday Book, where it is set down among the possessions of the See of Wells, that is to say, of Giso himself. That prelate actually held one-twelfth of the whole shire, more than was owned by any other landlord except the Abbot of Glastonbury:—

"*The same Bishop holds Banwelle. Earl Harold held it in the time of King Edward, and paid Danegeld for thirty hides. There is land for forty plough-teams. Of this there are in the demesne six hides. And there are three plough-teams and five serfs and twenty-three villeins, and twelve boors with eighteen plough-teams. There are one hundred acres of meadow. Pasture one mile in length and breadth. Wood two miles and a half in length and breadth.*

"*Of the land in this manor Serlo holds from the Bishop one hide, Radulph five hides and a half, Rohard five hides and a half, Fastradus one hide, Bono one hide, Elwi one hide. There are in the demesne nine plough-teams, and five serfs, and twenty-five villeins, and fifteen boors having eighteen plough-teams and a half. There are two mills belonging to Rohard, paying ten shillings. Ordulf one mill paying forty pence. The whole manor*

1 "Som. Arch. Pro.," vol. xxiii.

is worth fifteen pounds as regards the Bishop, and also fifteen pounds as regards the tenants."[1]

The Exeter Domesday adds that there were in the manor twenty goats and six wild brood-mares, *equæ indomitæ*.

Banwell was not originally included in the Royal Hunting Forest of Mendip. But under the Norman kings, and especially in the reign of King John, encroachments were made upon the lands and liberties of the smaller owners; and Banwell, with many other manors in the Mendip Country, was at an early period taken within the bounds. Henry III., by a Forest Charter of the year 1225, promised that all freeholders should have their lands restored, just as they had been at the coronation of Henry II. More than seventy years, however, elapsed before Edward I. carried out that promise of his father, "That all forests which our grandfather afforested should be viewed by good and lawful men." In March 1298, the King's Commissioners came down to Somerset. On the 10th day of May, after having empanelled a jury consisting of knights of

[1] A hide was a somewhat variable quantity, but it probably measured as a rule about 240 acres. Much of the Banwell land lying in the moor, where it was of no great value, the hide would, in this particular case, be larger than the average. A plough-team represented half a hide, or 120 acres. Serfs were mere chattels, and belonged not to the land, but to the landlord. Villeins, so called because they belonged to the vill or manor, were the highest of the classes which had no sort of freedom. Boors probably lived near the manor-house, and were the highest class of farm-labourers employed on the estate.—Eyton, "Domesday Studies."

the shire, gentlemen of the neighbourhood, foresters and verderers, they began the famous Perambulation of the Mendip Forest. In the end twenty manors, including Uphill, Hutton, Worle, and Banwell, were disafforested, and when the Commissioners had completed their labours it was found that the Royal Hunting Forest consisted of little more than the two manors of Axbridge and Cheddar.[1]

The manor remained the property of the Bishopric until the time of Edward VI., when Bishop Barlow sold it to the Duke of Somerset, Lord Protector of England, and most important personage in the country. But on the attainder and execution of that nobleman in 1552, the property once more reverted to the Crown. In 1553, the last year of his brief and troubled reign, the king granted part of the estate for twenty-one years to William St. Loe. Queen Mary, however, in 1556 restored the whole estate to the see, in whose possession the Manor of Banwell remains to the present day.[2]

In the "Itinerary" of John Leland, King Henry VIII.'s Antiquary, who visited Somerset in 1540 and 1542, are some brief allusions to Banwell. In describing Wells, Leland gives a list of palaces belonging to the Bishop, and the first he names is "Banwelle, 12. Myles by West from Welles in

[1] "Som. Arch. Pro.," vol. xxxvii.
[2] Collinson.

radicibus Mindepe." Farther on in his journal, while on his way from Keynsham to Sutton Court, he made a few notes about the place itself:—

"Banwelle is a 2. or 3. Miles from Wike, and there hath the Bisshop of Bath a goodly Lordship.

"There was at Banwelle in the tyme of Alfride King of the Westsaxons a notable Monasterie of . . .

"Banwelle standith not very holsomly, and Wike worse. The Fennes be almost at hande. Wood meately good aboute them."

Immediately upon the accession of Queen Elizabeth the King of Spain began to prepare for a descent upon this country; and England, for her part, took prompt steps to be prepared to meet him. The principal gentlemen of Somerset, like those of other shires, formed themselves into an association for the purpose of raising and arming troops for the national defence. The first return for Somerset was made in 1559, when the armed strength of the county was 4326. In the following year there was drawn up "The Certyffycathe unto the quenes Ma[tie] and here honorable Counsell of all syche abell men and armures as ys within the countey afforesayde whyche hathe ben ajowstred nowe yn the second yere of the quenes ma[ties] rayne"; and in this return it is recorded that Banwell was ready with 212 Hackbuttyers, under Commissioner Hew Broke, and Captayne Jas. Percyvall.[1]

[1] Green, "Somerset and the Armada.

In the Churchwardens' Accounts for 1560 are these entries:—

Pd. for 2 Bowes	5	6
Pd. for one Sheyffe of Arowes with ye cace .	2	3
Pd. for one sworde and 2 capps	5	8
Pd. for exspences at Bristowe when we bought the Harnes	0	10½

The special training went on, as did the hostile preparations in Spain, long after the Armada had been scattered. And in the Churchwardens' Accounts for the parish of Banwell, for the year 1599, is this further entry:—

It. paid to ye Furber for clensing of our armour for the hole year . . . . xvis.

It is interesting in this connection to know that in 1803, at the time when there was much talk of a French invasion, a company of light infantry was raised in this parish, called "The Loyal Banwell Volunteers," consisting chiefly of local gentlemen and yeomanry. "The dress and accoutrements of these patriotic Volunteers," wrote an admiring fellow-parishioner at the time, "are of the most handsome description, and they have volunteered their services at any part of Great Britain in case of any of those wretched and detestable slaves called Frenchmen, at the instigation of their abominable, bloodthirsty, and insatiable Tyrant, should ever attempt to invade the venerated and beloved shores of this land of real liberty."

The Bishops of Bath and Wells had a palace at Banwell at least as early as the reign of Edward II., but the date of its foundation is unknown. Nor, indeed, do we know much of its history. Perhaps the earliest allusion to it is in one of Bishop Drokensford's letters, relating to the establishment of a chantry at Stoke-under-Hamden. This document concludes with the words: "Dat. apud Banewell, 4 Non. Octobris, 1304," where the contraction "dat." stands for *datum*, "given," the origin of our expression "dating" a letter or document.

Thirteen years later, on the 20th of July 1317, in the chapel of the Episcopal Palace at Banwell, four ladies, Johanna de Gornay, Agnes Sant de Marays, Milburga de Derneford, and Bacillida de Sutton, by the solemn laying-on of hands by the Lord Bishop, were declared "Nuns professed" of Minchin Barrow Priory. In the year before this ceremony Johanna de Gornay, though not yet a Nun professed, had been elected Prioress of the Sisterhood. Her rule was not successful, though it lasted for some years. On the 3rd of May 1325, Johanna the Prioress was at Banwell again, accompanied by Agnes de Santa Cruce the Sub-Prioress, Bacillida de Sutton, and other Nuns, and then and there she resigned her office. "The Bishop forbade, on pain of excommunication, any Nun then present to disclose to any others what had taken place."[1] From the letters of Drokensford's successor, Ralph

[1] "Som. Arch. Pro.," vol. xii.

of Shrewsbury, it appears that he also often stayed at Banwell. The following is a translation by Mr. Thomas Hugo of part of an Epistle of Remonstrance addressed by Bishop Ralph of Shrewsbury to the Abbot and Convent of Muchelney :—

"We have lately discovered that certain monks of your House, who, according to canonical rule, ought to be content with cheap utensils, acting unlike the rest of the brethren in the refectory, presume to use costly and rich vessels in their repasts. Others whom, by the rule of their order, small cots might and ought to suffice, cause to be made for themselves couches or beds in the common dormitory, after the similitude of a tent or porch, and the like silly furniture more ornamental than the rest. Others, without discretion, too much affecting private retirement, separate meals, or other wantonness, do not come to repast in the refectory, as the profession of a monk demands. Others, wandering alone, ride about and disport themselves through the highways, plains, and fields. . . ." Dated at Banwell, July 10, 1335."[1]

The Episcopal Palace is said to have been rebuilt by Beckington, who was Bishop of Bath and Wells from 1443 to his death in 1465, and who did so much to improve the ecclesiastical buildings in various parts of his diocese. The statement appears to rest in the first place upon a passage in the "Itinerary" of William of Worcester, a traveller and chronicler who was born in 1415, and who is believed to have died about twenty years after Bishop Beckington. Speaking of the Bishop, and

[1] "Som. Arch. Pro.," vol. viii.

of his buildings and improvements, William of Worcester says: "He did the same at the Manor House at Banwell, ten miles from Bristol, and two miles from Uphill. The Bishop had it entirely restored. He resided there for the most part, and he laid out a very beautiful orchard of various excellent fruit-trees." This passage received striking confirmation by the discovery, during alterations at the Abbey, of a corbel, bearing the arms of Bishop Beckington.

When Collinson described the village, in the year 1791, some of the palace was still standing. "Great part of it," he says, "is ruinated, but there still remains the gateway, granary, and chapel, and the habitable part (which was then known as Banwell Court) has of late years been modernised." When Rutter wrote, in 1829, nothing was left of the old house except the chapel, in which, as may be seen from the Parish Register, marriages were celebrated as late as the year 1730. At a later period the chapel was turned into a cider-cellar, but it has since been restored; and it now forms part of the private residence called Banwell Abbey. During the construction of this building all fragments of ancient stonework that were found among the ruins were carefully worked into the modern masonry; and among these relics is one which shows that Beckington was not the only prelate who had a share in the building of the palace. This is a piece of stone cornice which was found under one of the floors, and which bears the name of Oliver King, who was Bishop of Bath and Wells from 1496 to 1503, that is to say, more than fifty years after Beckington's time. Mr. Bennett alludes in his notes on Banwell to the fish-ponds which, a few years before he wrote, could be seen in the field below the house. These, he adds, were drained about 1800. But the freestone archway in the wall of the Abbey precincts is no doubt the very one under which the Bishops passed on their way from the palace to the church.

The palace was, however, not the only episcopal residence in the parish. Godwyn, who was Bishop of Bath and Wells from 1584 to his death in 1590, built himself a summer retreat at Towerhead, three-quarters of a mile to the east of the church, at the foot of the northern slope of Banwell Park. Rutter describes the house as "a large substantial structure, in the Elizabethan style," adding that "it still retains much of its original character." The old house was, however, entirely pulled down about sixty years ago, and a new building erected to the south-west of it, among trees of remarkable beauty. Two of these standing close to the house—one of them a noble tulip tree—were greatly damaged by lightning during a storm in the spring of 1901. No doubt much of the material of Godwyn's summer residence was used in the new building. In the modern farmhouse, however, few vestiges of ancient workmanship can now be seen. There are some old stone doorways, and there is one oaken iron-studded door. But there is no panelling, no carved mantelpiece, no decorated ceiling. Almost the solitary relic left visible by the builders of sixty years since is the sculptured stone alluded to by Rutter, which may be seen in the outer wall of the house. It bears upon a shield the Bishop's arms, impaling those of Bath and Wells, with the motto over it, WYN. GOD. WYN. ALL. Near the house is a large walled garden, over the doorway of which there was until lately a finely carved lintel. The foundations of Godwyn's house can be traced in the short turf of the orchard to the north-east of the farm; and in the walls of some of the out-buildings are a few blocks of dressed stone. In one spot is a hollow, which has proved very difficult to fill up, and which is believed to mark the site of a well. Across the foot of the orchard, now buried under the turf, is an ancient road. Bishop Godwyn is said to have constructed a causeway from his house to the church, "for the more convenient attendance of his family."[1] This causeway, a high, raised foot-path, was demolished by the way-wardens in 1811 for the purpose of widening the road;[2] but some traces of it may still be seen behind the hedge during the first half of the way from Towerhead.

The Bishop cannot have spent long at this summer residence, for he lived only six years after he had been appointed to the see. But even that short

[1] Rutter. [2] Mr. Bennett's MS.

space sufficed to bring him into serious trouble, and to deprive him of a material part of his property. "He came to the place," says one of his contemporaries, Sir John Harrington, in his *Nugæ Antiquæ*, "as well qualified for a bishop as mought be, unreproveably without symonie, given to good hospitality, quyet, kynde, affable, a widower, and in the Queenes very good opinion. . . . If he had held on as cleare as he entered, I should have as highly extold him; but see his misfortune, that first lost him the Queenes favor, and after forc't him to another mischief." Harrington then goes on to relate how the Bishop, although "aged and diseased, and lame of the gowt," had married, as his third wife, a widow much younger than himself; how Sir Walter Raleigh, who before this time had tried to get possession of the Manor of Banwell, contrived that Queen Elizabeth, who much "mislyked such matches," should hear of it, and for his own part called upon Godwyn to give up the estate. The Bishop at first held out, and even braved "many sharp messages from the Queene, of which my selfe," says Harrington, "carried him one." Raleigh was not content with the unvarnished truth. "Never," says Godwyn's biographer, "was harmlesse man so traduced to his Soveraigne, that he had maryed a girle of twenty yeare old, with a great portion, that he had conveyed halfe the bishoprick to her, that (because he had the gowt) he could not stand to his mariadge; with such scoffs to make him ridiculous to the vulgar, and odious to the Queene. The good Earle of Bedford happening to be present when theire tales were told, and knowing the Londoners widow that the bishop had maryed, said merily to the Queene, after his dry manner, 'Madam, I know not how much the woman is above twenty, but I know that a sonne of hers is but little under forty.'" However, the mischief was done. Elizabeth still frowned. "So much the worse," was all she could say. And Godwyn, "to pacefie his persecutors, and to save Banwell, was faine to part with Wilscombe for 99 yeeres (I would it had bene 100), and so purchased his peace. . . ." "Setting this one disgrace of his aside," concludes Harrington, "he was a man very well esteemd in the countrie, beloved of all men for his great housekeeping; of the better sort, for his kinde entertainment and pleasing discourse at his table. His reading had bene much, his judgement and his doctrine sound, his government mylde and not violent, his mynde charitable, and therefore I doubt not but when he lost this life, he wonne heaven according to his word, win God, win all."

The Lady Sybil did not long remain a cause of contention. She died in 1587, and was buried, as we learn from the church records, beneath the Bishop's pew.

The Church of St. Andrew, which stands near the centre of the village, is not only the finest example of Perpendicular architecture in the district, but is in some respects unsurpassed by any similar building in the Mendip Country. The church shows to greatest advantage from the south, but there is a picturesque view of its noble tower from the main street of the little township, a view whose beauty is much enhanced by the reflections in the smooth waters of the mill-pool. The tower, which is a hundred feet high, was probably built in the early years of the Perpendicular period, perhaps about 1380, and it was regarded by Freeman as among the very finest of its class—the class "where the turret stands out very prominently, and its pinnacle soars above all the rest." In addition to the tower, the noteworthy features of the exterior are the fine proportions of the nave and aisles, the bold octagonal turrets containing the stairways to the Rood-loft, the noble windows, and the large south porch, which is remarkable in being of the same height as the aisle.

Above the western doorway, to right and left of the window, are canopied niches, each containing a figure carved in stone. These figures are believed to represent the Annunciation. That to the north of the window, a man holding a scroll, is the Angel Gabriel. That on the other side is intended for the Virgin Mary. The Lily Pot in the Virgin's niche is the symbol of Purity. The similar design with the other figure is modern, and, it may be added, meaningless. It was put up about the year 1825.

Over the south porch is a small chamber, called a Parvise, the exact use of which is uncertain. It may have served either as a lodging for a priest who came to officiate, or as a vestry, or as a chantry chapel—a place, that is, where prayers were offered for the repose of the dead. Such chambers were also used for the holding of short services, and for catechising those not to be admitted to the church itself. It was to such a room that Chaucer refers, when in the Prologue to the "Canterbury Tales," he describes—

> "A Sergeant of the Lawe, ware and wise,
> That often hadde yben at the paruis."

This particular Parvise may have been a chantry chapel. In Willis's "History of Mitred Parliamentary Abbies," is this entry:—

Pensions paid An. 1553, to Incumbents of Chantries, &c.
Banwell Fraternity.
To John LLoid Incumbent . . £3 6 8

The floor of the Banwell Parvise, which for some reason had been destroyed, was restored, and a blocked-up window reopened, in 1812, and the chamber is now the muniment room of the church. In it are preserved two old pewter Communion Wine Flagons, dated 1682, an old Lectern, a very curious Alms Chest, which in 1578 cost the parish 3s. 4d., and a still more ancient Communion Table, with regard to which there is the following entry in the Parish Accounts:—

1551. Paid Robt. Starkye for making the Communion Table 11 0

Within the porch, on the right, are the remains of the arch for the Holy Water Stoup. Over the door there formerly stood a Rood-loft, thus alluded to in the Parish Accounts:—

1548. Paid for takyng downe the Roode &c., in the porch 1 6

The interior of the church is of great and striking beauty. The nave is one of the finest in all Somerset, and it was Freeman's opinion that the proportions of the aisles and clerestory were absolutely perfect.[1] The chief features are the magnificent timber roof, the light and beautiful clerestory, the well-proportioned sculptured stone pulpit, the poppy-heads of the old oak benches, and the noble screen, which has few rivals in the county.

The history of the Church of St. Andrew is unknown. There are no records of the date of its foundation, or of its various alterations. Its story, like that of most West Country churches, can only be read from its own stones. Its oldest possession is the font, whose circular bowl, probably of late Norman workmanship, was at a later period decorated with lily-leaves like those in the Virgin's niche

[1] "Som. Arch. Pro.," vol. iv.

outside the tower, and with quatrefoils similar to those on the pulpit. The wooden font-cover is Jacobæan, of the year 1621. The oldest part of the church itself appears to be the north wall of the nave. Its original height was on a level with the sill of the clerestory window, and the line of the old roof can still be traced on the face of the tower, over the arch above the singing-gallery. The figure of St. Andrew, the Patron Saint of the church, represented with his characteristic cross in one hand and a net in the other, is now within the building, but originally it stood outside, above the roof of the nave.

Great changes were made during the Perpendicular period, which is the date of all the main features of the building. In Collinson's time, 1791, and as late as 1812, the arms of Bishop Beckington were to be seen in the east window of the north aisle, though they have since disappeared; and Beckington, who was Bishop of Bath and Wells from 1443 to 1464, and who not unfrequently resided at Banwell, has been spoken of as the rebuilder of the church. It has, however, been pointed out that the decorations of the pulpit resemble those of Bubwith's Chantry in Wells Cathedral, and it is quite possible that it was during Bubwith's Bishopric, which lasted from 1408 to 1424, that the south wall of the nave was built, the clerestory added, the pulpit set up, and the beautiful timber roof placed over all. The pulpit

Interior of Banwell Church

stair is modern, but the finely sculptured octagonal stone pulpit itself is a piece of admirable Perpendicular carving, resembling similar work at Kewstoke, Worle, and Hutton. The pillar to which it is attached has, like others in the building, been cut down from its original dimensions. A later alteration, perhaps of the following century, was the raising of the height of the chancel. The carved woodwork of the west gallery, under the tower, possesses a special interest. It formed part of the pew of Bishop Godwyn, the builder of Towerhead House; and in that very pew, which originally stood at the south-east corner of the nave, near the Vicar's reading-desk, the congregation doubtless often watched with curious eyes that "Londoners widow," by marrying whom in his old age the Bishop brought such a hornets' nest about his ears, and for whose sake he lost so much both of property and peace of mind. There is an added touch of pathos in the fact that she was buried at her husband's feet, and that her grave was beneath the Towerhead pew.

The Rood Screen, a particularly fine example of pre-Reformation art, was set up between 1521 and 1525, as appears from the following passages in the Churchwardens' Accounts:—

1521. Pd. for a paper to draw ye Draft of ye Rodelofte 0 0 4

Pd. for ye makyng of ye indentur and Oblygacyon for ye Kervar 0 1 8

Pd. to Jno. Shepol of Wolforshill . .	18	0	0
1522. Pd. to ye Kervar att Wylla Jervys howse	23	0	0
1525. Pd. to Rt. Hoptyn for gylting in ye Rodelofte and for steyning of ye Clothe afore ye Rodelofte	5	0	0

But even then the Reformation had begun. Only six years elapsed before the Crucifix—the Holy Rood of the Rood-loft, which was suspended by a chain held by the figure of an angel, which still stands above the chancel arch—was taken down and sold. What happened is briefly described in the Churchwardens' Accounts:—

1531. Rec^d. for ye Rode	3	0	0
Pd. for mete and drynke to take down ye Rode			10
Pd. for Careg of the Rode to Uphill . .	0	1	8
Pd. to ye bote men	0	1	0

Happily for us, the screen itself was spared. It consists of seven light and graceful arches—a doorway in the centre, and three compartments on each side, with wooden tracery much in the style of Perpendicular windows, and above the arches is a deep and beautifully carved cornice. Robert Hoptyn's gilding remained bright and perfect, so Rutter says, until 1805, when the screen was restored; but even by the time he wrote, in 1829, the new work had "already considerably faded." The whole was finally regilt and decorated in 1865. After the Reformation, an organ was placed on the top of the screen in place of the Crucifix, and it remained there till early in the eighteenth century. In 1830, a new Barrel Organ was placed on the screen. In 1865, this was taken down and altered, and moved into its present position.

In 1767, a gallery, supported on four fluted Ionic columns, was put up across the west end of the church, and remained there until it was taken down by the late Vicar, the Rev. W. H. Turner. Two of the columns now form part of a porch at the Grange, in Banwell, and two are put to a similar use in the village of Blagdon.

The only ancient glass in the church is in the east windows of the aisles. In Rutter's time it was in the screen, having been collected from various parts of the building and placed in the arches of the woodwork in 1813. In the vestry is some modern Flemish glass, presented to the church about fifty years ago by Mr. Turner's father. The great east window of the church was put up to the memory of Bishop Law, and four out of the five chancel windows are memorials of the Bishop's family. In the north aisle is a stained window to commemorate the late Vicar's fiftieth year as parish minister.

In the floor of the church are many old memorial stones, whose inscriptions are now in many cases quite illegible. And although several fine brasses still remain, it is clear, from marks on some of the sepulchral slabs, that a good many have disappeared. Mr. Bennett, writing nearly a hundred years ago, quotes an epitaph from the north side of the nave, in which, even then, the full name could not be made out:—

Here Lyeth the Body of . . . Wife of Wm. Goodridge Deceassed this Life the 23 of Aug. 1672.

"Death is a debt that is due;
I have paid it, soe must you.
You must pay it soe well as I,
For all that live must surely die."

One of the most interesting possessions of the church is the Memorial Brass of John Martok, which, in order to preserve it, has been taken up from its original place on the tomb at the east end of the south aisle, where its outline can still be seen, and which now, fastened to a modern slab of stone, leans against the vestry wall. This brass represents the deceased doctor (who died in 1503), dressed as a monk, and it is accompanied by this inscription:—

Here . Lyth . Buryed . the . Body . of . Mastir . John . Martok . Phisician . which . Decessyd . the . xxxi . day . of . August . in . the . Yere . of . Oure . Lorde . mcdiii . on . whose . Soull . Almyghty . Jhu . haue . Mercy . Amen.

Partly hidden by the reading-desk is a stone which bore the brass effigies of John and Elizabeth Blandon, the former of whom died in 1554, and of their four children. The figure of the woman, the head of the man, and the two brasses representing

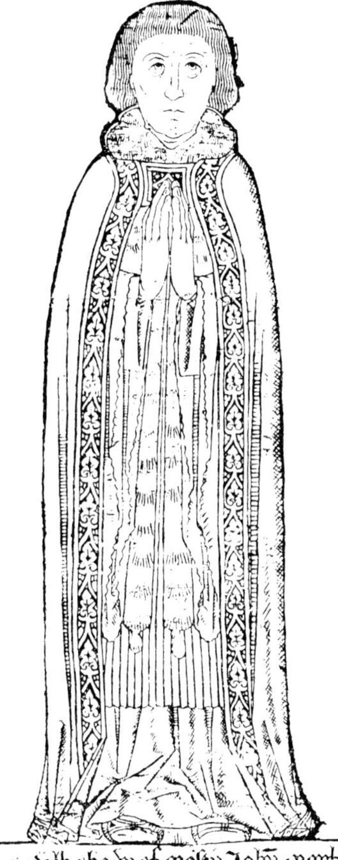

THE MARTOK BRASS

children, have disappeared, but the epitaph is still clear :—

Pray for the Soulls of John Blandon and Elizabeth his Wife Whose Body Lyeth Here Buryed which John Decessed the Seconde Day of Sep[r] Anno M:V[c]liiii. on whose Soulls Ihu haue Mercy Amen.

On another stone near the Blandon Brass are two small brass effigies of a man and a woman. The brass which bore their epitaph has been removed, but, to judge from the costumes of the two figures, this is one of the oldest memorials in the church.

The ringing-chamber under the tower has a beautiful roof of decorated stonework, with fan-tracery and carved foliage. Banwell Bells are among the largest and most musical in the Mendip Country. There are six of them, all modern. A seventh, a Sanctus Bell, which was recast in the eighteenth century, also hangs in the tower. The six bells formerly hung in the top story, but their swinging caused cracks in the masonry, and in 1743 they were removed one stage lower.[1] The bells of the peal are thus inscribed :—

1. THIS BELL WAS RECAST BY JOSEPH DYER SIMPSON, ESQ., 1844. W. H. TURNER VICAR THOMAS BLACKBARROW AND GEORGE BENNETT CHURCHWARDENS. JEFFERY AND PRICE BRISTOL.
2. MR. EDMOND SHEPPARD & MR. IOHN LANSDOWN CHURCHWARDENS. 1734.
3. Ditto.

[1] Mr. Bennett's Manuscript.

4. IOHN HAYNS AND JOHN HUNT CHURCHWARDENS. THOMAS BILBIE 1742.
5. The same as 2 and 3.
6. MR. EDMOND SHEPPARD AND MR. IOHN LANSDOWN CHURCHWARDENS. 1734.
RING TO THE PRAISE OF GOD.
I TO THE CHURCH THE LIVING CALL
AND TO THE GRAVE I SUMMON ALL.

The Communion Plate consists of five pieces:—

1. A silver gilt communion cup, undated, but Elizabethan.

2. A large silver paten of Queen Anne's time; probably the one presented to the church in 1706 by Thomas Moore, of Winscombe.[1]

3. A silver flagon of about the year 1845.

4. A silver cup given by Bishop Law to William Beard, in 1825, and by the latter presented to the Vicar for the use of the church.

5. A small silver paten.

The Church Records of Banwell are of great interest. The Registers go back to the year 1569, while the old books of Churchwardens' Accounts, which have unfortunately been lost sight of for some years, were a most valuable possession, commencing as they did in 1516, the seventh year of the reign of King Henry VIII. In the year 1603, the first year of the reign of James I., an Ecclesiastical Mandate enacted that a parchment book should be provided in every parish in the kingdom, in which should be entered

[1] Collinson.

the day and the year of every christening, wedding, and burial which had been in the parish since the time that the law was first made in that behalf, so far as the ancient books thereof could be procured, and also, that this new register should be kept in a "sure coffer," with three locks and keys. This was done at Banwell, in the year directed, and the old Registers, which apparently had been commenced in 1569, were all re-copied. Between 1642 and 1653 there are no records. The reason for this is given in a note:—

"Through the troubells of the tymes and negligence of the Clerk Littell or nothing hase bin Registered since the year 1642 Untill an Acte of Pa'lm't bearing date the 24 of August 1653 in which sayd Acte Registers was chosen in every p'ish, and for Banwell was elected and chosen by the P'sh'ers alsoe with the consent of Mr. Robert Morgan and Wm. Coles Esquire, to justices of the peace for the county of Somtt. Gyles Hemin Junior, And sworne at Wrinton Before the said Justices."

Accordingly the first entry in the new book is as follows:—

"Giles Hemin of the Parish of Banwell, approved and sworne Register of the sayd Parish accordinge to the Act of Parliamt. in that case provided 24 August 1653. GL. HEMINS."

The Registers contain few points of special interest; but in the old books of Churchwardens' Accounts, which, as already remarked, have disappeared for some years, are many curious entries. The following extracts are taken partly from Rutter's "Delineations," partly from notes made by Ernest E. Baker, F.S.A., and partly from a copy made by Mr. Bennett:—

1516. Pd. for 58lb. of Wexe agen Crysmas	01 11 03
Pd. for making of the High Cross light agen Crysmas	00 01 05
Pd. for the making of the Paschall agen East^r^	00 00 01

"Paschall" in this case no doubt means either the recess in the wall or the chest in which the Easter Representation was arranged. "Making" it was cleaning or repairing.

Pd. for Rychard Webbe ys Dyryge . .	00 01 00
1517. Pd. John Keyncote for his mete and drynke for 6 daies with the plomer . .	00 01 00
Pd. for mendyng of the belys of ye orgons .	00 00 04
1519. Pd. John Morse for mendyng of the poly [pulley] of the clocke	00 00 01

This is the first of many allusions to the clock, which must have been more than three hundred and fifty years old when, in 1884, it was replaced by a new one, given to the church by Miss Fazakerley, of Banwell Abbey.

1521. Rec^d^. of Robart Cabyll for the lyyng of his Wyffe in the Porche . . .	00 03 04
Rec^d^. of Robert Blandon for the lyyng of his Wyffe in the Church	00 06 08

1522. Pd. John Wylde to helpe rede the boke of counts 00 04

1523. Rec[d]. of John Blandon for candyll of the trendyll 00 00 04

Trendall, or Trental, is said to mean thirty days' masses for the dead. This John Blandon was no doubt the man whose brass, dated 1554, is in the floor of the church. What he bought was probably the candle ends left over when the masses were finished.

1523. Rec[d]. of John Ree for a boschell of Whete 00 00 11

The price of wheat was at its highest in this country in 1801, during the French war, when it stood at 15s. a bushel. It is now, 101 years later, about 8s. a bushel—less in proportion to the altered value of money than it was in 1523.

1568. Pd. John Payne for the Kooken Stool 00 17 00

The Kooken Stool or Cucking Stool was a chair in which a scolding wife or a fraudulent brewer or baker was tied, and then thrown into the water. Banwell Pool would be a most convenient place for the infliction of such a punishment.

1600. It' paid to John Baber cunstabell for Easter for the Ospetales . . . . iiis. vid.

The Hospital so often referred to in the Churchwardens' Accounts of the various parishes in the district was at Woodspring, as has been already pointed out.

1712. It' paid The Hospitall money for three quarters of a yeare	00 15 04
1731. Pd. the hospitall the year . .	01 00 00
Spent at paying it several times . .	00 01 09
1730. Pd. for painting the orlidg . .	02 06 00
" " John Loxton for putting him up	00 04 00

"Orlidg" stands no doubt for Horologe, and in this case means probably the face of the clock. That the wardens concerned themselves with the morals of the parish no less than with its more ordinary business affairs is shown by such an entry as this :—

"1727. That no inhabitant, licensed or unlicensed, or any other person, shall appoint horse raceing, cudgel play, or any other unlawful gaming.

On one of the free seats in the north aisle is the carved figure of an axe. There is a tradition in the village that this was intended as a memorial of a man who was executed as a rebel after the Battle of Sedgemoor. There is no record that any Banwell man suffered for having followed the ill-fated Duke of Monmouth, and the rebels were, moreover, hanged and not beheaded. The axe is more likely to be the emblem of the man who, in pre-Reformation times, made and decorated the benches. The Masonic signs which are to be seen on corbels to right and left of the south door of the church, and again on the leaves of a book held by a figure over the north door inside the building, are modern, and were carved in the year 1813 by a mason, who, to make room for the emblems, cut away the ancient heads from the fronts of the corbels.

Near the south porch there once stood, Mr. Bennett says, a very large and ancient yew tree, and the whole churchyard, he adds, was formerly nearly surrounded by a double row of ash trees, which were all cut down before 1810. Near the porch is the tomb, surmounted by a small portrait-bust, of William Beard, who received from the Bishop of the diocese the title of Professor in recognition of his zeal in exploring the Banwell Bone Cave. The silver tankard which the Bishop gave him at the same time is now, as has been already noted, the property of Banwell Church. It was originally inscribed :—

GIVEN TO MR. BEARD, OF BANWELL,
BY GEORGE HENRY LAW, LORD BISHOP OF BATH AND WELLS,
AS A SMALL TOKEN OF ACKNOWLEDGMENT
OF HIS CARE AND SKILL IN EXPLORING THE
ANTEDILUVIAN REMAINS, DISCOVERED AT BANWELL.
A.D. 1825.

When the cup was given to the church, the following words were added :—

PRESENTED TO THE
PARISH CHURCH OF BANWELL BY THE ABOVE NAMED
WILLIAM BEARD, AS A REMEMBRANCE OF HIMSELF
AND THE RIGHT REVEREND DONOR.

Bishop Law also gave Mrs. Beard a silver snuff-box, bearing the words:—

PRESENTED TO MRS. BEARD BY GEO. HY. LAW
LORD BP. OF BATH AND WELLS. 1825.

Beard was an indefatigable cave-hunter, not only at Banwell, but at Sandford, Burrington, and elsewhere, and science owes him no small debt of gratitude. A lifelike portrait of him, in a frame decorated with specimens from his famous cave, and dated 1831, is in the possession of Thomas Castle, Esq., of Winthill House. The cottage where Beard lived, on the right of the road leading from Banwell to Christon, and still called Bone Cottage, may be recognised by two large ammonites built into the wall at the gate.

In the middle of Banwell, opposite the Bell Inn, there formerly stood a covered Market-Cross, probably like those at Cheddar and Shepton Mallet. In 1754 a plain freestone cross was substituted for it. But even this was considered by the authorities to be an obstruction to the traffic, and it was finally demolished in 1798.[1]

For nearly two centuries at least Banwell has been provided with apparatus of some kind to aid in the extinguishing of fires. Until the year 1812 there hung in the north aisle of the church two Thatch Anchors, like gigantic boat-hooks, which, in days when most houses were covered with straw, were

[1] Mr. Bennett's Manuscript.

used for pulling the thatch from the roofs of burning buildings, so as to prevent the fire from spreading. In 1812, these most curious and ancient implements, which bear the date 1610, were removed to the church tower, and in 1887 they were placed in a shed behind the Fire Brigade Station, where they are now preserved. These Thatch Anchors, of which very few other examples are now known, are very massive and heavy oaken poles, twenty feet long, and each furnished with a ponderous wrought-iron head, like the head of a great boat-hook, or one fluke of an anchor. Near the head of each are four stout iron rings, and one of the poles has two more rings at its opposite extremity. To these rings ropes were fastened, so that when the Thatch Anchor had been hoisted on a burning roof, and its pointed end buried in the thatch, the blazing straw might be torn off by the united efforts of many men. These primitive appliances were supplemented, in 1810, by the gift to the town, by one of the Emerys, of an almost equally primitive Fire-Engine, which like the Thatch Anchors, was kept under the church tower until 1887, and is now, with them, preserved in the shed at the back of the engine-house. Small as it is, filled by buckets, mounted on four small solid wooden wheels, and adapted only for manual hauling, this old engine has in its time done good service, and has been called for even to fires at Weston-super-Mare in days when that town had no engine of its own. In those

2 F

times the Fire Brigade consisted of bellringers and of other men more or less connected with the church, and it was under the command of the sexton. In the year of Queen Victoria's Jubilee the Banwell Fire Brigade was remodelled, and equipped with a fine modern engine and other appliances, largely through the efforts of Miss Fazakerly, who also gave to the brigade a cottage at the gate of the Abbey, for a fire-engine station.

A service of which the Banwell men have just reason to be proud was on the occasion of a fire which, a few years ago, broke out at Paywell Farm, not far from Charterhouse. When the call for help was received, the brigade were at the engine-house. The scene of the fire was seven miles away, on one of the highest parts of Mendip. But the engine was on the spot in an hour, and as there was an ample supply of water, the brigade were able to render efficient service, although the fire by that time had made great headway.

Two other local institutions, of much interest in their day to certain sections of the community, have long ceased to exist. One of these was the Lock-Up, a square building, erected about the year 1825, to the right of the road a little below the Ship Inn. "As to its propriety and usefulness," writes Mr. Bennett, in his manuscript History of Banwell, "we shall say nothing; but as for the look of it, it is anything but ornamental to the village." A relic still preserved in the neighbourhood is an oaken staff, with brass mountings, inscribed: "Banwell Constable, 1828."

The other building was a "Workhouse for the Employment of the Poor," which was established about 1806. Writing seven years after that date, Mr. Bennett observes that the institution had by that time "dwindled into a mere Poorhouse, no kind of work whatever being provided for the inmates." Whether or no this house was first established in 1806, it would appear that there had been an institution of the kind before. West of the church there formerly stood a Public Brew-House, to which there are allusions in the Churchwardens' Accounts:—

1530. Received of Jelyan Shore for greyns	0	0	4½
Received of Rychard Scheppard for the Brewing House	0	1	2

This Brewing House was afterwards converted into the Parish Hall, and at a later period was used as a Poorhouse.

The Free School was established by public subscription about 1767, when the sum of £250 was invested on behalf of "eight or ten of the children of the second poor of the parish." A new schoolhouse was erected in 1824.

Banwell Castle, at the top of the road that rises steeply to the south of the village, is altogether modern, and was built about 1845 by Mr. Simpson, on the site of an old farmhouse, from stone which had been quarried on the spot. Banwell Tower is a few years older, having been built by Bishop Law between 1835 and 1840, not of limestone, but of Knightcott lias with freestone dressings.

Until nearly the end of the eighteenth century the hill to the west of the village was an open common, and on the top of it was a Racecourse, two miles in circuit; and the knoll called the Heughings, which now forms the base of the Tower, formed a most convenient vantage-ground from which to watch the races. An Act of Parliament passed in 1796 for the enclosure of waste lands led to the erection of walls on the hill and to the consequent closing of the course. The last race, which, Mr. Bennett says, was attended by an immense concourse of people, was held on the 12th of October 1796. The woods round the Tower were planted by Bishop Law, chiefly in the year 1825, and the work of planting and of laying out walks and drives, with the express object of providing a park for the people of Banwell, was continued by his son, Mr. Chancellor Law (Chancellor of the Diocese of Lichfield), who also greatly extended the allotments on the hill. The cottage which the Bishop built during the exploration of the Bone Cave was, in 1833, much enlarged and altered by his son, who called the house by its present name of The Caves. Near its site there was found, in 1822, the skeleton of a man, which was afterwards reinterred by the side of the track leading up to the Tower, and the spot marked by a large stone, on which is inscribed the following epitaph :—

> " Beard with his kindness brought me to this spot,
> As one unknown and long forgot ;
> He made me a grave and buried me here,
> When there was no kind friend to shed a tear.
> My bones are here, but my spirit is fled,
> And for years unknown numbered with the dead.
> Reader, as I am so shall you be ;
> Prepare for death, and follow me."

Of more interest than these lines, however, is the small rapier or dagger, with the gold-inlaying still bright upon its blade, which was found near the skeleton, concealed in the middle of a dry stone wall, and which is now in the possession of Thomas Castle, Esq., of Winthill House.

There was a good deal of mining on the hills near Banwell, especially of Calamine and Lead, though neither has been worked for more than fifty years. There are also a number of Ochre-Pits, which have been in operation more recently. Forty years ago a good deal of Heavy Spar or Baryta was dug in pits near Hillend to the north of the Tower ; and Manganese has been mined at points nearer the top of the hill within the last five-and-twenty years. It is a curious fact that small pieces of Coal are occasionally thrown up by the spring that fills the pool in the village. And, as been noted in a previous chapter, the Shipham Dowsers or Water-finders claim to be able to trace the course of the Banwell spring from near the spot in Longbottom valley, where, in 1813, a shaft was sunk in search of coal.

Banwell Caves are at the western end of Banwell Hill, near the late Major Law's residence, where there are some imitation Cromlechs and other so-called Druidical remains. The first of these caves was originally discovered by miners towards the close of the eighteenth century, while sinking a shaft in search of Ochre or Lead. Traditions of a great cavern or "Leer," as the miners called it, remained current in the district; but it was not until 1824 that William Beard, a farmer of Wint-hill, hearing of Buckland's discoveries in caves, began his explorations, in company with two other miners named Colman and Webb. The original shaft was by that time filled up, but it was reopened, and at the depth of about a hundred feet the entrance of the cave was found, and at this point there still remained some pieces of candle, left by the explorers of thirty years before, and now covered with a thin film of stalactite. Beard and his companions continued their excavations until they found themselves in a great subterranean chamber, about 150 feet long and 35 feet high, from whose vaulted roof hung beautiful stalactites and half-transparent draperies of stone, while the floor was strewn with masses of fallen rock, more or less encrusted with stalagmite. At the farther end of the cavern was a great stone, no doubt fallen from the roof, and now covered with stalagmite. This stone, from its striking resemblance to a roughly-hewn throne, and in compliment to Bishop Law, who at a later period took great interest in the exploration of the caves, was called by Beard "The Bishop's Chair." On attempting to make an easier way into the cave, by following up a fissure in a quarry at the western end of the hill, the men came upon a second and much smaller chamber, almost filled with earth and sand. This deposit was found to contain an immense quantity of bones, many of them of extinct animals, or of species not now found in England, such as the Cave Bear, a gigantic creature, far larger than any species of bear now living, the Wolf, Glutton, Arctic Fox, Reindeer, Bison, and Wild Ox, the latter the huge animal known to science as *Bos primigenius*. The most important of these remains have been removed from the cave, which was called by the men employed in the work the "Bone House," and are now in the Museum at Taunton; but many bones are still to be seen on the floor of the cavern. How the remains got into the cave is less clear than is the case in other Mendip Bone Caverns. At Wookey, for instance, it was evident from tooth-marks on many of the bones that the bodies had been dragged into the cave and devoured by Hyænas. But there are no tooth-marks on the Banwell bones; and it is believed that the carcasses of the creatures which they represent were washed into the hole by water.

Scattered at intervals over the low-lying moor which occupies so much of the northern part of Banwell parish, and which, like the Tower Hill, was enclosed by Act of Parliament in 1796, are a number of small hamlets or clusters of houses, with several of which are connected interesting historical and other associations. Puttingworth, a single farm-house, north of Puxton Station, preserves the altered name of Potingthrop, where by a licence dated at Evercreech, October 1, 1399, Bishop Ralph of Shrewsbury gave leave to Richard de Clyvedon to establish a private chapel, for the use probably of his family and tenants. Puttingworth Farm was no doubt the manor-house, and contains some fine woodwork. The railway station, though called Puxton, is in this parish, and before the opening of the Cheddar Valley branch in 1869 it was called Banwell Station. Its name was then altered to Worle, but when at the completion of the Weston loop-line in 1884 Worle got a station of its own, this station was finally called by its present name. Sandford and Banwell Station is in the parish of Winscombe. Close to Puxton Station is the little hamlet of St. George's, where in a field still called Chapel Hay there formerly stood a chapel dedicated to the Patron Saint of England. In the Banwell Churchwardens' Accounts for 1521 is this entry, alluding perhaps to a Church Revel or Festival, when collections were made in aid of the parish funds :—

Rec^d. of St. Georgy's stocke 2 16 4½

Mr. Bennett found passages in old Parish Books which showed that this chapel was converted into a cottage for some of the poor, and that it was used for this purpose for many years before its destruction in the reign of Queen Anne. Where the chapel stood, to the right of the road north of Puxton Station, skeletons have been found from time to time, and the late Thomas Castle of Worle had some pieces of armour which had been dug up on the same spot.

The two small villages of Rolstone and East Rolstone formed at one time the Manor of Worlestone, and Collinson gives details of its ownership so far back as 1272. Rolstone belonged for a time to the Percivals, and the Earl of Egmont, whose family name is Percival, is also Baron of Rolstone and Tickenham. West of Rolstone are Weywick and Westwick, two spots that are named not from the Scandinavian *Wik*, "a creek," like Wick St. Lawrence, but from the Saxon *Wic*, "a dwelling." Mr. Isaac Taylor derives Rollestone in Staffordshire from Rolfestun, "the farm of Rolf"; and Rolstone in this parish may have had a similar origin.

Wolvershill, whose name is more likely to be a corruption of that of some early Saxon owner than to have anything to do with wolves, is on the Worle Road, about two miles from Banwell. It is known in the district for its Lias and its Brown Lime, though the hamlet itself is on the Rhætic Beds, and the actual quarries are nearer to Knightcott. Little seems to have been done to explore the Rhætic formation here, but the Lias contains a few fossils. The most remarkable of these are remains of Saurians —skulls, ribs, and vertebræ; fish, sometimes in fine condition; bivalve shells, such as *Ostrea liassica*, a small oval oyster, and the large and highly polished *Lima gigantea*; together with numerous poor ammonites of the species *planorbis*. Between 1840 and 1850, some men at work in a field close to the road, on the left-hand side on the way to Worle, about half a mile from Banwell, came upon a number of buried skeletons. The skulls and principal bones, which were of exceptional size, nearly all bore marks of wounds, as if these were the remains of men who had fallen in battle; while their position, with their feet to the east, further suggested that they were Christians. Shortly after they were exposed to the air the skeletons all crumbled away. With them were found a curious enamelled brooch of bronze and some Roman coins. Most of the latter were in poor preservation, but there were two fairly good second brasses, one of Maximianus and one of Constantine. The brooch, which is in the form of the Pelta Shield and still has its pin attached to it, is of a pattern different from any in the British Museum. The neighbouring village of Knightcott, at the four cross-roads a mile out of Banwell on the way to Weston, has probably nothing to do with knighthood. It may have received its name at a time when *Cnecht* meant a "serving-man," and we may perhaps translate Knightcott as "The Village of Labourers." The principal part of the chief house at Hillend was built in the reign of Charles I., and in a stone over one of its doorways is the date 1635. Towerhead, on the north slope of Banwell Park, has been already alluded to. "Tower" is here a corruption of Ture, the ancient name of the stream that rises near the spot, and whose name, in a very old list of Banwell boundaries, is given as Ture Broc.

On the south side of the hills are the little hamlets of Winthill and Yarborough. The latter is named no doubt from the Lox Yeo, the winding stream which here forms the parish boundary. About 300 yards to the south-east of Yarborough, in one of the long and narrow fields running down towards the river, is a great stone, five feet broad and nearly eight feet high. It may have been intended for a boundary-mark, for it is within a short distance of the spot where three parishes meet—Banwell, Christon, and Winscombe.

Various origins have been suggested for the word Winthill. Some authorities have it "The Hill of Battle." Others think that the first syllable means "fair," or "open," or "level," and see in the name an allusion to the flat country which here, as in Winterhead and Winscombe, and indeed throughout the whole Hundred of Winterstoke, in all of which the same root appears, stretches away from the foot of the hills. Rhodyate, or Roddy, as it is more commonly called, means "The Road at the Gate," or the entrance road. Mr. Bennett says that, about the year 1800, two skeletons were found at the top of Banwell Roddy. And he adds that it was the belief of the time that these were the remains of a man and his wife, who, having murdered their mistress at Hutton, and having afterwards set fire to the house, were convicted on the dying evidence of their victim, and were executed and buried at this spot. In 1813 another human skeleton was found near the same place, lying buried in the middle of the road, and with its feet to the east.

Although there has never been any systematic exploration of the spot, there is some ground for thinking that there was a Roman settlement near the hamlet of Winthill. The second large field on the left hand, after passing the Castle on the way to Winthill, on the old Roman road, is called Chapel Leaze, and the field adjoining it to the west is called Chapel Close—names that in themselves suggest human occupation. At the top of Chapel Leaze, close to the road, is a large level space, to which tradition points as the site of a building. It appears from Mr. Bennett's notes, that remains of buildings were still visible in this field in 1815. In a hollow in the Chapel Close, lower down the slope, are well-marked lines which appear to be traces of old foundations. Fragments of dressed freestone may still be seen here; and there are persons still living who can remember a ruined cottage which had evidently been constructed from the remains of a much more ancient and important building. In both fields there have, at various times, been found skeletons, Roman coins, and other relics. A stone coffin dug up many years ago in Chapel Leaze was long used at a neighbouring farm as a pig-trough, but it has now disappeared. There is a tradition that this was the original site of Asser's Monastery, that the house was burnt by the Danes, and that it was afterwards rebuilt in the village of Banwell. Of this, however, there is no real evidence. And when we consider the sheltered character of the spot, the proximity of the Roman road, and the nature of the remains which have been found here, it seems more probable that in these fields there once stood a Roman villa.

Many Roman coins have at various times been found both in Chapel Leaze and Chapel Close. Of these about eighty are still preserved in two small collections, one made by the late Mr. George Bennett, and the other by Mr. Thomas Castle of Winthill. Mr. Bennett's collection includes about forty of the small coins known as Third Brass, many of which are much worn, and bear no legible inscription, and two silver Denarii, one of them of Julian, often called the Apostate, who was Emperor of Rome from 361 to 363. Mr. Castle has also about forty Third Brass coins, one First and one Second Brass, and one Denarius, all of which have been found during the last forty years in the

Chapel Leaze and the Chapel Close. A brass signet-ring, bearing a shield, charged with what look like three casks and two staves, and probably mediæval, was also picked up in the former field about forty years ago.

The Geological Features of the neighbourhood of Banwell are more varied and interesting than those of any other parish in the Sea-board of Mendip. The two principal hills are of Carboniferous Limestone, and the famous caves, like all those in the district, are in this formation. The hills are surrounded by a fringe of Dolomitic Conglomerate, broadest to the south of Banwell Tower. Outside this again lies the Red Marl, on which the village of Banwell stands. Knightcott is in the centre of a narrow band of Rhætic or Penarth Beds, and a broader patch of the same stratum lies round Wolvershill. Between these two places is a broad belt of Lower Lias. The low ground to the north of the parish, and a small patch between Yarborough and the Lox Yeo, on the other side of the hills, is Alluvial, with some peat and in some places a good deal of clay—used for brick-making about a mile north of the village—lying underneath it. When the Gas-Works were in course of construction, about thirty years ago, many bones, chiefly those of Deer, were found deep below the surface, together with remains of tree trunks, cones, and hazel-nuts.

The Flora of the neighbourhood includes a great variety of plants. The Arbutus Trees of Banwell

Tower Hill, planted probably by Bishop Law, are among the features of the parish. By the roadside, on the way to Woodborough, grows the Everlasting Pea, and near the same spot is one of the very few places in the district where the Soapwort is found, a beautiful flower with pale rose-coloured blossoms. At the foot of the northern slope of Banwell Park, Primroses have many times been gathered on New Year's Day. In the late Dr. Pooley's list of the Diatomaceæ of Weston-super-Mare, Banwell is put down as the locality for many species of these tiny plants.

The Fish of the various Banwell waters are much the same as those of the Mendip Country in general. In the rhines there are Eels, and both Nine-spined and Three-spined Sticklebacks, and there are Flounders in all streams and rhines that are connected with the sea. The Lox Yeo contains a good many Trout, and no doubt there would be more if it were not for the Pike which have of recent years so increased in this little river. In this stream, small as it is, Salmon have been taken. It is even possible that "Lox" is connected with the Scandinavian *Lax*, "a salmon"; but since the obstruction caused by the flood-gates on the Axe at Bleadon, these fish have been rarely seen. There are also in the Lox Yeo Minnows, and Loach, and Miller's Thumbs. A more remarkable species is the Lampern, the lowest down in the scale of all the British fishes, a creature of whose life-history very little is at present known.

The Banwell game-preserves attract many Birds, and a number of interesting species have been shot here at various times. On the 1st of January 1901, a Buzzard, with a grey head and neck, and therefore probably in its first or second year, was killed near the village. The Park is one of the few places in the district which are frequented by the Nightingale, and among the woods and the scattered timber along the bases of the hills such birds as Woodpeckers, Nuthatches, and Wrynecks find congenial surroundings. The fields that border the Lox Yeo are a favourite haunt of Shrikes, Sedge Warblers, and Reed Buntings, and the wayfarer by the footpath that loiters with that wandering stream may at times catch a glimpse of a Kingfisher, or startle a Water-rail from the sedges, or put up a stray couple of Wild Duck. Otters, too, are still occasionally seen. Here the Herons of Brockley watch and wait in solitary corners, leaving the sign-manual of their broad feet on sandy shoals along the banks, among the light footmarks of Water Rat and Sandpiper, of Wagtail and Moorhen.

Here, along the winding shore, grows a wealth of wild flowers—Bogbean and Marsh Orchis, Meadow Sweet and Comfrey, great double Daffodils that have wandered away from the farm precincts, and the tall, goat-scented St. John's Wort, an alien, too, but well established. Here and there among the fields grows the graceful Meadow Rue. More rare is the beautiful Marsh Epipactis, whose exquisite flowers are lovelier than those of many a highly prized tropical orchid.

It is a pleasant path, this slight track along the wandering stream. An angler's path, a stream like Songo River:—

"Never schoolboy in his quest
After hazel-nut or nest,
Through the forest in and out,
Wandered loitering thus about."

It is a place of moods, a scene that the axe of the woodman or the billhook of the hedger too often robs, though only for a time, of half its beauty. The carrying off to distant water-works of most of a powerful spring higher up the valley, together with a long succession of dry summers, has sadly shrunk the volume of the stream; but at its best it is a spot to charm the nature lover, a place

"Where timid Rail and Moorhen hide
In the tufted sedge by the river side;
Where dusky Coots, with careless oar,
The silver pools drift idly o'er;
Where the grey Heron looks silent down
On the Trout that flash through the shallows brown;
Where fiery marsh-flowers stoop to lave
Their golden bells in the whirling wave."

A CONTRIBUTION TO THE FAUNA OF THE MENDIP COUNTRY.

BIRDS, which are the most familiar of wild animals—partly because there are so many of them, and partly also because of their habits—are with few exceptions fond of sunshine; and the more light there is, the more likely they are to be abroad. Our wild mammals, on the other hand—the creatures which we often call "animals" to distinguish them from birds, and perhaps also from reptiles and insects—are all lovers more or less of twilight and of darkness. About forty different kinds of them, all told, inhabit this country, and some of them are very common. But unless we are specially looking for them, and unless, which is more important, we know just when and where to look, there are only a few which most of us are ever likely to see, while there are some which even a man well skilled in woodcraft will probably never see at all. Some of the Bats, for instance, are so rare, that we cannot hope to set eyes on them, except in a museum. Few of us have seen, or ever will see, a real Wild-Cat. Even creatures which are really common, such as Voles and Wood-Mice, of which there are scores in every country hedgerow, hold themselves so aloof, and hide themselves so well under cover of the darkness, that they are comparatively seldom seen; and it is only by trapping that we can be sure of their existence in any particular locality. How many people have seen a Harvest Mouse or a Pygmy Shrew, although both animals are believed to be widely distributed throughout England? How many have even seen a live Mole, though mole-hills are common objects enough?

Still, there are a good many wild animals in England which we may see if we will, provided always that we choose the right place and the right time, and that we set about the quest in the right way. Whittier has drawn a masterly picture of an old man who, though

> "Innocent of books,
> Was rich in lore of fields and brooks,
> Holding the cunning-warded keys
> To all the woodcraft mysteries;
> Himself to Nature's heart so near
> That all her voices in his ear
> Of beast or bird had meanings clear."

Some men no doubt are gifted with keener vision than their fellows, with senses more awake to country sights and sounds. But with good eyesight and the power of observation, and above all with a real interest in the subject, any one who will may see a good deal of the ways of even the shyest birds and beasts. Go alone; move quietly and slowly; pick out the soft places to walk on; avoid treading on stones or dry sticks; when you have reached the place of observation keep absolutely still; and never forget that patience and solitude, silence and stillness, are master-keys of woodcraft.

MAMMALIA OF THE MENDIP COUNTRY.

Noctule, or Great Bat.
Pipistrelle, or Common Bat.
Long-eared Bat.
Greater Horse-shoe Bat.
Lesser Horse-shoe Bat.
Hedgehog.
Mole.
Shrew.
Pygmy Shrew.
Water Shrew.
Fox.
Polecat.
Stoat.
Weasel.
Badger.
Otter.
Squirrel.
Dormouse.
Rat.
House Mouse.
Harvest Mouse.
Wood Mouse or Long-tailed Field Mouse.
Water Vole, or Water Rat.
Field Vole.
Bank Vole.
Hare.
Rabbit.
Bottle-nosed Whale.
Porpoise.
Grampus.

Fourteen or perhaps fifteen species of Bats have been observed in Britain, though of these there is one of which only a single example has been recorded. The Noctule is the large Bat that comes out early in the evening, generally flying very high. About thirty years ago, sixty of these Bats were seen to issue from the interior of a hollow tree near Congresbury. The Long-eared Bat, distinguished by the great length of its ears, which are nearly as long as the animal's head and body together, is a common species, and oftener seen out in the day-time than any other bat. The Horse-shoe Bats, which have most curious leaf-like membranes round the nose, have frequently been found hanging to the roof of Goatchurch Cave at Burrington. The cry of the Bat is pitched in so high a key that there are persons who cannot hear the sound at all. Hedgehogs are common throughout the whole Mendip Country. They are mainly insectivorous, but they destroy snakes, frogs, and mice, and even birds and young rabbits. They have also been taken in traps baited with hens' eggs. The Hedgehog is in the main a silent animal; but when caught in a trap, or when being killed by a dog, it sometimes utters a loud and most pitiful scream, like the cry of a wounded hare. The Mole is a common Mendip mammal, and white specimens have several times been seen in the district. Opinions are still divided on the value or otherwise of Moles as agriculturists. They kill a great many earthworms; but worms are the friends, not the foes of the farmer. And there is no doubt that mole-hills give a good deal of trouble in hay-time. Shrews are very common, especially in woods and hedgerows. They do not always hibernate, for the writer has frequently seen them abroad when the ground was covered with snow. The Pygmy Shrew is the smallest European mammal, with the exception of a relative found in Tuscany. Ten full-grown specimens weigh exactly one ounce avoirdupois. The writer has found only two examples, both in the parish of Winscombe. Water Shrews are common among the ditches, or rhines, as they are called in the district, and they are most charming animals to watch, especially as they swim round and round and frolic on the surface of the water. Foxes are common, though they are seldom seen, and they often leave their marks on unprotected poultry-yards among the hills. The Polecat has been almost exterminated. The writer has seen two alive and two dead in the course of forty years. Stoats and Weasels are both common. The latter is a harmless little animal, and renders good service in the destruction of rats and mice. Badgers are probably much more numerous than is generally suspected. They are doubtless to be found in most woods. They have been killed at Uphill, and they are known to inhabit the Hutton woods; and the writer knows several spots in the Mendips where Badgers have regular holts. The Mendip Country is not well suited for Otters, but they have been seen on the Axe, the Cheddar Water, and the Yeo, and one was killed not long ago at Puxton. Squirrels are abundant and widely distributed. Cores of cones which they have gnawed are to be seen in every fir-wood, though the creatures themselves keep mostly out of sight among the tree-tops, or are passed unnoticed because the colour of their fur harmonises so well with that of the bark of their favourite trees. The Dormouse is an animal of which we see very little. Hedgers sometimes find them in the winter, and the writer has been offered them for sale under the name of Seven Sleepers. The Brown Rat and the House Mouse are as common as the Harvest Mouse is rare. The only examples of the last-named which the writer has seen were obtained at threshing-time, when ricks were being pulled down. The Wood Mouse is a very common and a very destructive, yet a very pretty little animal. The Water Rat, or Water Vole, as scientific men prefer to call it, is also both abundant and pretty, and has the merit of being quite harmless. It is strictly vegetarian in its diet. Water-side Rats that kill ducklings or take eggs are real Rats, not Voles at all. The Field Vole and the Bank Vole are two very destructive little creatures; and the former is the most mischievous of all rodents to the farmer. The damage done by these marauders to fields in Scotland ten years ago amounted to hundreds of thousands of pounds. Hares, never common in the district, have become still rarer since the passing of the Ground Game Act. Rabbits, which, unlike Hares, are not really native to this island, are very abundant in some parts of the Mendip Country. Three kinds of marine mammals have been stranded on the shore near Weston. A Bottle-nosed Whale, about eighteen feet long, was left by the tide on the beach near Knightstone in 1860. It was alive, but naturally did not live long. Dead Porpoises and Grampuses have been found on the shore, and both have been seen alive by the fishermen.

BIRDS OF THE MENDIP COUNTRY.

The following species, except those marked †, have been seen, either living or dead, by the writer or his friends. Those marked * are, or were, in the collection of the late Arthur Tanner, of Oakridge, Sidcot.

Misselthrush.
Songthrush.
Redwing.
Fieldfare.
(1) White's Thrush. One shot at Langford, 1871.†
Blackbird.
Ring-ouzel. Seen on migration; also during the breeding season on Callow and at Burrington.
Wheatear.
Whinchat.
Stonechat. Found throughout the winter.
Redstart.
Black Redstart. A good many seen at Weston-super-Mare, and one obtained in the winter of 1884. Said to have nested near Worle.† Sidcot*
Redbreast.
Nightingale. Rather more common than forty years ago.
Whitethroat.
Lesser Whitethroat. Much rarer than the preceding.
Blackcap.
Garden Warbler. Not a common species.
Goldcrest. Very common in all fir-woods.
Chiffchaff.
Willow Warbler.
Wood Warbler. Not common.
Reed Warbler,
Sedge Warbler. Both these birds are found on the moors, and the writer has seen nests of both near Weston-super-Mare and other places.
Grasshopper Warbler. Not common, but heard every year at Weston and Winscombe.

Hedge-sparrow.
(1) Alpine Accentor. At Wells.†
Dipper. At Cheddar, Frome, and Banwell.
Long-tailed Tit.
Great Tit.
Coal Tit.
Marsh Tit.
Blue Tit.
Nuthatch. Common in many parts of the district.
Wren.
White Wagtail. Not common.
Pied Wagtail.
Grey Wagtail. Not common.
Yellow Wagtail. Not common.
Meadow Pipit.
Tree Pipit.
Rock Pipit. Common on the coast.
(1) Golden Oriole. Near Frome. †
Great Grey Shrike. A winter visitor; very rare.
Red-backed Shrike. Abundant, especially on the moors.
(1) Woodchat. Shot at Hale Well, Winscombe, about 1860.*
(1) Waxwing. Shot at Hale Well, Winscombe, about 1860.*
Spotted Flycatcher.
Pied Flycatcher. Shot at Hale Well, Winscombe, 1889; another seen there in 1901.
Swallow.
Martin.
Sand Martin.
Tree Creeper.
Goldfinch. Much increased in numbers of late years.
Siskin. A winter visitor to Max Mills and other parts of Winscombe. Seen feeding on alder-cones and nettle-seeds.
Greenfinch.
Hawfinch. Commoner of late years.
House Sparrow.
Tree Sparrow. Not common.
Chaffinch.
Bramble Finch. Not common. A flock of about ten in a garden at Weston, and even on the window-sill, in the winter of 1881–82.
Linnet.
Lesser Redpoll. Not common. Eggs found near Winscombe.
Twite. A winter visitor to the sand-hills on the coast.
Bullfinch.
Crossbill. Small flocks at Sidcot, about 1860. One specimen there in the summer.
Corn Bunting. Not common. Most often seen on the moors.
Yellow-Hammer.
Cirl Bunting. Not uncommon.
Reed Bunting.
(1) Ortolan. Shot near Sidcot, about 1860.*

Snow Bunting. A winter visitor to the sand-hills near Uphill.

Starling. Now very numerous. Old men say it was rare sixty years ago.

Rose-coloured Pastor. Very rare. Twice. Winscombe and Axbridge. †

(1) Chough. A specimen formerly at Sidcot said to have been shot in the neighbourhood.

Jay. Much less common of late years.

Magpie. Common, especially at Weston-super-Mare.

Jackdaw.

Carrion Crow.

Hooded Crow. Rare; a winter visitor. Five at Cheddar in 1900.

Rook.

Raven. Not uncommon. Two regular breeding stations are known to the writer.

Skylark.

Woodlark. Not common.

Swift.

(1) Alpine Swift. Near Axbridge. †

Nightjar.

Great Spotted Woodpecker. Rather rare, but occurs in several places in the district.

Lesser Spotted Woodpecker. Occurs in many places.

Green Woodpecker. Widely distributed.

Wryneck. Common in Winscombe parish.

Kingfisher.

(1) Roller. Seen near Frome. †

Cuckoo. Very common. The writer has seen five together.

Barn Owl.

Long-eared Owl. Not common.

Short-eared Owl. A winter visitor.

Tawny Owl.

(1) Hawk Owl. Shot near Yatton. †

(1) Tengmalm's Owl. Shot near Winscombe, in the winter of 1859. †

(1) Marsh Harrier. Shot at Brean Down. †

(1) Montagu's Harrier. Trapped at Brean Down, 1864. †

Buzzard. Rare. One shot at Banwell, Jan. 1, 1901.

White-tailed Eagle. Shot at Brean Down. † Seen at Winscombe.

Sparrow-hawk. Decreasing in numbers.

Kite. Not seen for many years.

Peregrine Falcon. Breeds both on the Steep Holm and at Cheddar. Rather rare.

Hobby. Once bred on the Steep Holm. † Seen at Hutton.

Merlin. A winter visitor for the most part, but seen in Winscombe and at Burrington in the breeding season.

(1) Red-footed Falcon. Shot in Cheddar Wood about 1860.*

Kestrel. Common.

Cormorant. Seen at Uphill.

Shag. Seen near Brean. †

Gannet. Shot off Brean Down, 1895.

Heron. Heronries at Brockley and at Mells.

Little Bittern.†

Bittern. Not unfrequently shot in the winter.

Greylag Goose. Rare.

Bean Goose,

White-fronted Goose. Both these geese sometimes occur off Brean in hard winters.

Canada Goose. A flock at Winscombe, 1892.

(1) Barnacle Goose. Shot at Cheddar about 1860.*

Brent Goose. Shot at Weston-super-Mare.

Whooper. Shot at Uphill.

Bewick's Swan. Several shot at Uphill at various times.

Black Swan. Two shot at Weston-super-Mare in 1884.

Sheldrake. Breeds in increasing numbers on Brean Down and Sand Point.

Widgeon,

Pintail. Both these birds are winter visitors; the latter very rare.

Wild Duck. A few breed.

Teal. A winter visitor.

Shoveller Rare, and chiefly in winter.

Tufted Duck. Seen near Frome. †

Scaup. A very common winter visitor to the sea-coast.

Pochard. A rare winter visitor.

Golden-eye. A winter visitor to the coast.

(1) Long-tailed Duck. Shot at Weston-super-Mare in 1890.

Scoter,

Goosander,

Red-breasted Merganser,

Smew. Winter visitors, chiefly to the coast. A Goosander shot at Banwell about 1877, and a Red-breasted Merganser at Cheddar about 1860. *

Ringdove.

Stockdove.

Rockdove. Breeds at Brean Down, Cheddar, Burrington, and elsewhere. The writer once counted sixty in a flock at Cheddar.

Turtle Dove. Much more numerous of late years.

(1) Pallas's Sand Grouse. Seen at Worle in 1888.

Pheasant.
Red-legged Partridge.
Partridge.
Quail. Thirteen eggs found at Sidcot, Winscombe, June, 1876.
(1) Red Grouse. One shot on Black Down, 1885.†
Black Grouse. Breeds on Callow, Wavering Down, and Black Down.
Water Rail. Not uncommon, especially in winter.
Spotted Crake. Rather rare. Occurs mostly in the winter.
Corncrake. Much decreased of late years.
Moorhen.
Coot. Not common.
Stone Curlew. Not common. Believed to breed on Callow.
(1) Collared Pratincole. Shot near Weston-super-Mare.†
Golden Plover. A winter visitor.
Grey Plover. A winter visitor.
Ringed Plover. A few breed on the coast.
Dotterell. Has been seen in May, on the coast, and on Mendip.
Lapwing.
Turnstone. Seen on the coast, on migration.
Oyster-catcher. A few breed. Eggs taken near Brean in 1865.
Grey Phalarope. An autumn visitor to the mouth of the Axe.
Woodcock. Not very common. Has bred.
Great Snipe. Shot at Weston-super-Mare.†
Common Snipe.
Jack Snipe.
Dunlin. A very common winter visitor.
Little Stint. Shot at Weston-super-Mare.†
Purple Sandpiper. A winter visitor to the coast. Formerly bred on Birnbeck.†
Knot,
Sanderling. Both winter visitors to the coast.
Sandpiper. A few breed.
Green Sandpiper. Seen during the breeding season near Winscombe.
Redshank. Chiefly in the winter. Eggs have been taken on the Black Rock.
Spotted Redshank. Two shot at Weston in the autumn.†
Greenshank. Autumn visitor.
Whimbrel. Chiefly in the spring.
Curlew. Not known to breed.
Arctic Tern.†
Common Tern.
Little Tern.†
Black Tern.† Terns of any kind are rare on the coast.

(1) Ivory Gull. Trapped at Weston-super-Mare.†

Kittiwake. Common in winter on the coast, and sometimes seen inland. A few breed on the Steep Holm.

Glaucous Gull,†

Iceland Gull. Two rare winter visitors, shot at Weston-super-Mare.†

Herring Gull. A few breed on the Steep Holm.

Lesser Black-backed Gull. A few breed on the Steep Holm.

Common Gull. A winter visitor.

Great Black-backed Gull. Rare on the coast.

Black-headed Gull. Common on the coast in winter.

Little Gull,

Sabine's Gull,†

Pomatorhine Skua,

Richardson's Skua,

Storm Petrel,

Leach's Petrel,

Wilson's Petrel,

Manx Shearwater,

Fulmar,

Great Northern Diver. All these have been recorded at Weston-super-Mare. Storm Petrels have been shot at Cheddar.*

Little Grebe, or Dabchick. Not uncommon.

Razorbill,

Guillemot. Both these are occasionally seen off Weston-super-Mare. The writer found a dead Razorbill, quite fresh, at Brean Down.

Little Auk. Sometimes occurs in winter on the coast.

Puffin. Sometimes seen off Weston-super-Mare.

† "Som. Arch. Pro.," vols. i., xvi., xxxix., xl.

REPTILES AND BATRACHIANS.

Viviparous Lizard. Not uncommon, chiefly on the hills.

Slow-worm. Common. The largest specimen measured 18 inches.

Adder, or Viper. Common. The longest specimen, out of 117, measured 2 feet 3 inches.

Grass Snake, or Ringed Snake. Common. The longest measured 3 feet 9 inches.

Frog.

Toad.

Newt.

Palmated Newt.

Triton.

FRESH-WATER FISH.

Perch.
Bass. Tidal water, at the mouth of the Axe.
Miller's Thumb.
Three-spined Stickleback.
Nine-spined Stickleback.
Flounder.
Eel.
Carp.
Gudgeon.
Roach.
Rudd.
Chub
Dace.
Minnow.
Tench.
Trout. In the Yeo, the Axe and its tributaries, the Chew, &c.
Salmon. Formerly, and perhaps still occasionally, in the Axe and Yeo.
Pike.
Lampern. In the Lox Yeo.

MARINE FISH.

The following are all the Marine species of whose occurrence the writer has been able to obtain definite evidence. A great many more have been recorded for Bridgwater Bay.

Sea Bream.
Gurnet.
Sea Angler, or Fishing Frog. Once at Uphill. A specimen taken in Bridgwater Bay weighed 80 lbs.
Sword Fish. Once, in Weston Bay. Its "sword" now in the Museum.
Spotted Goby.
Grey Mullet.
Cod.
Haddock.
Whiting.
Pollack.
Coal Fish.
Hake.
Ling.
Turbot.
Halibut.
Plaice.
Dab.
Flounder.
Lemon Sole.
Sole.
Eel.
Conger.
Herring.
Sprat.
Common Dog-fish
Skate.
Thornback.

Snipe Fish. Once, at Uphill.

Salmon. Occasionally in the nets off Weston-super-Mare.

Sea-Trout. Near the mouths of the Axe and the Yeo.

LAND AND FRESH-WATER SHELLS.

The following species have been found by the writer or his friends:—

Unio pictorum. Naturalised in the Weston Rhine and the Lox Yeo.
Unio tumidus. Ditto.
Sphærium corneum.
Sphærium lacustre.
Sphærium ovale.
Pisidium amnicum.
Pisidium fontinale.
Pisidium nitidum.
Pisidium pusillum.
Pisidium roseum.
Carychium minimum. Sometimes, but not always, very abundant in Weston Wood.
Ancylus lacustris.
Ancylus fluviatilis.
Limnæa auricularia.
Limnæa palustris.
Limnæa peregra.
Limnæa stagnalis.
Limnæa truncatula.
Planorbis albus.
Planorbis carinatus.
Planorbis complanatus.
Planorbis contortus.
Planorbis corneus.
Planorbis nautileus. Very abundant in some rhines in early spring.
Planorbis nitidus.
Planorbis spirorbis.
Planorbis vortex.
Physa fontinalis.
Physa hypnorum.
Amalia marginata.
Limax flavus.
Limax agrestis.
Limax arborum.
Limax maximus.
Limax cinereo-niger.
Arion ater.
Arion hortensis.
Vitrina pellucida.
Zonites alliarius.
Zonites cellarius.
Zonites excavatus.
Zonites crystallinus.
Zonites fulvus.
Zonites glaber.
Zonites nitidus.
Zonites nitidulus.
Zonites purus.
Zonites radiatulus.

Bulimus acutus.
Bulimus montanus. Callow and Churchill.
Bulimus obscurus.
Helix aculeata.
Helix arbustorum. Callow and Cheddar.
Helix aspersa.
Helix caperata.
Helix concinna.
Helix ericetorum.
Helix fusca. Callow.
Helix hispida.
Helix hortensis.
Helix nemoralis.
Helix lapicida.
Helix pomatia. Found in 1902 on Callow and near Cross. Perhaps descendants of specimens introduced in 1878.
Helix pulchella.
Helix pygmæa.
Helix rotundata.
Helix rufescens.
Helix rupestris.
Helix sericea. Once, in Weston Wood.
Helix virgata.
Pupa marginata.
Pupa ringens.
Pupa secale.
Pupa umbilicata.
Vertigo edentula.
Vertigo pygmæa.
Balea perversa.
Clausilia biplicata.
Clausilia rugosa.
Clausilia laminata.
Cochlicopa lubrica.
Cochlicopa tridens.
Achatina acicula.
Succinea elegans.
Succinea Pfeifferi.
Succinea putris.
Neritina fluviatilis. The Axe and Lox Yeo.
Cyclostoma elegans.
Acme lineata.
Bithinia Leachii.
Bithinia tentaculata.
Paludina vivipara. Found dead on the shore. Others naturalised at Winscombe.
Valvata cristata.
Valvata piscinalis.

MARINE SHELLS.

The following have been seen by the writer :—

Common Mussel.
Oyster.
Pecten varius. Rare.
Tellina balthica. This is the very abundant and many-tinted little bivalve whose empty shells are so conspicuous on the sands.

Tellina tenuis.
Scrobularia piperata.
Cockle.
Pholas candida.
Melampus bidentatus. Formerly classed with fresh-water species.
Limpet.
Trochus umbilicatus. Rare.
Natica islandica. Rare.
Littorina obtusata,
Littorina rudis,
Littorina littorea. Three kinds of periwinkle.
Rissoa striatula.
Hydrobia Ulvæ.
Hydrobia ventrosa.
Assiminea grayana. Formerly classed with fresh-water species.
Cowrie, Cypræa europæa. Rare.
Murex erinaceus.
Purpura lapillus.
Whelk.
Cylichna alba.
Chiton squamosus, the Sea-Slater.
Cuttle-fish or Squid.

BUTTERFLIES OF THE MENDIP COUNTRY.

The following species, except those marked *, for which Newman is the authority, have been taken by the writer or his friends :—

Silver-washed Fritillary.
Dark Green Fritillary.
High Brown Fritillary.
Pearl-bordered Fritillary.
Small Pearl-bordered Fritillary.
Greasy Fritillary. Rare. Formerly more common.
Comma. Many in 1902.
Small Tortoiseshell.
Large Tortoiseshell. Rare.
Peacock.
Red Admiral.
Painted Lady.
*Purple Emperor. Twice near Brockley.
Marbled White. Rare. Brean Down.
Speckled Wood.
Wall Brown.
Grayling.
Meadow Brown.
Large Heath.
Ringlet.
Small Heath.
*Duke of Burgundy, Weston-super-Mare.
Green Hairstreak.
Purple Hairstreak.
Black Hairstreak. Rare.
Copper

Silver-studded Blue.
Brown Argus.
Common Blue.
Clifden Blue. Rare.
Chalk Hill Blue. Rare.
Adonis Blue. Rare.
Little Blue. Very abundant in Winscombe and Shipham parishes.
Azure Blue.
Large Blue. Rare.
Clouded Yellow. Very abundant in 1865, 1876, and 1900.
Pale Clouded Yellow. In the same years.
Brimstone.
Orange Tip.
Green-veined White.
Small White.
Large White.
Black-veined White. Now very rare.
Grizzled Skipper.
Dingy Skipper.
Chequered Skipper.
Large Skipper.
Small Skipper.

The recent publication of "The Flora of Somerset," by the Rev. R. P. Murray, M.A., seems to render the addition here of a list of Mendip Plants unnecessary. Species of special interest or rarity have been alluded to in the body of this work.

Sea Front Weston-super-Mare.

Sea Front Weston-super-Mare.

The Scaurs Worle.

Upper Worle.

Worle Observatory.

Uphill Village.

Uphill Wharf.

Kewstoke Village.

Foot of Brean Down.

Bleadon toll-gate.

Bleadon Village.

Hutton Village.

Banwell.

INDEX

INDEX

INDEX

INDEX

INDEX

INDEX

INDEX

INDEX

INDEX

INDEX

INDEX

INDEX

INDEX

THE END

Printed by BALLANTYNE, HANSON & Co.
Edinburgh & London